"*Angel Walk: Nurses at War in Iraq and Afghanistan* is the HBO documentary *Baghdad ER* put into a complete and succinct book with numerous stories of the heroic role, compassion, dedication, psychological stress, and mental aftermath of war, with numerous references on how to get psychological support and help."

—MG ELDER GRANGER,
U.S. Army (Retired), MD; FACP; FACPE; FACHE; CMQ; Ph.D. (hon);
President/CEO of THE 5Ps, LLC Healthcare and Education Consultants

"This is an extraordinary read for citizens of all nations that have ever been engaged in armed conflict, and especially for those who have, or have had, loved ones serve at such times. To know the caliber and heroism of nurses that care for our soldiers brings much comfort to those of us waiting for their safe return."

—REV. LAURI J. GIST,
Senior Minister (Unity Church of Citrus County, FL) and mother of an Army ranger

"The stories of the experiences of these military nurses are compelling and powerful; as intriguing as they are difficult to read. The situations are unfathomable to the civilian nurse, and yet, the relationships and emotions the military nurses describe are familiar. This book offers a captivating look at one of our country's most important jobs in nursing. A must-read for military and civilian nurses alike."

—MARY O'CONNOR,
Ph.D.; RN; FACHE; Assistant Professor; Coordinator Graduate Program in Leadership
in Nursing Administration, College of Notre Dame of Maryland

"*Angel Walk* is an important book for several audiences. It is clearly a book to be read and appreciated by those in the nursing profession, especially those who have served, are serving, or will be serving in any of the military services. It will also be appreciated by everyone else who has served in the military. Just as significantly, because of the insights it provides into the work and lives of nurses in war settings, this is an important "must-read" book for the families of nurses and other medical personnel in the military, and indeed, for the families of all who serve their country in any military capacity. Finally, this is an important book for everyone in the general public to read. The glimpses this book gives us into the poignant stories of the men and women who serve their country under harshly adverse circumstances are both eye-opening and moving. Dr. Richie-Melvan and Dr. Vines deserve thanks and applause for telling us about the work of nurses under combat conditions, and for highlighting the impact of such work on those nurses. I heartily recommend *Angel Walk* to all potential readers!"

—R. EDWARD DODGE, JR.,
MD; MPH; author of The Ten Secrets of Exceptional Health

" . . . What a terrific read! Not in the medical field, I was so moved by the first-person accounts of the challenges of caring for wounded soldiers in the field. What role models for the next generation of military nurses and indeed for all student nurses. My heart ached when I read of the challenges these incredible caregivers had when they returned to 'the normal world' . . . without ways to deal with the stresses they experienced. I was extremely impressed with the catalog of resources that Sharon and Diane provided. . . . Thanks for giving me a preview of what I am certain will be an important contribution to nursing education and literature about the untold stories of war."

—MARSHA (MARTY) J. EVANS,
Acting Commissioner of the LPGA; Rear Admiral, U.S. Navy (Retired); former chief executive of the American Red Cross

"*Angel Walk* is a thought-provoking, heartrending book that masterfully depicts the effects of war on the mental, physical, and spiritual nature of mankind! This book offers a new beginning or a continued journey for all of us who have been involved in the dying and healing processes. ANC professionals are 'boots on the ground' in the war zone, as well as stateside facilities, and continue to assist warriors, families and, yes, themselves to survive the aftermath. The physical, emotional, and spiritual toll are almost indescribable; yet *Angel Walk* offers descriptions and uncovers the pain, while maintaining the pride and dignity of the valiant men and women who served and gave their all. Families will find useful resources that will ensure quality of life, as they continue their individual 'angel walks' throughout the remainder of their lives."

—COL GWENDOLYN FRYER,
U.S. Army (Retired); RN BSN; MSN; First Active Duty Polytrauma/Seamless Transition Liaison 2005-2006, James A. Haley Veterans' Affairs Medical Center, Tampa, FL

"As a Vietnam veteran and career military officer, I understand the tremendous importance of the 'angels' profiled in this extraordinary tribute. The authors have vividly described how the best of humanity can be found even in the most inhumane of circumstances. The authors of *Angel Walk: Nurses at War in Iraq and Afghanistan* are themselves extraordinary nursing professionals. Their many contributions to nursing, military nursing, and nursing education have provided a unique perspective to the challenges that our military nurses face and to the skill and dedication that have contributed to their success. Well done."

—JOHN F. EBERSOLE,
President of Excelsior College (home of America's largest nursing education program); Commander, U.S. Coast Guard (Retired)

"The bond between combat nurse and wounded soldier
has never been so movingly described."
—PATRICIA L. WALSH,
Vietnam civilian nurse, author of River City: A Nurse's Year in Vietnam

"*Angel Walk* is a brilliant guided tour into the experience of the warriors' nurse.
It offers an insightful understanding and a wealth of resources. Nurses and their
professional associates, families, and friends will read it and revisit it again and
again and again."
—REV. MILTON A. CLARKE,
Faculty, Inner Visions Institute for Spiritual Development; retired regular Army social work officer

"When the United States military mobilizes for combat, it encompasses
considerably more than just the ultimate combat operations. One of the most
vital, and largely invisible, aspects is the immediate care, sweat, and tears with
which a wounded soldier is treated. Invisible, that is, unless you are the wounded
soldier! In that case, you are the eternally grateful recipient of the incredible
care given by the nurses and doctors charged with your care; indeed they are
angels and *Angel Walk* is their story. *Angel Walk* is a story most deserving to be
told. It is the riveting story of unsung heroines and heroes who selflessly served
their wounded fellow soldiers—and their country—under the most difficult and
emotionally wrenching circumstances. Their stories will capture you and move
you. Here is the story of angels—and 'angel' is most certainly the correct choice
of a description."

—DAVE CAREY,
*Captain U.S. Navy (Retired); motivational speaker, consultant, trainer,
and author of* The Ways We Choose: Lessons for Life from a POW's Experience

"Transcending time and locale, the gripping first-person interviews of *Angel Walk*
poignantly capture the emotions, sacrifices, and special bond shared by military
nurses at war. The book's forthright and painful personal account of military
nurses caring for the dying and the wounded bares a degree of compassion,
courage and commitment that is truly inspirational. After reading *Angel Walk*,
one will fully understand the human toll of war and never again view it in the
abstract. As a father of a Marine, I believe the most important lesson of *Angel Walk*
is that America's sons and daughters are never alone on distant battlefields, thanks
to the military nurses who are always at their side to treat and comfort them."

—COL CURTIS V. EBITZ,
*U.S. Army (Retired), twice combat-wounded veteran and Purple Heart recipient of the Vietnam War; served as
an infantry platoon leader and airborne infantry company commander; father and father-in-law of Marine Corps
officers who served a total of three tours of duty in Iraq*

"This book really hit home! It was my divine appointment to confront the past again and finish dealing with it. Thanks for the tools and the resources."
—WARRANT OFFICER JOHN MARQUA,
Vietnam helicopter pilot, earned a Distinguished Flying Cross for Valor, a Bronze Star, an Army Commendation Medal, and an Air Medal with 25 Oak Leaf clusters

"*Angel Walk* reminds us all of the heroic role of nurses in wars, past and present. Equally important or perhaps more so, we are made acutely aware that these noble caregivers need care. This book (with its appendices) provides resources that both caregivers and their patients can use."
—LOUISE T. BECTON,
RN, BS (Nursing Education), military spouse; and LTG Julius W. Becton Jr. U.S. Army (Retired); former FEMA director; former president of Prairie View A & M University; author of Becton: Autobiography of a Soldier and Public Servant

"Dr. Richie and Dr. Vines have added to the literature that chronicles the compassion and professionalism that are the hallmark of Army nursing, and that is, more importantly, through the first-person accounts skillfully elicited and retold in the context of two wars forty years apart. While there are sections that provide guidance on navigating support resources and dealing with issues such as PTSD, the human touch of the stories told, alone, makes this a valuable read."
— LTG JAMES B. PEAKE,
U.S. Army (Retired); former Secretary of the Department of Veterans Affairs; former U.S. Army Surgeon General

"A truly beautiful, moving, much needed book about the first-hand . . . experiences of Army nurses who served in the military combat zone. Two very talented and caring psychiatric nurses have done all of us a huge service with their contributions in *Angel Walk*."
—JANET A. RODGERS,
Ph.D.; RN; FAAN; Professor and Dean Emerita Hahn School of Nursing and Health Science, University of San Diego

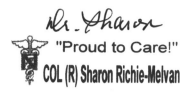

"Proud to Care!"
COL (R) Sharon Richie-Melvan

"Proud to Care!"
Prof. Diane Vines

ANGEL WALK

Nurses at War in Iraq and Afghanistan

by

Sharon I. Richie-Melvan, Ph.D., MSN, RN
Colonel, U.S. Army *Retired*

&

Diane Vines, Ph.D., RN
Associate Professor, School of Nursing, University of Portland

Arnica Publishing, Inc.
Portland, Oregon

Library of Congress Cataloging-in-Publication Data

Richie-Melvan, Sharon I.
  Angel walk : nurses at war in Iraq and Afghanistan / by Sharon I. Richie-Melvan
and Diane Vines.
       p. cm.
  Includes bibliographical references.
  ISBN 978-0-9816822-0-4 (pbk.)
  1. Iraq War, 2003—Medical care. 2. Afghan War, 2001—Medical care. 3.
Vietnam War, 1961-1975—Medical care. 4. Iraq War, 2003—Personal narratives,
American. 5. Afghan War, 2001—Personal narratives, American. 6. Vietnam
War, 1961-1975—Personal narratives, American. 7. Nurses—United States—
Interviews. 8. United States. Army Nurse Corps—Biography. 9. Combat—
Psychological aspects. 10. United States. Army—Military life. I. Vines, Diane,
1945- II. Title.
  DS79.767.M43R53 2010
  956.7044'37—dc22

                          2010005237

A portion of the proceeds (or royalties) for this book is being donated to the scholarship programs of
ANCA, MOAA and The ROCKS, INC., and the Unity of Citrus County.

Portions of this manuscript have been previously published by the U.S. Army War College and are
approved for public release and unlimited distribution. Portions have also been published in the
professional journal *Military Review* and are used here with permission.

The views expressed in this manuscript are those of the authors and do not necessarily reflect the
views of the Department of Defense or any of its agencies.

Arnica Publishing, Inc.

3880 SE Eighth Ave., Suite 110
Portland, Oregon 97202
www.arnicacreative.com

We dedicate

ANGEL WALK
Nurses at War in Iraq and Afghanistan

to the memory of these three psychiatric Army Nurse Corps Officers.
While preparing to deploy to Iraq, they were killed on November 5, 2009,
at the Fort Hood, Texas, Soldier Readiness Center.

LTC Juanita Warman • CPT Russell Seager • CPT John Gaffaney

We know that all gave some for their patients;
but these nurses gave all trying to serve.

See our appendix to learn more about their careers, service,
and devotion to Army nursing.

DEDICATIONS

This book is dedicated to wounded warriors around the world. Know that Army Nurses Corps (ANC) officers are standing watch, waiting to care for you.
You will never be alone!

It is also dedicated to the ones who stand watch everyday. ANC Angels, my Heroes and Sheroes, who serve on yesterday and today's battlefields, overseas and at home.
I know you will continue to serve where you stand.
I am so very proud of each of you.
Lean on Me!

To my partner, my general, and my dear husband Michael D. Melvan who keeps me on task, keeps us organized, and surrounds me with love and laughter.
You are my rock!

Finally, it is dedicated to Unity Prayer Chaplains around the globe who keep The High Watch for me in all that I do to serve my God.
Thank you!

—Dr. Sharon I. Richie-Melvan

Before working on this book, I spent many years working as a therapist or psychiatric community mental health nurse with victims of traumatic experiences. These were civilians of all ages who were victims of child abuse and neglect, rape and sexual abuse, elder abuse, PTSD, and natural disasters. They were homeless on the Bowery streets in New York City, in housing projects in the South Bronx, in South and South Central Los Angeles, in impoverished areas of Boston, on the streets in Portland, Oregon. I cofounded the sexual abuse treatment team at Boston Children's Hospital and worked with the child abuse treatment team. In my private practice, I treated women survivors of rape and sexual abuse including incest. I adopted two children with all the symptoms of PTSD—one who survived as an orphan for several years on the streets of San Salvador and the other who lived in drug houses as a very young child.

Many of these victims were in crisis but many were also in a constant state of stress that lasted many years. We ascribed different labels, such as reactive attachment disorders or agitated depression, to their reactions but their symptoms were similar or identical to wartime stress reactions.

I dedicate this book to those victims and especially to the brave and dedicated nurses who have served in wartime and in civilian disasters. And to the many who are working to help these victims recover their strength and joy of life. May God bless them and give them the patience and dedication to help those who are suffering. As the Library of Congress Military Medicine Web page states, "No one in war has a purer mission than nurses."

—Dr. Diane Vines

TABLE OF CONTENTS

FOREWORD

BG (R) Clara L. Adams-Ender, Chief, Army Nurse Corps 1987–91

Angel Walk: Nurses at War in Iraq and Afghanistan is an important book. It is important because it is written by two members of an undervalued profession—nursing. It is also important because it is written about war, a subject about which there are heroes who are often glorified in our highly civilized society. Yet, when the authors, two nurses of distinction, make a substantial case for the resultant ugliness and aftermath of war, as reported by those who actually experienced them, their work seems to be an equalizer for both the value of nursing and the insanity of war in a modern society. The authors are also specialty nurses in psychiatric nursing practice, which makes them eminently qualified to discuss, assess, analyze, and report upon the behavioral states of military troops and the military nurses who care for them.

The stories as related to the authors came from Army nurses who voluntarily left their places of record to join the Army. Their mission was to provide nursing services to the troops in times of peace, low-level conflicts, and war. The stories included in the book are those related by nurses who were returning from overseas duty about their experiences while caring for wounded warriors in the combat zone. The reader will soon learn that those who care for troops who are experiencing pain and suffering are likely to experience some of the same emotional crises themselves. As their stories are related, you will discover that their experiences in a combat zone left an indelible mark on their memory and that they were forever changed.

Direct combat, or coming face-to-face with another person (enemy) for purposes of doing bodily harm or killing that person to win, is held out to be the ultimate challenge in war fighting. With more than thirty-four years of experience as an Army nurse, I have constantly contended that there are many challenges in war and that direct combat is but one of them. Those who must wage battles, often seemingly unending, to save the lives of those wounded or injured in wars are challenged repeatedly for the sake of the entire team.

All who participate in military conflicts of any kind experience situations and circumstances that affect them in different ways. At the end of the day, they are never the same as they were before they had the experiences of military conflict. Vernon Baker, the lone African-American soldier to receive a Medal of Honor in 1997, which he had earned during World War II, stated in his memoir that, "War, however, is the most regrettable proving ground. For the sake of my nineteen comrades, I hope no man, black, white or any color, ever again have the same opportunity to earn the Medal of Honor. War is not honor. Those who rush to launch conflict, and those who seek to create heroes from it, should remember war's legacy. You have to be there to appreciate its horrors. And die to forget them."

Angel Walk is about some Army nurses in a combat zone; what happened to them, how they perceived what happened to them, how they responded to their experiences, how they see their situation now, and how they may cope in the future.

The final chapter is the real essence of what *Angel Walk* is all about. It contains the process of healing experienced by the troops and nurses, the availability of resources to help these deeply traumatized professionals, and some major lessons learned.

I believe it is not only important but very necessary to emphasize some of the major lessons learned. Moreover, emphasizing these lessons may create increased dialogue about the use of war as a means of problem solving between and among other nations.

One of the lessons learned is that war changes people, especially those who participate in battles and receive injuries. It also changes the caregivers, especially nurses, who bear the major responsibility for planning, assessing, intervening, and evaluating the care of these warriors. Because of their experiences, many of which highlight crises on a daily basis, these troops are never the same as they were before these life-changing encounters.

A second lesson is that war often creates problems that are interminable. As a result of wartime experiences, warriors are often left with challenges with which they must live for the remainder of their lives, both mental and physical. Many of these challenges would never have occurred had they not been involved in war. In some instances, some of these challenges increase in magnitude because of the warrior's age and physical ability or disability.

A third lesson is that leaders have a responsibility to be cognizant of and understand the vast expenditure of human capital that is made during war. Consequently, it is incumbent upon both political and military leaders who decide to engage in war to understand that the insanity of war must only be undertaken when there are no other options to resolve conflict.

The authors of *Angel Walk* have made a tremendous contribution to the body of knowledge about troops and their reactions and responses to combat-zone experiences. They describe the ugliness and aftermath of war in great detail through the eyes of those who lived them and were willing to tell their stories of fear, fright, strength, courage, and survival. I am grateful that the authors heard the voices, wrote this book, and shared these stories with us.

Clara L. Adams-Ender, RN, BSN, MSN, FAAN, CNAA, PhD (hon)
Brigadier General, U.S. Army, *Retired*

Author of *My Rise to the Stars*

FOREWORD

BG (R) Dorothy B. Pocklington, Assistant to the C, ANC for Reserve Affairs 1988–1992

Wow! *Angel Walk* is a "must read" book. Some time ago I was sent a projected Table of Contents and a short synopsis of this book. All I had to do was look at the Table of Contents and I wanted to buy the book "sight unseen" because I knew that *Angel Walk* would be a groundbreaking book.

I encouraged Dr. Sharon to be a scribe for those nurses who could not speak for themselves because of system prohibitions or because of an inability to cope with their memories and experiences. I also recommended that she not seek "official sanction" for this book so that she could proceed toward publication without arbitrary delays and restrictions that are inherent when dealing with official protocol or regulations.

The result is a gripping, graphic, and honest account of Army nurses working and living in a combat zone. Throughout the interviews it is apparent that these nurses had intense respect for, pride in, and love of their patients and members of their health care and combat support teams. The interviews also document those who returned and did not vocalize to families, friends, spiritual leaders, neighbors, or professional colleagues their sometimes horrendous experiences.

As an Army nurse on active duty and in the reserves for thirty years, I have had the privilege of caring for combat casualties stateside, but never in a combat zone. I have also had the privilege of working with many Army nurses who experienced nursing in a combat zone. Reading *Angel Walk* made me realize that I had totally missed the opportunity to offer a listening ear or a helping hand to my fellow nurses who "survived" the combat zone, but who may have had wounds of their own in spirit and mind.

Perhaps my intuitiveness could not have broken through their zeal to be a "soldier" and admit that what they experienced in a combat zone would forever haunt their memories and that silence was not their best friend. I know better now. As a number of the nurses related, there is an emotional component to serving in a combat zone that must be recognized, shared, and put on the table for discussion. I know I could have been more of a support to them, but their silence lulled me into believing that "all is well."

I was glad to see the acknowledgment of the military and civilian nurses who were not in combat zones, but in stateside military hospitals. Faced with the unrelenting presence of returning injured warriors, these nurses provided a safe haven away from war and expert care, often within days of an injury. With little recognition they also selflessly kept long work hours with determination, skill, and grace so that these warriors could recover in body and spirit. The acknowledgment of the burdens that these nurses worked under brings to light a caregiver who is so often ignored and forgotten when warriors return home. Our pride for their contributions is no less than our pride for those nurses privileged to care for warriors on the battlefield.

Though the "Angel Walk" in the title of this book refers to our fallen warriors and the "movement of the escorted casket between the lines of soldiers saluting their flag-draped casket" on the flight home to their families, I took the liberty to give it an additional definition for purposes of my final comments. After reading this book I also look upon the Angel Walk as the path our military nurses take when they answer the call to care for the wounded and dying in combat. Their journey is not a final one, but one fraught with danger. Yet they overcome their fears and ensure that no comrade in arms will suffer or die alone.

Our nation can rest assured that when a decision is made to go to war, nurses will always be in the wings ready to take their own Angel Walk and go where needed to provide compassionate and expert care for our warriors. This book is a stark reminder that there must be helping hands along that walk so that these "Angels" can stay on path and are not wasted on the wayside with frayed wings, unable to fly in the future.

Lastly, mea culpa to our colleagues who returned from war zones unwilling or unable to share their experiences and to those who did not receive the help they needed. Let this book be the igniter to sensitize those of us who did not share those experiences. I urge them to utilize the resources and guidelines provided in this book to mend the wings of their colleagues who took the Angel Walk. Surely future nurses who take their own Angel Walk will be eternally grateful for the recognition of their own special needs and the insight this book can give them to persevere in a combat zone.

Dorothy B. Pocklington, BSN, MSN, FAAN
Brigadier General, U.S. Army, *Retired*

Editor of *Heritage of Leadership: Army Nurse Corps Biographies*

PREFACE

"Sometimes we'd have soldiers in the hallway crying and breaking
down at the loss of one of their friends. We would have a little
service to honor him, then go to the morgue and let them say their
good-byes to give them some kind of closure. Then we always had
our Angel Flights to say the final good-bye. Everyone would stand
along the road leading to the heliport. When the helicopter landed,
they'd bring the body in the body bag to the helicopter. We'd all
stand there with the wind of the helicopter blowing, trying to stand
up straight and salute. Sometimes we had a hundred people at a
heliport saluting, saying good-bye to the soldier. . . I always thought,
'What a heartfelt way to say good-bye.' You could see all the love
that we had for our fellow soldiers when you just glanced around
and saw the tears on their faces and the hugs. We actually do love
our soldiers—every one is your brother or your sister."
—CPT Nichole, Army Nurse, Iraq

This book is filled with heartwarming and heart-wrenching stories of active-duty
Army Nurse Corps (ANC) officers who have returned from overseas duty caring
for their "wounded warriors." Their battlegrounds were the bloody emergency
rooms, busy operating rooms, detainee camps, civilian casualty wards, and the
helicopters that evacuated critically wounded patients. These Army nurses served
overseas in Vietnam, Iraq, and Afghanistan and then returned home to continue
caring for wounded warriors in military, veteran, and civilian hospitals. All but two
of the Iraq/Afghanistan nurses interviewed are still serving on active duty or in the
reserves. Few of these nurses have discussed the details of their deployments with
anyone who has not served in a war zone. When asked why, they could not answer
except to say, "They would not understand."

As Dr. Sharon interviewed more and more nurses and shared some of their stories in workshops and in her Army Nurse Corps Association (ANCA) column "Lean on Me," she began to receive responses of gratitude for helping them to tell their story, enlightenment from those who had not served, and remembered pride for the extraordinary work they had accomplished. The ANC volunteers who shared their stories included men and women, young and old. A diverse group of Caucasian, Black, Hispanic, Asian, and Islanders talk about their unifying experiences of serving with America's finest veterans. Over time, she also heard from soldiers and family members who wanted to know more about warrior-patient care and the Army nurses who provide gold standard, evidenced-based care under the most trying circumstances.

It is our intention to provide a look at, and contrast the experiences of, Army nurses who served forty years apart: during the sixties in Vietnam, and those who have served in Iraq and Afghanistan. We will explore in detail the daily patient workload caring for injured soldiers, insurgents, civilian bystanders, and innocent children, and the day-to-day personal activities of these nurses. How did they relieve the stress on that precious one day off, and maintain the critical connections with their family and friends? The fierce camaraderie and unconditional love they shared with one another is a little-known reward for those serving in the Army Nurse Corps. Of utmost importance to most of these dedicated soldiers is the spiritual nourishment that lifted them up and supported them on a daily basis.

For those who have served on active duty as an Army nurse and have not yet deployed to a battlefield, these stories will help you to learn and appreciate what many of your colleagues have experienced. If you have deployed and have not yet shared your story, we hope that you will be comforted by some of the shared experiences and learn new coping mechanisms. If you are a wounded warrior or the family member of one, be encouraged, knowing that the ultimate level of care, expertise, love, and concern will be experienced under the care of an Army nurse.

For the rest of the civilian world out there we want you to know that you could meet one of these "Angels of the Battlefield" today in your church, at a school board meeting, or while shopping for groceries. If you do, we want you to have a better understanding of who they are, what they have endured, how they have coped, and how they are now thriving. We want you to be enlightened, humbled, awed, and appreciative of our "forever family," the extraordinary men and women of the Army Nurse Corps.

PROLOGUE—
THE PROFESSOR

Sharon Richie-Melvan and I have been friends since 1982 when we served as the first ever nurse White House Fellows since the program's establishment in 1964. We started talking about this book several years ago. It was not our first collaboration; we wrote an article together during our time in Washington, D.C. I wanted to work on the book with Dr. Sharon because my generation of nurses had never truly reconciled the events of the Vietnam War and the terrible struggles of the nurses and warrior vets after serving in Vietnam. In 1967 I received my bachelor's degree in nursing and was then eligible to volunteer for military service but I was in love and wanted to marry instead. The Vietnam protests were not only aimed at the policy makers but also at the returning nurses and warriors. My brother had just returned from a year in the Army in Vietnam as a forward observer and aerial observer. These were the people who called in fire on enemy troops. He talked very little about the war or his experiences until one Christmas Eve when my other brother and he had a heated discussion about the war that ended up with my mother in tears and my brothers agreeing not to talk again about the war.

I had friends who were drafted and returned as very damaged people. One friend was totally disillusioned by the experience and ended up in activities that required him to disappear. One day years later he called to tell me that he would never be in touch with me again and that I should not try to find him. Several years later I called his mother who told me that she did not know where he was. My husband was about to be drafted; he joined the Navy pilot program at a time when they were losing so many pilots over Vietnam that they were continually extending their duty. At that time it was a six-year commitment. Because he had physical problems at high altitudes, he ended up on board a ship as an enlisted man for most of the first two years of our marriage, cruising off the coast of Vietnam.

These experiences inspired me to contribute to this book, from the perspective of how people can help, including educators like me, who are preparing military nurses who will likely end up in these war zones, and the civilian nurses and other health care providers who may care for these emotionally and physically wounded warriors at home in the United States.

The meaning of this book's title, *Angel Walk*, is twofold. First, military nurses have long been called angels—by wounded warriors. And second, the remains of a United States soldier from Iraq and Afghanistan are also called angels; the procession of the escorted casket between the lines of soldiers saluting the flag-draped casket on its way to an angel flight to be returned to their families in the United States is called the "Angel Walk." The honored walk is often arranged by military nurses as the final, emotional salute of gratitude to the heroic soldier. If possible, the walk is accompanied by the emotionally wrenching sounds of bagpipes. We want to honor both these angel nurses and the fallen angel warriors with this book.

We hope you find this book compelling—in fact compelling you to action on behalf of these health care champions and our warrior heroes.

PROLOGUE—
THE OFFICER

I cared for my first soldier at the age of five. It didn't matter that my patient was my brother and we were under a pup tent in the midst of a fierce cowboy and Indian war in the bowels of Tasker Street Government Housing Projects in South Philly. He was injured and I was determined to bandage his wounds with the supplies from my very own nurse's kit. For as long as I could remember I knew I was destined to be a nurse.

My five-year-old mind knew that the only way to become a nurse was to buy one of those ninety-nine-cent nurse's kits. It might as well have been one million dollars since I didn't have the money and my mom and dad certainly didn't have it. I was one of seven sisters and brothers and we lived on my dad's ninety-nine-dollar-per-week salary. It was just enough to pay for the bills and spend twenty-five dollars each week for groceries at the outdoor Italian food stalls on 9th Street. I spent each weekend as the "only child" of my godmother, Aunt Mae, and godfather, Uncle Ernie. I discussed my problem with her, and she suggested that I earn the money shining the shoes of her residential boarders. I did, and thus a battle-tested Army nurse was born.

Fast-forward to the end of my sophomore year at Wagner College. I was faced with having to drop out because my school funding package of scholarships, grants, work-study, and loans was to be cut by 10 percent. Again, it could have been a million because I didn't have another penny and I couldn't work any more part-time hours without jeopardizing my grade point average (GPA). My deal of a lifetime arrived that afternoon in the form of an Army Nurse Corps recruiter who offered me money to pay for tuition, books, fees, room and board, and a monthly stipend that allowed me to quit working part-time. All of this was in exchange for a three-year, active-duty commitment. Additionally, my active duty time would also decrease my student loans by one-half for each year served. I only asked, "Where do I sign?"

I met my first soldiers, wounded Vietnam veterans, during a student nurse clinical rotation at a veterans hospital in New York. I was interested in their wounds. They were awed that I was already a second lieutenant and hadn't yet been to basic training; that I was a black officer; and that I was going to be their nurse for the day. One fellow said, "In all of my time in 'Nam, I never saw a black officer. I just want to shake your hand." The other soldier told me how the Army nurses had cared for him in Vietnam and that he thought that they were the best nurses in the world. Their comments gave me pause for two reasons: first, I'd never thought about the racial composition of the officers in the armed forces and second, I'd never felt so appreciated in my life. Nursing took on another dimension that grew as I acclimated to military life.

There was some trepidation and fear of the unknown as I headed off to basic training. But, within one week of studying, dancing, saluting, marching, and meeting great folks from around the country, I was sold and tried to sign up for the "twenty-year plan." The personnel officer told me there was no such thing, but I was undaunted. I loved nursing, I loved the Army, and I was going to be the best psychiatric nurse they'd ever seen. I also was prepared to go to Vietnam, but as it turned out, the soldiers returned to the United States one month before my report date to Vietnam. I never got to serve in Vietnam and my fellow nurses seemed reluctant to talk about their time over there. Their deafening silence was broken by occasional jokes or a passing reference to pictures in a footlocker . . . "I'll show them to you one day."

They never did show me the photos. The closest that I came to field nursing was during a six-week training exercise in Texas called "Border Star '85," when some Canadian troops flew into the side of the mountain range. I heard nonstop French broken by English cuss words as we set broken bones and admitted thirty-two solders to the 8th EVAC hospital within a four-hour time period. As the chief nurse, I was proud of the nurses who worked quickly and efficiently throughout the next forty-eight hours. I wondered what would have been different had it been forty-eight days instead of forty-eight hours. What would have been different had it been a real combat zone and not a Texas suburb?

With the backing of the U.S. Army War College, the Military History Institute, and the Army Nurse Corps, I found the answers to some of those questions in 1986 by interviewing active duty Army nurses who had served in Vietnam. Later, I followed up that study with other studies in which I interviewed physicians and medics who had also served in Vietnam. I learned of their fears, hopes, and dreams; their clinical workloads, living conditions, and exposure to violence and most important, their camaraderie and love for their patients and one another. I was able to share this information in workshops, and consoled myself with the thought that maybe I didn't go to Vietnam because one of my life missions was to be an oral historian and to teach about the experiences of others. This thought held me for a while, but deep inside I knew it wasn't enough. I wanted to apply this knowledge and actually serve in a combat zone.

At the start of the first Gulf War, I was a colonel and the chief nurse of Letterman Army Medical Center at the Presidio in San Francisco, California. I thought to myself, "This is my last chance to finally be deployed and serve in a combat zone." I called the Chief of the Army Nurse Corps, Brigadier General Clara Adams-Ender, and *begged* to be selected to go. She said, "No. No sitting chief nurse would be deployed." Instead, she deployed most of my active duty nurses and back-filled Letterman with reserve nurses from across the country. She felt strongly that each sitting chief nurse needed to remain in place to ensure the stability of stateside medical centers with the influx of new staff and the departure of the deploying nurses.

I was sorely disappointed by her response, but I was comforted by the knowledge that my best friend had been recalled to active duty and she would be assigned to work with me at Letterman. I had met Tina during the first few months that I was on active duty. Over the next twenty years we were either stationed at the same place or trailed one another across the country and to Germany and back. We were "forever friends and family," as we supported each other through life's challenges and celebrations. Tina retired from the Nurse Corps only to enroll in the seminary and become a Unity minister. She was in the midst of her seminary training when she was recalled during the first Gulf War for one year of active duty service. Not surprising, LTC (almost a reverend) Tina Dixon-Bartlett turned out to be a blessing to me and the other "slick-sleeved nurses" left stateside.

I didn't fully appreciate the meaning of "slick-sleeves" until fifteen years later when I met a few disappointed, exhausted, and demoralized active duty nurses who had not yet deployed to Iraq. They somehow thought that others believed that they were "less than . . ." those who had already been deployed. The "slick sleeves" did not have the concrete evidence—that badge of honor sewn onto their uniform sleeve that automatically conveyed to the world that you were brave, dedicated, loyal, and skilled. It didn't matter that the "slick sleeves" *also* were brave, dedicated, loyal, skilled, and cared for the same patients sometimes within twenty-four hours of their leaving Iraq.

For a few, I saw the hidden pain and unwarranted shame of being "slick sleeved." However, for most of the others left behind, including the civilian nurses, and for the returning "warrior" nurses, I saw the visible exhaustion and emotional numbness that came from caring for multiple severely wounded patients. I realized then that perhaps another personal life mission was for me to teach and counsel people about how to armor up against compassion fatigue and how to develop battle plans for better time management.

Now, twelve years after retiring from what I considered the best job in the world, a U.S. Army Chief Nurse, I still get to meet with active duty nurses around the world. I conduct oral histories about their experiences working in Iraq and Afghanistan, write a column entitled "Lean on Me," teach workshops, and serve on national nonprofit boards, which champion soldiers, nurses, veterans, and their families. I am privileged to be their confidant, coach, cheerleader, comforter, scribe, and self-proclaimed "Forever Global Chief Nurse."

This book is my attempt to share these stories, highlight the lessons learned, console the isolated, heal some invisible wounds, and celebrate the triumphs of more than thirty-seven Army nurses (about one-third males and one-third persons of color) who served during the Vietnam, Iraq, and Afghanistan wars. It is my hope that it will enlighten their friends and family members, who are still asking, "What happened?"

Each nurse volunteered to share their experiences. Some might call this a convenience sample. I prefer to think of each person as having kept a divine appointment in their desire to help others. I honor their thoughts and recognize that their memories are unique and may not be shared by others who served alongside them. Given that these nurses are still serving on active duty or in a reserve unit, and in an effort to preserve their privacy, I have changed their names and given each a pseudonym.

Ultimately, I pray that this book will give insight and comfort to the families of our soldiers. Whether you are a wife, husband, child, mother, father, sister, brother, aunt, uncle, or distant cousin, know that your loved one received the "gold standard of care" and that they were touched by the hands of caring, compassionate, and supremely competent Army nurses. If your soldier made the ultimate sacrifice, know that in the end they were not alone and that each received a heartfelt last salute as they made their final "Angel Walk."

VIETNAM...
ECHOES FROM THE PAST

"...I would tell them about some of the funny things that
happened. And for most of those people that was enough because
they didn't know enough to ask me anything else... I could get
away with that, but I never told them about the rest of it."
—Lieutenant Colonel Helen, AN, November 1987

"Those people" to whom LTC Helen referred were anyone who had *never* deployed to a combat zone. In 1987 that included 4,150 Army Nurse Corps (ANC) officers, family members, friends, and many community leaders back in the "world." This section about the combat nurse's experience in Vietnam provides "the rest of it" through the voices of seven Army nurses as they describe their professional challenges and successes, personal disappointments and delights, and lessons learned during their year deployed overseas. Two of the greatest challenges noted by each nurse during their year in Vietnam were dealing with the periodic overwhelming number of critically wounded patients admitted at one time and coping with the Spartan living conditions.

IN COUNTRY WORKLOAD AND LIVING

"The workload was the biggest stress. Clinically I felt confident." LTC Nadia had already been to Vietnam. This time she was serving her second tour in Japan. "I was only twenty-five years old when I went to be head nurse [of] a 208-bed building with four wards. . . . I had twelve nurses to cover three shifts a day until we went to twelve-hour shifts. . . . We got casualties right out of the field . . . there was a horrendous . . . movement of patients in and out [trying to get the stabilized patients back to definitive care in the states]. I can remember trying to move eighty-five patients out of that building [in] one day . . . [and] we would easily have fifteen to twenty to prepare to go to surgery the next day. That was the average. . . .

"I had not been in Japan long when the Tet Offensive of 1968 happened . . . we actually opened up another building overnight and in twelve hours, another 120 beds were set up. . . . It was volume—that was the big thing—the volume that we were trying to get a handle on."

LTC Nadia was an experienced trooper for that second tour. For the others, it was a twenty-four-hour adjustment to a new and frightening world. LTC Helen explained: "The door opened and this young captain in full combat gear and two or three troops got on the plane. They explained that they were taking ground fire and the plane would not be shutting down its engines. They would be taking off soon and we were expected to literally run from the airfield into this little covered hut."

LTC Elaine received the same introduction and described it as culture shock. "They deplaned us in a rapid fashion and we had to run across the tarmac in our high heels and our class-A uniforms, with a guy on either side trying to hasten our speed. I don't recall being frightened. I was probably in culture shock."

LTC Helen was more specific: "Particularly when you first get there, you think about how you would define yourself. It's how anyone would define themselves. It's where they work, what they wear, what they do, and what they own. But, when you first get in country all of that is gone—you don't have a place—you don't have a real job. You don't have any of the clothes or things you faintly remembered. It was like starting new. You have to have a pretty good grip on who you are, even if it changes."

Assignments were made once the nurses arrived in country, but it usually took a few days. Most found themselves guests of the 90th Replacement Battalion in Bien Hoa. COL Glenda, a major in 1967, described her first few days in country: "It was terrible. It was crowded. It was hot. I think I had about three hours sleep and one full meal in those three days with nothing to do except wait. Mostly it was spent trying to occupy one's time gainfully is the midst of having absolutely nothing to do except wait. "Some of the worst times were getting to the latrine in the dark. There were no lights. There were a lot of fire at night, a very narrow pathway, and people were falling off the pathway and getting hurt. It was a dirty latrine. I guess with so many people there wasn't a lot of cleaning being done. All in all, I looked at it later on as being very positive. It was very good psychologically because after that, you were so glad to get out of the 90th Replacement Depot that anything would look good."

COL Patti might not have agreed with that assessment while she was a captain in Vietnam and was reassigned to different quarters after having only been in country for two weeks. She was moved from a "civilized" apartment complex at

Qui Nhon to an old wooden hootch (a small building or large tent with beds that served as their living quarters) in Chu Lai. She explained: "I shared it with nine nurses. We had beds or bunks; just odds and ends. That was it. That was what a hootch consisted of. Later on in the tour, they were able to give us a metal locker, but you had to put them together yourself . . .

"We had to go out because you had no indoor plumbing at Chu Lai. We had no bathroom. We walked down quite a distance from our hootch and they had these three- or four-hole community bathrooms in there. . . They were actually outdoor toilets. Across the way, we had a shower. The shower consisted of a showerhead hanging up there and you pulled this chain and the water came out of the tank on the top of it. If the sun was shining, you had warm water. If the sun didn't shine like during the rainy season, you had your cold showers." Captain Patti accepted an offer to move to different quarters (military housing) for a very important reason: "I moved there for one month just before my PCS (permanent change of station) because I was able to go to the bathroom and flush the commode."

Housed in the servant quarters for Madame Nhu's old summer villa in Qui Nhon, LTC Nadia had the luxury of indoor facilities for her first two weeks in country: "There was one bathroom between two rooms so there were about four-to-eight to a bathroom. That was the most interesting experience. They said never lock the bathroom door . . . 'one in the shower, one on the pot, and one at the sink.' That's the way we lived."

Living also included sustaining oneself with food. For LTC Nadia, it was the high point of her ship voyage to Vietnam: "There was a lot of 'down' time. We lived for meals. We lived to go to breakfast; we lived to go to lunch; and we lived to go to dinner. There wasn't a lot to do on the ship because it was so packed."

Mealtimes proved to be more difficult once she was on shore. After the two-week stint in the servant quarters with mess hall privileges, LTC Nadia moved to a tent eight miles out of Qui Nhon. She described her first attempt to return to the mess hall: "We went back one day and this captain who was in charge of the compound came up to us and said, 'Ladies you can eat here this time, but don't come back.' As I think about it, I guess that was the closest I ever came to picking up my plate and throwing it in somebody's face. That was my first reaction, but then I calmed down . . . I know that there were problems with getting food and we'd go in town and eat at the mess hall because it obviously had better food than the B-rations or whatever it was that we had out in the 'The Valley.'"

The Spartan living conditions at the reception station and in their quarters at their base hospitals were deemed as little more than inconveniences or hassles easily handled. That was not the case with incoming mortar rounds.

INCOMING ROUNDS, CAMARADERIE, AND CASUALTIES

LTC Helen's first look at security came at the Long Binh reception station: "They explained that since I was a female, I would get to stay in one of the trailers. In front of the trailer was a six-foot-high stockade fence with a guard shack in front. I can remember saying to myself, 'Well, this is more like it. I feel a little better.' The problem was that when you opened the guarded stockade fence and went around to the back of the fence, it was not finished."

She said, "The little fellow explained to me that they would get around to finishing it—if they weren't too busy. I wasn't quite sure about this because in our first briefing someone explained to us that the local Viet Cong command had been given permission to take the post if they could."

LTC Helen did not take any hits at Long Binh, but LTC Elaine did at Cu Chi. She described it as one of her most frightening experiences. "During that night we took over 120 rounds into the hospital compound and the entire base camp of the 25th Infantry. There was a huge fire over to the north of us. Having been there before, some of the other nurses looked to me for direction. In my strongest voice I said, 'Don't worry about it. They won't let anything happen to us. If they overrun us, they'll land the Chinooks in the middle of the compound and take the nurses and the most seriously injured patients out.' What I didn't know was that the large fire on the other side of the base camp was the Chinooks—all ten of them."

She went on to describe the scene: "Sappers had taken [us] out by cutting through the wire. In fact, the Viet Cong had overrun our perimeter [in] several places. Many of the men with injuries that night were shot in the back going in to support the bunkers. [But] the Viet Cong had [already] taken the bunkers. . . I think that's the first night I really thought that I could have gotten injured by one of those rounds, when it whistled overhead. . . . Rockets are a rather impersonal thing; you figure that if they get you, they don't have your name on it. If you get hit by a piece of shrapnel, it was just your time. It was just when small arms fire began to come into camp now and then, that you felt, 'WOW!' That's real personal because they're aiming at *you*."

Needless to say, security of the area was crucial and one important part of that was the bunker. But that did not mean that the nurses liked them. COL Patti described her feelings: "What I hated most was going into the bunkers. I didn't know how safe the bunkers would be. They were sanded up; they had rats in them and the banks had holes in them. You clumped a whole group of maybe fourteen nurses in a bunker. That is where my friend got into problems because she had a phobia. She would not go into the bunkers. She was reprimanded and they were going to give her an Article 15 (military punishment that goes on your permanent personnel record) for not going into the bunker. Maybe it was her life if she chose to die out in the open."

COL Patti still questions the relative safety of the bunker: "How many of the mass group would be hit in comparison to staying out and maybe only one or two people would be hit? It seemed like bunker life was an every night drill for us, but it was not a drill. There were actual mortar rounds coming in. There was a time when we would have to hit the bunkers almost every night. Then, after the bunker routine, we would have to take care of the casualties."

Danger was not just for nights in the hospital compound. LTC Isaac served on a thoracic team during 1968 and frequently went on medical missions to the field. He was grateful for the bunkers the day the coordinates were switched. "They were dropping them on us instead of putting them where they were supposed to . . . That was probably the worst experience for me because there were probably four or five Vietnamese in that bunker . . . that was the only place that could protect you from . . . this stuff coming in."

LTC Elaine also flew to neighboring villages for medical assistance visits. On her second tour in Vietnam, she noted: "It was a very strange sense of foreboding every time we would go out. I felt a lack of security that I had not felt on the first tour. When I went to a Cu Chi subsector village, if the kids weren't waiting around the MEDCAP Building, we would do a rapid turnaround and get right back to post because that was indicative that the Viet Cong were around somewhere. If we stayed there, we would have put ourselves in jeopardy." Were their different reactions due to the different threats or were their different reactions because of a different perception of the same threat? COL Glenda has wondered about that over the years: "I'm not sure, but I think that I perceived a much less personalized response to danger by the females than the males. When we would be going on these MEDCAPS, on helicopters to these odd places out in the hills, one of the first things the men did getting ready to go, was to get themselves a personal weapon. That was never the first reaction of the females. They were annoyed when they had to get into their helmet and flak jacket and get into the bunker. But, there was never a sense of impending doom or feeling expressed that the world was going to fall apart because I'm over here. They seemed to be other-directed, in those instances; much more other-directed than the men."

When asked to speculate on the "why" of what she perceived, COL Glenda first thought of external factors, like the fact that most of the male nurses were married and had children to worry about. Focusing directly on the situation she continued: "If anything happened, it might be because they saw themselves as the one who would have to carry the weapons and fight to the last barrier . . . It might have been something they were brought up to expect in themselves, that made them look at all of this very differently."

It may never be known whether there was a difference between males and females because of their gender, but there was certainly a difference over time for LTC Nadia. Stationed at the 83rd EVAC as a lieutenant, she noted: "Our hospital was moved because of the threat. We were about eight miles out of Qui Nhon and General Westmoreland came to see us and did not like our security. They had not put up bunkers and we were only 300 yards from VC Village. Of course, you have to realize that this was very early in the war [fall 1965]. "They built bunkers and things like that and a couple of weeks later, Westmoreland came back. He said it was still not secure enough, so he made an engineer unit in town give up their space. They were to move out there and we were to move back into town . . . Seventy-two hours after we left our location in 'The Valley,' it was hit by a mortar round.

"They say that we probably would have easily lost 70 percent of our physicians and males nurse because it hit right where their tents sat. Later, a MACV advisor told me that he was just amazed that we were never attacked. He never wanted to tell me while we were out there, but he felt the VC did not have the ammunition to waste on us and that was the only reason we were not hit . . . I can honestly say that at twenty-four, I came to grips with my own death. I think that I realized that I was not indestructible. You usually come to that realization as people your own age die. That's how I have thought about life ever since so I enjoy every day for what it's worth, because that may be all you have."

And what did they have day after day in the way of support? The bottom line was each other. COL Glenda called it, "the cohesiveness of the group." Everyone in her unit had come from the same stateside hospital to help establish the 91st EVAC in Vietnam. As a head nurse, she worked hard to ensure that the ties established in the states continued in Vietnam. She recalled: "We got over there early enough to help with painting the wards, putting in the wiring, opening conexes (large storage and moving boxes for equipment and supplies), putting the furniture out. . . . I think that strengthened the ties between the enlisted personnel and the nurses."

Teamwork, camaraderie, cohesiveness—words used over and over again by the nurses. They are descriptive of a positive working relationship but there was more. LTC Helen explained: "Whatever was happening somewhere else, it didn't matter. I was very aware of that when they sent me the hometown paper. Initially, I got it and read it all. Then it would come and it would sit for days and days and days, but I never opened it and finally threw it away. When I really thought about it, it was because nothing in there had any importance to me. It didn't relate to me at all.

The people I cared about, the people who meant the most to me, everything, my whole life was right there."

COL Helen was talking about more than the professional relationship that we now share with our hospital colleagues. She was talking about a family that supported one another.

Support went across that chain of command with peers and it also went down the chain. Sometimes the support needed was lighthearted, like finding a home for a horse before the hospital commander learned of the new mascot. At other times the support needed was more in the form of protection. Senior nurses stepped in to help subordinates with everything from unwanted sexual advances from senior officers to unwanted party invitations after a twelve-hour shift.

As a head nurse, MAJ Glenda frequently met with her younger nurses to discuss their problems. She had expected and prepared for the physical and emotional demands of patient care. Not expected was the responsibility for the emotional health of her charges. Now a colonel, Glenda remembers this as the most demanding part of her year: "I was just trying to support them, trying to keep them out of mischief, and trying to help them get to where they wanted to go. Probably also intervening between them and the administrative staff. They were young and had a lot of energy and the administrative staff was a little bit older. They didn't always understand that, or if they did, they really didn't do too good a job of explaining to us why certain things needed to be the way they said they needed to be."

Support also crossed hospital department lines and military service lines. COL Elaine used the word "cherish" to describe her feelings about her most vivid memory of Vietnam: "The teamwork and camaraderie that came with all the staff in the facility and in the EVAC hospital. That extended out into the helicopter unit, the dust-off unit that was attached to the hospital and the other line units around us. It gave you a genuine respect for one another and it really made the whole tour of duty, the whole experience, not only tolerable, but enjoyable. Not in the task we had to do, but in the *pride* we felt in doing it. It was what we went there to do, and that was to take care of our troops."

Not everyone found the close relationships experienced by Glenda and Elaine. LTC Nadia faced officers who "objected to our being there. One officer explained to me that it was better to fight a war without women around. However, some time later he told me that a friend of his had been injured and had survived because of the nurses and that changed his attitude."

LTC Charles described another problem: "People who operated under a kind of martial law, a biggest-man-on-Bunker-Hill concept. It was everything for themselves. They didn't care about the group as a whole, or your personal problems. You could be hurting very much inside. It made me cry." And cry he did. Not because of the humiliation of receiving a public tongue-lashing from a physician, but because of the frustration that came with working with an insensitive man who showed little respect for other people.

Eventually LTC Charles stood back and reassessed the situation: "I sort of forgave him. It was helpful to me too. You can't go around being upset all the time. You have to keep going, keep on living."

And what was daily living for these Vietnam nurses? COL Glenda summed it up: "It was either very intense pushes with a lot of casualties coming in, or a lot of people with very acute medical conditions."

COL Glenda's hospital was enlarged to 400 beds and designated a Civilian War Casualty Program (CWCP) hospital. She described their patient workload and the staff's response: "Sometimes during the year we took in more civilians in the hospital than we did military casualties." When asked if this caused a problem for the nurses assigned to Vietnamese patients, the response varied depending on the nurse and their assignment.

COL Glenda spoke for the staff in her medical intensive care unit: "We were too busy to be worried about those kinds of things." LTC Elaine found the situation more difficult when she was in the ER (emergency room) and two badly wounded troops from the Americal Division were brought in: "The Viet Cong came up on them and gouged their eyes out with bamboo sticks. The screams of these young men as they lay in the emergency room seemed to penetrate the whole base. Anger then came through. Not just the frustration and helplessness, but anger and it was frightening. I found myself having to watch the troops, the doctors, and myself when the Vietnamese came in so that we wouldn't do things we would be sorry for later."

She went on to describe a confrontation with an American soldier. "He wanted to know why . . . we would rush as much for the Vietnamese as we did for our own troops. And the response I gave him was that once they came to the emergency room, once they got to our door, our professional commitment said that we had to care for them, and that we would care for them as best we could. If they didn't want that or they didn't expect that, then they need not come to our door."

That was true for COL Glenda but COL Patti described a different response: "We had a little animosity feeling on everybody's part. We got kind of worn out a little bit whenever we took care of the enemy. The Viet Cong—we did what was acceptable medicine for them, but it was not done with the vim and vigor or the ambition that they had for the other troops."

Even for the American patients, acceptable nursing care was difficult at times in the face of minimal supplies and the most basic equipment. In nursing school, COL Nadia had been taught to give injections with a disposable needle, preferably one that was as small as possible to minimize the pain. She soon found that the rules had changed in Vietnam: "We would have four or five needles that we would rush back to CMS, Central Material Service, to re-sterilize. Sometimes [all we had] was a 16-gauge [big] needle to give the IM [intramuscular] shot."

The supply problem was not much different for medications. For LTC Nadia's first three months in country, the overall drug supply level was inadequate. She had to ration out antibiotics because of time constraints in administering the medicine. "We were giving massive doses of antibiotics, particularly penicillin, and I remember mixing little 100,000 unit bottles of penicillin. We wanted to give each patient two to four million units and still your were doing everything else [other patient care]. We would say, 'Well this guy's wounds don't look too bad, we will give him one million.' We had to do this because we couldn't keep up with trying to mix all of those bottles for so many patients four times a day."

The supply problem eased after those first three months, but COL Nadia's concern about one's ability to improvise in such situations has stayed with her, her entire career. She fears that the disposable world of today will not allow the fulfillment of COL Glenda's tenet: "Know how to make do." Thankfully LTC Elaine had three years of civilian nursing experience under her belt when she reported for duty in Vietnam and was expected to improvise and "make do" immediately.

Just out of basic training, LTC Elaine described her first night of duty and initiation to military nursing: "I worked on a ward that contained eighty-eight patients and we were on twelve-hour shifts. I reported to duty that first night to find myself the only nurse on duty with three corpsmen. The orientation that I got was by the good graces of the night nurse, who donated four hours of her time to show me the paperwork and tell me what was expected of me as the only nurse on the floor."

Those were the routine days, but what happened during a push with multiple casualties? What happened during the biggest push of all, the Tet Offensive when the Viet Cong overran the city in January 1968? Exposure to violence took on a very personal meaning.

LTC Isaac had only been in country one week when he wandered into the operating room on his day off. "When I got in there they were working on a guy who had arrested a couple of times. They were thumping on his chest about the third time when somebody leaned in the door and said, 'They've just hit the embassy.' Everybody said, 'Yeah, right.' 'No,' he said. 'Forget this case, we have plenty more to go.' The marathon started at that point."

Isaac had been taught how to triage patients in basic training—you categorize the patients by the severity of their wounds. He found that learning and doing were not the same. "It just *wasn't working*, so for the first couple of days we took all of them. We were doing cases that should not have been done. Nobody had been through that kind of an experience before. It took a lot to get adjusted to it.

"I had worked in a south Philadelphia hospital and the most I had ever seen were two or three shooting victims at one time. There, it was just people everywhere.

"We had a piece of butcher-block paper that ran the whole width of the triage area, with names of people waiting to go to surgery. I think finally the reality sunk in. The Chief of Anesthesia started to do some of the triage and tell the people that there was no way we could work on all of them, even though in a normal situation, the expectants (those with injuries so severe that they are not expected to live without extraordinary efforts) possibly could have been saved. But, we didn't have the supplies, the manpower, or the operating room space to work on them. That was the cold fact that it came down to the second day of the offensive."

Isaac went on to describe his work for the next forty hours: "They wouldn't let us out of the OR. They'd bring food in for us to eat. We just worked until we were dead exhausted or we ran out of supplies." COL Patti also worked in the operating room and recalled the Tet Offensive: "We did something like twenty-two amputations in less than twelve hours, all Americans. They were multi-amputations of arms and legs on twenty-two different patients."

LTC Isaac lost track of his exact numbers, but vividly remembers the scene: "They brought in a deuce and a half that was full of bodies. The MPs went in to try to bring out a bunch of officers who were stuck in a BOQ [Bachelor Officer Quarters]. They got into the street and claymores were fired into the truck and they just towed it behind another truck with all of the bodies still in it. There were probably twelve or fourteen people just in the one load. Only a couple of them were dead—a lot were really hurt."

His normal patient census ran around 200, but he was told at that point that they had at least 500 patients in-house and over 600 bodies in the new OR building that had been turned into a morgue. With patients coming in hour after hour, day after day, relief was relative to the situation. LTC Isaac remembered: "We sort of got our break from the OR once in a while; we went outside to help in the triage area between cases. I think that was kind of a relief. Nobody intended it to be a relief. . . . We would go outside to see if it was either daylight or it was dark, just so we would know."

Environmental relief came in different forms and at different times. For the combat troops, sometimes it was being in the hospital. LTC Charles explained: "Some didn't want to go back to the combat zone. What I thought was a terrible place was heaven to some of them. [The hospital] was the best place they had seen during their entire experience." But, for the nurses something more was needed. For LTC Isaac, it was the orientation of a look out of an ER window. For COL Patti, it was the rejuvenation of a couple of hours sleep or a care package from home, shared with the staff. LTC Charles found solace with his oil paints and occasional Sunday outings.

A day off might mean the beach or it might mean another workday at the orphanage in the next town. LTC Elaine explained: "The first five months that I was working as a med-surg nurse, we had one day a week off. I donated most of my time. Actually I enjoyed most of my time off traveling from Long Binh, which was the large military post there, to Bien Hoa, which was the nearest village. At Bien Hoa there was an orphanage that was run by Vietnamese nuns. It was there that I spent most of my off-duty time. I worked both in the labor and delivery area of the hospital, which was connected to the orphanage, and the orphanage itself."

LTC Helen turned to her colleagues after work: "There was a time when you would get off work at 7 or 8 o'clock, go over and take a shower if you could because the VC used to blow up the pumps from the water station pretty regularly. Along about 7 o'clock you could find yourself with a head full of shampoo and no way to get it out. So, you learned quickly that you did that first or you were out of luck. Then you went to the club.

"We drank pretty heavily until 12 or 1 o'clock in the morning when they closed the place up and we all sang "God Bless America" and cried a bit. Then we got up the next morning and went to work. Most of the time we worked seven days straight; sometimes six when it was lighter. But it was usually twelve hours a day, seven days a week. Making out a time schedule was easy because everybody worked all week and nobody was off. We did do things together. We had parties and looked forward to R&R [rest and recreation—a vacation]."

Everyone is entitled to R&R right? Wrong! Approvals for R&Rs were given out on a priority basis. COL Glenda quickly learned the basic guidelines for hospital personnel: "The higher the rank, the less your priority. Since I was a major, I had less priority so I didn't get my R&R." That was what happened after her first request. She knew that R&R was not granted with less than thirty days remaining in country so she quickly processed a second request, which was also denied. A reprieve came later in the form for a command decision to reverse the previous disapprovals.

Finally COL Glenda joined the ranks of the vacationing few trying to get to Australia. The only female in the airport, she said that she was met by, "Two American males in civilian clothes who escorted me down the steps into the airport. We went though a couple of offices and out into a waiting area where we got an orientation on how to 'be good' on R&R. I never did figure that one out. Later on someone said it might have been because at that time, all the troops coming into Australia were being searched. I guess my escort was somebody's gesture to assist the lone female to make sure that she was not searched." COL Glenda returned after eight days of leave, for her last few weeks in country. Shortly after her return, the medical intensive care unit became a surgical intensive care unit, and the casualties kept coming.

Each nurse I spoke with expressed the pain and frustration of working on a soldier only to have him get well and return again the next week. The only thing worse was to have him come in the first time and *know* that he was going to die. It was LTC Isaac's most difficult experience: "Spending time with the expectants."

YOU'LL NEVER BE ALONE

Other members of the hospital staff shared LTC Isaac's feelings of helplessness. In the operating room COL Elaine looked on at the terror and frustration in the eyes of the physicians. "Because with all of this training they had and all the knowledge they had and all that we could give, we still couldn't give this man a chance."

LTC Isaac explained it further: "I think it was real hard for me to see somebody that could have been my brother, same age, not a whole lot younger than I was, that was talking to me and we knew that he was going to die. After it was all over, it was like that door shut, and you did something else. I never held still the whole time I was there. If I stopped, I would have to think and I just didn't want to think."

Isaac called this denial and said that it worked for a while, only to be replaced by anger and depression when he got home. Our interview in 1988 was some twenty years after Vietnam and he had never spoken about his experiences to anyone that had not been there.

The pain was very evident. When asked if he had visited the wall, the Vietnam Memorial, he didn't answer for a while as tears rolled down his cheeks: "I went down there about three years ago. My wife and I went down. It was real tough. I know some of the people on the wall. Most I don't remember. This is real hard."

The question was equally difficult for LTC Helen. Her tears started with the same question about visiting the wall. She had not been, and had no plans to go.

Helen's year in Vietnam had been a tough one. Also one she has never discussed: "I would tell them about some of the funny things that happened. And, for most of those people, that was enough because they didn't know enough to ask me anything else. I could get away with that, but I never told them about the rest of it."

She has carried the memory longer than the patient's life span of eighteen years, and it still hurts. LTC Helen explained, "He had been seen in the surgical hospital up country and had a severe abdominal wound. By the time we got him, he was really pretty sick but there was really very little we could do for him. All day he was very alert, calling for his mother. This boy was Catholic and I tried to get the chaplain, but couldn't reach him. He was down in the village. They were building an orphanage or whatever, which is all well and good, but we needed him then. We were calling all day for the chaplain and this kid was calling all day for his mother [tearful]. . . I had forgotten some of this, I'm sorry.

"Along about six o'clock that night he died. I stood there and wept. I can remember thinking that nobody else knew he died but me. Somewhere he had a mother and a sister or some family who were probably talking about him and expecting him home. There were lots of incidences like that but that one stayed in my mind the longest because there really wasn't anything I could do for him."

LTC Elaine recalled a nineteen-year-old who never made it to the operating room: "I remember trying to wrap his head so that his brains would not be lying on the litter. He looked up at me and said, 'Well, how does it look?' I had to tell him, 'It doesn't look good, but you won't be alone.' That really was all we had to offer him."

The phrase "you won't be alone" may well have been the only comfort that the then young lieutenant Elaine could offer her patient, but it was not an insignificant gift. It meant that someone else would be there to support you and see you through. She did this many times for the patients who came through the hospital, and once for her best friend: "She was a lieutenant. We had done a lot of MEDCAP visits together and had been invited to the Vietnamese Army's celebration for Tet in '67 as guests of honor. She became so ill she had to be air evaced out, but first we had to stabilize her for a while. She had severe headaches and they asked me to sit with her to try to identify whether or not she would be seizing. . . . I think that was probably the most emotionally draining time because it involved someone I knew. There were a couple of times when the married nurses at the hospital would have their husbands brought in. . . . Those things that involved us personally were the most draining."

When asked what sustained her through that ordeal, LTC Elaine sat forward in her chair with a smile on her face as she reflected: "It was the support from my chief nurse COL Kay [pseudonym]. COL Kay had had experience as an Army nurse in

World War II. Now looking back on her, she was my role model; a person that I emulate as an Army nurse to this day. She genuinely cared about her nurses. She calls us her girls even now even though we've all married and have children of our own. It was her genuine compassion for everyone and the fact that she was there and she understood. Not that she was soft on us. She expected us to do the best we could and we knew that the best we did would be good enough. Those things are what sustained us through all those periods."

COL Glenda had thirteen years of civilian nursing experience when she went to Vietnam and she knew the importance of a caring leader. When asked what advice she might give to nurses preparing to deploy she replied, "I'd want to talk to the older ones and tell them to really look out for the younger ones. They have an obligation to them, not only to provide nursing supervision, but they have an obligation to provide them with the support of one who is grooming an officer as well as a nurse.

"I was so fortunate with the people that I dealt with there. They opened themselves up. That might have been a function of maturity because many of them weren't just out of school and they helped each other. They cared for each other as much as they cared for the patients. They supported each other as much as they supported the patients."

COL Glenda and LTC Elaine both addressed the external support supplied by the chief nurse and/or other senior nurses. Social support from colleagues helped much of the time, but the nurses told me of another source of strength. LTC Charles looked internally: "You have to have a lot of inner strength. How an individual goes about having inner strength, each one has to decide for himself."

PRAYER ON THE BATTLEFIELD

LTC Charles explained further: "Spiritual strength is probably one of the most enduring strengths because the good Lord is always with you no matter where you are, even if there is no one else around who cares. He is always there.

"If a person doesn't know that, because they haven't been taught that, or they haven't lived in the right kind of growing up environment, then they might find themselves extremely lonely and very likely to give up if things are really down and bad."

Recalling her time on a critical care ward, LTC Nadia also highlighted the connection between spirituality and inner strength: "I am not a religious fanatic, but I have a deep faith in God. I would do everything in my power to help somebody survive and if they died, then that was beyond what I could control. I think that belief helped me survive losing patients. Some nurses got into problems emotionally because they believed they had made a mistake if the patient died. I never felt that way . . . I have no doubt that that helped me to survive."

LTC Elaine switched from being a Protestant during the war to the Catholic faith in 1979 and now calls herself a "Christian person." She summarized: "I feel like whether you're a Protestant or Catholic or even Jewish, that there is a religious and spiritual component to our being that you have to pay attention to. It is the essence of health care in providing for the whole person, both for the injuries and for the spirit."

Remember when LTC Elaine provided for the emotional and spiritual well-being of the nineteen-year-old troop who was not expected to live and she had to tell him, 'It doesn't look good but you won't be alone'? The soldier died with LTC Elaine by his side, and LTC Elaine lived on with God by her side.

She explained: "That was generally who I talked with when I was trying to find a meaning for the things that were happening. In the beginning, we might not know what it meant or why it was happening, but we will eventually find meaning and substance for the things that have happened to us.

"Being in Vietnam made me a better person; made me a better Christian. I don't embrace a corporate religion because I think that too often that's false. I think that religion comes from within the person. However they believe, and however they choose to demonstrate that belief."

Intrigued by the nurses' reference to spiritual support, I searched the literature and found a little known but very significant study entitled *The American Soldier: Combat and Its Aftermath* (1949).

In this case study, Samuel Stouffer (1949) surveyed more than 4,000 enlisted men in four divisions in the Pacific and Mediterranean theaters to find out what sustained those enlisted men in combat. Seventy percent of the men in the Pacific and 83 percent of the men in the Mediterranean theater said that "prayer helped a lot." That response was their first choice of the five available answers. For the officers charged with caring for the enlisted men in their command, prayer was the second choice after "Not letting the troops down." Stouffer also found that the amount of stress a soldier was subjected to during the war proved to be a significant factor in the use of prayer when he compared Infantry troops with those in other branches (Stouffer et al, 1949, p. 176).

He identified several factors that influenced the amount of stress experienced by the troops. In turn, these factors influenced how much prayer helped them. The more combat time, the more intense the combat, the more likely that the soldier said that prayer helped. Coinciding with that, Stouffer discovered that these men were more likely to have seen close friends become casualties, to have been strafed (fired upon) by their own planes, or to have been replacements and therefore more isolated in their unit (Stouffer et al, 1949, p. 183).

Comparing the experiences of the Vietnam nurses with the World War II troops, I found that they shared many of the same deployment circumstances noted above and in turn, factors of stress.

For the Vietnam nurses, the constant overwhelming workload along with the intense pushes with multiple patients arriving all at once spoke to the intensity and frequency of stress they faced on duty in the hospital. LTC Isaac is the only nurse who was strafed during his MEDCAP (Medical Assistance Program) visit. All of the nurses experienced the isolation, although not necessarily while serving in Vietnam. For many, the isolation came when they returned home.

TIME TO SAY GOOD-BYE

Before facing that isolation, they had to say good-bye. Most of them were prepared for the sadness that naturally accompanies loss and separation, but few anticipated the ambivalence. LTC Helen described her first confrontation with such feelings and the help she received from a Special Forces helicopter pilot: "The ambivalence was incredible. I wanted to go, but I didn't want to go. And when I thought about what I was afraid of, it was that I realized that I had changed a lot and I really wasn't sure how I was going to manage that. I was a very different person. There was no judgment as to whether it was better or worse—just different.

"I remember trying to explain that to him [the pilot]. Based on his experiences, since this was his second tour, he said, 'Helen, let me tell you something. When you get home, you are going to be very impatient with people, because they don't understand. They really can't understand what you are trying to tell them.' And he was absolutely right! Incredible as it may seem, I was impatient and became upset when they didn't understand. At the same time, it didn't matter to me whether they did or not. Those two emotions were there at the exact same time."

LTC Isaac's initial isolation ended on a hunting trip with his brother who had also been to Vietnam. "He saw something and fired. I just hit the deck, rolled, came up, and pointed the weapon at him. Then both of us sat down and talked about what it was like there." Isaac could not explain the unspoken agreement with this brother not to talk about Vietnam the previous year. But he did have thoughts about why he has never discussed the topic with those of us who have never been to Vietnam.

"You are probably the first person I have talked to that has *not* been to Vietnam. There is still a feeling that you wouldn't understand. There are some things that happened that were funny but there were different mores. They are not funny now. I look at in the context of today and it was kind of bizarre. If you weren't there you couldn't understand how things happened the way they did. I guess that is part of the reason why it is hard to talk to somebody else.

"My uncle was in Korea, at the parallel. After I came back he talked to me about it. He had never said anything about it before. He was kind of curious to find out what experiences I had, compared to what he had. I think that is kind of true for people who have been through a war, when you see the casualties of war. We saw it. Not because we saw the people get hit. We saw the wounds. We saw how destructive the war was. I think that is real hard to have somebody understand. Intellectually, I know you can understand it, but I have a hard time bringing that out, on a feeling level. This is a test for me."

BOTTLED UP INSIDE

LTC Isaac described the disconnect between knowing something intellectually and knowing it on a "feeling" level. His disconnect was with *other* people understanding his Vietnam experience. COL Helen experienced the same disconnect in understanding her *own* Vietnam experience. She explained: "When I first came home, I said it didn't really bother me. I had put this all out of my head. But then I went to the movie *Deliverance*. There was a scene in it where there was this body coming down the river and it has been going through rock and whatever, so the arms are out of joint. I was sitting in that movie and had to leave because it was instant *déjà vu*. I could remember being back in the emergency room in Vietnam.

"I went looking for something in this big ER room. There was a curtain in the back and I went to get something out of the cupboard. I pulled the curtain up and on the floor was a body. His one leg was disarticulated, so that when you looked at him one leg was down and one leg was back up over his head. I didn't know what I was looking at, at first. I got what I wanted and left and was down the road there doing things before I realized what I had seen. I just didn't have time to stop and think about it. I didn't think about it again until that night in the movies. And seeing that, it was instant, I couldn't stay. I had to leave. I couldn't even explain what the problem was."

Initially, LTC Elaine couldn't explain the problem either. Looking back, she now calls it denial and comments on how some members of the Army Nurse Corps have reacted to Vietnam: "They are refusing to admit that there is, or could be, or will ever be, an emotional component to their time in Vietnam."

LTC Elaine's own admission of that emotional component came years after her return from Vietnam. She had responded to a call from a stateside Army emergency room. "I got there rapidly, went into the room where the troop was, and saw him lying there. He had lost his right arm midway between his elbow and his shoulder and he had lost his face from just below his eyes to just above his chin. I had to turn quickly and lean against the wall outside because I nearly fainted. It was like a rote-type of behavior that took over and I just began to do the things that need to be done. That afternoon, when it was over and for a number of weeks thereafter, I was really depressed."

Elaine was caught short by another nurse's assessment that maybe her reaction was connected to Vietnam. It had been more than ten years and she thought she had adjusted well.

When she got to her next duty station, Elaine sought other Vietnam nurses. "We got together and realized that we needed to work some things out. In 1979 or 1980, we had a couple of meetings on our own and then the chaplains sort of adopted us and sponsored a weekend seminar. They brought in an outside facilitator and we did a lot of healing and sharing with one another.

"Some of the things that I remember today are things that I had not thought about or remembered since that meeting. I think that we've made a better transition from all that we went through."

LTC Elaine went on to speculate about the difference in adjustment between those that remained in the military and those that went back to civilian life. "We who stayed on active duty continued to retain the purpose for doing what we did. The folks that got out of the Army were on their own. They had to identify within themselves, why they did what they did. Maybe they overidentified with the people yelling 'baby killers' and internalized a whole lot of guilt that really didn't belong to them.

"I think there are a lot of women out there, whether they're using denial or sublimation or whatever they could benefit by recognizing that they are not alone in the feelings that they have. I think there are a lot of us in the Nurse Corps who went to Vietnam, [who] never recognized that there are problems and that having problems doesn't mean that you are weak or inefficient or ineffective. It just means that you are human."

Post-traumatic stress disorder? Yes, for a very few. Based on Stretch, Vail, and Maloney's study of 700 Army nurses in 1985, the answer would be yes, for 3.3 percent. For the nurses who remained on active duty, it seems that their reaction to their tour in Vietnam was to bear an emotional pain that was survivable, but mostly buried.

I'd like to share a letter I received from an active duty Army Nurse Corps Lieutenant Colonel in response to a presentation and article (Richie 1989) written about these interviews. (We'll call him Pete.)

> *Colonel Richie . . . I can certainly relate to and concur with the feelings expressed. Particularly the section "You Won't Be Alone." It brought my heart up into my throat and tears (behind closed doors of course). I have never talked about my experiences. I thought I had successfully repressed the negative, painful part anyway until my high-school daughter [sic] asked me if I would talk to her World Studies class about Vietnam.*
>
> *I thought about it and agreed. I asked Joe (another Army nurse) to join me and we put together a slide presentation with a tape for background music of the times. When we got to the class, I started to "try" to do my presentation. I lost it and couldn't go on. I guess it was the first time, some fifteen years later after the fact, that I was confronted with my real feelings. Since that day I have reverted to suppressing the feelings. I even apologized to my daughter for not doing well for her. Her response was, the kids thought I was great. Maybe because they saw the pain I obviously was showing.*
>
> *I won't ever do it again, though. The tears are running, even as I write this. When I take visitors to the wall, I can hardly stand it. I try to hide my tears and get out as fast as I can avoiding any conversation. The pain is real . . . Thanks for listening. (Pete)*

Looking back twenty-one years later and hearing the echoes of the Vietnam Army Nurse Corps officers, I ache for the pain and isolation so obviously experienced by some, and I celebrate the triumphant survival, overcoming of obstacles, and thriving of most of the Vietnam nurses. I garnered more hope with the next generation as I listened to the voices from the Iraq and Afghanistan Army nurses, depicted in the next section. Listen to their voices and hear the similarities and the differences in Army nurses at war.

As a preview, I am honored to share below excerpts of a speech a senior ANC leader, LTC Tamora (a pseudonym), gave at a celebration of the 105th Army Nurse Corps Anniversary in 2006. She wanted to compare the experiences of her nurses then deployed to Iraq with the anticipated experiences of those nurses who had served in Vietnam.

LTC Tamora welcomed her nursing staff, other health care workers, and guests to the ANC anniversary celebration: "We are making history. We currently have fifteen Army nurses deployed to Iraq and ten nurse reservists backfilling those positions. The current focus on deployments encourages a look at past operations that the ANC has supported. The following excerpt, written in 1968, is taken from an orientation letter sent to nurses preparing to deploy to Vietnam. MAJ Q, Chief

Nurse, 71st Evacuation Hospital, Pleiku, Vietnam, writes in hopes of inspiring the young nurses who will soon staff her hospital."

> *Nursing in a combat area has many unusual features—some good—some bad. The philosophy of nursing you bring with you will have a lot to do with how this year in the Republic of Vietnam will affect you. You cannot come to your DEROS [departure date to return to the United States] the same individual you were on the day you arrived in country. You will be either a better or worse nurse—a better or worse person. The outcome will depend primarily upon you.*
>
> *Let us look at some of the plus signs for personal and professional growth and development. One of the biggest blessings encountered over here is that the American Soldier who comes under your care is the most wonderful patient in the world. His ability to accept the misfortune that brings him to the hospital and to continue to be combative against the forces of pain, infection, disfigurement, and frustrating helplessness is phenomenal. More remarkable, however, is the fact that he will try to make you feel you are "the greatest" because you care for him in his hour of need. That you do care, really care for him not only as a patient but as person is essential if your work is to remain meaningful and satisfying.*

LTC Tamora then shared some of her e-mails from her currently deployed nurses: "I asked the nurses in Mosul and Tikrit to describe their experiences which, not surprisingly, correlate closely with the experiences of Army nurses thirty-eight years ago. For example, for professional and personal growth, MAJ G says that the mature theater in Mosul has everything a real-world hospital has with the benefit of a truly appreciative population. 'The in-country care is saving more lives. The soldiers have said they feel comfortable going outside the wire because they know that we are there to take care of them.'"

LTC Tamora continued: "And ready they are. CPT W shared a recent patient encounter. He works in EMT [emergency medical trauma room] and he received a call that they had four patients coming to them after an IED [improvised explosive device, a homemade bomb] attack. There were three KIA's [killed in action] on site so they knew the injuries would be significant. He recalls how everyone just snaps into action. 'We prep the trauma bays while we are waiting; the medics are at my side and spiking warm normal saline bags. I check the suction and airway tray, get antibiotics, tetanus and the RSI [rapid saline intravenous] kit, and place it next to me and ensure that my ACLS [advanced cardiac life support] drugs are behind me. The other section personnel are notified and begin to come to the EMT . . . radiology, the surgeon, ortho, pharmacy, the EMT physician, and our interpreters.

The wait seems long and I'm going over my primary and secondary survey in my head even though I have done it hundreds of times in the past. The ambulance arrives, litter teams go get the patients, and the controlled chaos begins!' He goes on to mention how they saved them all."

LTC Tamora then went back to Major Q's Vietnam letter: "Another facet of life in South Vietnam is the realization of how much stamina you possess. Long hours, tense days and nights, heavy workloads and close day-to-day contact test your mettle and the moment of reckoning must be faced by all. The unusual and sometimes awesome task of handling mass casualty situations not just once but time and time again sharpens your ability to organize the available resources and to improve all your nursing skills."

LTC Tamora resumed her commentary about her nurses in Iraq and Afghanistan: "Once again, my present-day nurses say the same thing [as the Vietnam nurses]. MAJ B says: 'We must be very versatile. The last trip I took, one of our Strykers [an ambulance that can hold six patients lying on litters] started throwing fire out of the exhaust and died. I had to dismount with the others and help provide security while they hooked up a tow bar. A small crowd gathered about fifty meters away, so I had to pull out my weapon and chamber a round just in case an insurgent popped up and fired on us. It goes to show that even though we are noncombatants, we still have to carry weapons and be prepared to use them if necessary." As I read this portion of LTC Tamora's talk, I couldn't help but reflect back to COL Glenda's perceptions about gender difference in Vietnam; that most female nurses did not carry weapons and most male nurses did carry a weapon when they went on medical assistance visits to the villages. Clearly the rules changed in Iraq and Afghanistan where weapons were mandatory for everyone when you left the hospital building.

LTC Tamora continued with excerpts from her staff's e-mails: "MAJ D endures frequent MASCALs and describes things that she says we don't always hear on the news. She was working EMT the other night when a call came in about eight burn-and-blast patients who were injured in an IED blast on a major highway from Mosul to Baghdad. The blast was a daisy chain [sequential, multiple explosive devices] and caused major damage to the main supply route. The first people on site were an Army supply convoy returning to their Forward Operating Base. The eight injuries were two families of Iraqis returning from visiting family. The major burn victims were women and children.

"The Army personnel went into the burning vehicles while taking direct fire to help those family members. Those daisy chains were meant for the U.S. convoy and the U.S. is not responsible for the care of the civilian casualties. But these solders were so concerned about these people that they picked them up and took them to the closest Army supply base down the road. All of these family members were then flown out to the Combat Support Hospital for treatment. They saved four out of the eight and the heroic actions of these young soldiers will never be known outside of that dark roadside incident. So when MAJ D asks herself, 'Am I making a difference?' The answer is *yes!*"

LTC Tamora then went back to the last portion of MAJ Q's Vietnam letter to her inbound nurses:

Many times you may be hampered in this work by enemy activity, curfews or disinterest among the people you would like to help. By doing what you can, when you can, you will leave something worthwhile behind you when your tour is up. You may find yourself developing ambivalent feelings about the patient load as the weeks and months progress. If the hospital is busy, the time passes faster and after a hard day's work you can go to your hootch tired but with the feeling you are needed and being here is really necessary and worthwhile. However, this means men are facing the enemy in frightful conflict and for some, release from battle will only come with death. If the wards are quiet, time drags, boredom sets in and tempers grow short. But then you are aware that during these quiet times, there is a respite from the fighting and people are not being brutally wounded or killed.

LTC Tamora concluded with another e-mail: "MAJ D said they were very slow right after the elections. She goes on to say, 'That was a good thing, but many of us came here to make a difference and if we are not busy doing what we love to do or at least trained to do, we feel guilty and underutilized. It reminds me of that part in *White Christmas* when Bing Crosby sang 'What do you do with a general when he stops being a general?' Well, we sing, 'What do we do with a trauma surgeon when we have no trauma?' We remind ourselves that if we aren't busy, that means that soldiers, sailors, and marines are living and the Iraqi Army is doing their job! It also means that imaginations run wild. The weather has been cold and rainy and MAJ D is thinking about selling the mud as a beauty aid, 'From the cradle of civilization. . . Cleopatra's Miracle Mud.'"

The similarities between Vietnam and Iraq are striking and the differences surprising. Continue on now to hear the voices of those who have served in Iraq and Afghanistan from their arrival in country, through the incoming rounds, the camaraderie and comic relief, the loss of their comrades, and talks with their Lord; until they touch down again in the United States.

IRAQ & AFGHANISTAN...
VOICES FROM THE FRONT

BOOTS ON THE GROUND AND FULL BATTLE RATTLE

Most traveled about 6,729 miles from the east coast of America to get to Iraq. Some traveled with their unit as a group, and some traveled off-cycle and alone as a replacement for someone who had to return to the states. Either way the journey was about twenty-four hours of grueling travel via automobile and airplane, then either helicopter, truck, Humvee, or for some, a rhino (armored bus).

CPT Marissa recalled her feelings about traveling and trying to get to the hospital the night of her arrival. She'd landed at Baghdad International Airport (BIAP) around midnight with three duffel bags and a rucksack and no notion of how to get to the 28th Combat Support Hospital (CSH). With the help of a captain from the 14th CSH and some other seasoned soldiers, she was manifested on a rhino to take her to the hospital.

The departure times were classified (they could not be shared with the soldiers), so once she was manifested she just had to sit there through the night and wait until one showed up. CPT Marissa didn't move fast enough when it arrived and she found herself in the last available seat on the rhino, next to the driver, next to a window. Given that everyone else rushed to the back of the rhino, she had a feeling that it was not the safest place to sit on the bus.

Just as they were leaving the airport to travel through Baghdad, CPT Marissa realized that her helmet was fastened too tight. "I never had to wear it in Kuwait and I just needed to adjust it. When I put it on, it was squeezing my head so tight I had the worst headache in my life and I wanted to take it off. But I was too afraid." She thinks the ride was only about forty minutes, but it was an eye-opener for her. "That's when my heart started beating really fast. It's dark but even then, I could see these bombed out buildings on the left or right of you. In Kuwait they taught us what to look for, for IEDs." CPT Maria echoed those same sentiments. "It was kind of spooky how they would transport us. Everything was so clandestine. It did kind of make you feel like you don't know what to expect, so you're more alert."

Most soldiers stopped in Kuwait for a few days on the way to their final duty station in Iraq. The Kuwait stop was for acclimation, in-country administrative processing, and for some additional training. CPT Maria reported, "It was so hot. It got up to 148 one day. The climate is so different compared to what we're used to. You would walk a few feet and then the whole bottle of water you just drank, just came out of you, and you go to another building."

CPT Dalton agreed, and elaborated on the time spent there. "When we got to Kuwait, we lived in this giant tent city. Things there were actually kind of slow. It was just basically a stopping, resting point to collect yourself and the rest of your unit and to get all your gear put together to go to your duty site, which was Baghdad. We were there for two weeks basically. You try to rest as much as you can, get acclimated to the weather, and prepare to move out. We did very little training. You're so disoriented because of the twelve-to-fifteen-hour time change and there's so much daylight in Iraq, it just disorientates you and you're exhausted from the flight."

LTC Mary arrived in Kuwait with her unit and they prepared to move out to Baghdad in stages. While in Kuwait they slept on cots, lived with about thirty folks per tent (separate male and female quarters), and dined quite well. "There was more food than you ever care to imagine. You could eat yourself right out of the Army over there with [the] great dining. There were four hot meals [to include] midnight chow. . . . I was a lot of things, but hungry was not one of them."

Not all of them stayed in Kuwait. MAJ Donna and her unit were immediately loaded up on buses and traveled about two hours to get to Camp Virginia in Tikrit. She described their arrival: "Everybody was tired, everybody was anxious, and nobody knew what to expect. They told us to drink all of this water. People got off the bus and they put everybody in formation. There were people who had to go to the bathroom and I remember one of the nurses ran. She just couldn't hold it anymore and she ran and peed over [behind] the sign in the sand dune. I remember going 'You can't do that!' The whole thing was so funny. At the time, we were exhausted. You guys have to allow people the ability to go to the bathroom, but accountability was such an issue at that time.

"When we got there, we were dead tired but we had to go swipe our cards to get through. Then we had to unload the military vans that brought over stuff. Then we just got in long lines and [were] sort of unloading the equipment and all the duffel bags. And we just did it for an hour or two, unloaded the luggage. We were just numb. I think that was pretty much it. When they gave us our beds, we laid out our stuff and tried to sleep. We're in this big huge room all full of people, where before we were in the barracks where, you know at my rank as Major, there were just two of us in a room. So now we're in open, big barracks where people are snoring. People got sick, the usual things that happen. It was a little bit of an adjustment period, but I think everybody did well."

MAJ Donna also commented on the environment and questioned whether she could make it for a year: "You got off the buses and I mean it was clean and they had everything there—but all you could see for miles were sand dunes— nothing growing, not even a blade of grass. It was so desolate and so stark with white tents and shower trailers. It just reminded you of prison camp. I mean, there was just nothing to it. You could even have gone with the old Army tents; but they were big and long, they looked like Quonset huts, only they were made out of light, heavy plastic or something and you just looked at miles of this stuff. You just kind of went 'Ahh! I don't know if I can do a year here.'" CPT Maria also listed grass as one of the things she missed most while in Iraq: "I would always say, 'Where's the grass? Somebody plant one blade of grass for me to look at.'"

The accountability issue was important for safety and security reasons and sometimes you had to take responsibility for it yourself. While in Kuwait, CPT Marissa struggled with that: "They bussed us through and we got there. Then they said, 'Okay. Everybody get in formation and get a battle buddy.' Of the people in my [replacement] group, which is 3rd MED, I was the only female and there were four males. I felt kind of —I don't know what the word is—it's not alienated—but I just felt like, 'Wow, I guess, I don't have a battle buddy' . . . So, walking to the showers and back, or walking to the DFAC [dining facility] and back; the challenge was to find somebody. Usually I just did it alone. It (DFAC) was right outside and I knew my surroundings."

Eventually she realized that this was not the safest choice and she joined forces with the two enlisted soldiers in her group. "They looked out for me. Those were my battle buddies. They'd come pick me up. Once I finally met them, they'd come pick me up from my tent and walk me to the DFAC or we walked to our classes together. So I felt like I had somebody then—somebody to look out for me and take care of me."

CPT Madeline remembered in-country briefings and live fire range training; as well as PX (post exchange) shopping, reading, relaxing, and exercising at the gym during her six days in Kuwait. In 2004, CPT Dalton did some of that training and preparatory work with the 31st CSH at their mobilization site in Fort Bliss, Texas, before he left the states. "We stayed there a couple of weeks. That's where you get field maneuvers, buddy listings, field carry. You wanted to make sure you were as trained up as possible before you left. We actually left from an oil field at Fort Bliss to go to Frankfurt, Germany. From there, we went to Kuwait City, then to Baghdad International Airport. [Then] we convoyed into the green zone. At the time that's what it was called and that's where the hospital was."

Boots on the ground in Afghanistan was a pit stop in Kurdistan (next to the Soviets) and then on to Bagram where some staff members were selected for placement in a smaller unit known as a FOB (Forward Operating Base). CPT Frank was sent to just such a unit in Salerno to support the 3rd Brigade of the 10th Mountain Division. He remained there for about three months and then moved to an even smaller unit known as an FST (Forward Surgical Team) to support an upcoming mission called Operation Mountain Lion. "There were five of us. Of course we called ourselves the elite. I think that's where I had the best experience. If I ever deploy again, I would rather go with an FST. . . . When things happened, it just went. You never expected it, it just kept going. You could be working twenty-four hours straight . . . We all helped each other out. It was a small group. I don't like too big of a crowd because then politics start to get involved and that kind of screws up the morale of the group. So a small group is what I like and I fit right in. That's where I wanted to be. I didn't want to leave." CPT Frank's team consisted of one OB (obstetrics) physician, an OR (operating room) nurse, an LPN (licensed practical nurse), himself (an ICU nurse), and their commander, a CRNA (certified nurse anesthetist). They joined the depleted staff of the original FST, which consisted of one orthopedic doctor, one OB physician, one OR nurse, and one ER (emergency room) nurse.

CPT Frank was more than qualified for the demanding and independent work required at an FST in Afghanistan. Prior to that deployment, he had deployed for two months with the 14th CSH to help the 2005 Katrina victims in New Orleans. "We set up an eighty-four-bed hospital next to the airport there. We stayed there for about three weeks or so. . . . Then, after that we packed up, broke down the hospital, and moved downtown to the Convention Center . . . and set up a smaller hospital there for another two or three weeks before the 121st CSH came and relieved us."

CPT Frank heard rumors while in New Orleans that the unit might be deployed to Afghanistan when they returned. The rumors proved to be true and the 14th CSH was sent to Fort Benning for one month of readiness training prior to moving out to Afghanistan in 2006. The readiness training would provide a refresher for specific clinical skills needed in a combat zone and specialized classes so that the nurses could protect themselves and their patients.

Already specialty-trained by the Army to be an intensive care nurse (ICU), CPT Frank received even more certifications. "We did mostly BLS (Basic Life

Support) courses, we did ACLS (Advanced Cardiac Life Support), and we did TNCC (Trauma Nurse Course Certification). Most of those I already had, my certification for BCLS and ACLS, and burn life support. We also did weapons training and also some detainee-type training with the MPs [military police] . . . just in case we were caught in a situation where you had to search any enemy. Any encounter that we might have there, then at least you knew what to do. Hopefully, you would never have to get into that situation." One could hope, but they also had to be prepared.

Remember LTC Tamara's e-mail from MAJ B who had deployed to Iraq? MAJ B greatly appreciated that field training when his Stryker (an eight-wheeled infantry carrier that can be configured for six patient litters) "started throwing fire out of the exhaust and died. I had to dismount with the others and help provide security while they hooked up a tow bar. A small crowd gathered about fifty meters away, so I had to pull out my weapon and chamber a round just in case an insurgent popped up and fired on us. It goes to show that even though we are noncombatants, we still have to carry weapons and be prepared to use them if necessary."

A combat medic, SGT Dolly traveled the same route as CPT Madeline into Iraq. "I just remember the convoy into Iraq. Most people were out in the street; they were watching us as we passed through. Sometimes they would steal equipment—anything that was left out—they were taking. I didn't see any people with guns out on the street or act in a threatening way. You always made sure you were in a safe climate when you passed through. You were also moving quickly through the areas." Once she arrived in Iraq in 2003, SGT Dolly lived in a burned-out building that had once housed animals. "At that point, it was very early on, so not as many people lived in that area."

For SGT Dolly, boots on the ground also meant guard duty along with her normal job of working in the medical clinic helping the brigade nurse and doctor with sick call.

"During guard duty, we usually sat in a tower to guard the post and watch the sheep herders that would bring their flocks out during the day. We could see for miles so it was really a good point to be at because we were in the countryside in Iraq. There weren't any walls per se like in the city where someone could just walk by and throw a bomb or anything over it. We could see them coming, so we were fortunate in that respect. But you just never knew about the sheepherders coming every day, who might have a bomb or anything like that. We didn't have any incidents while we were there. If anybody got too close to our point, we would call up and whoever was on duty would send a unit out to check out the situation. But that didn't happen too often. The sheepherders kind of knew their distance; [they]

had to be so far from us that they just let their sheep graze all day and when they were done, they would just leave."

Guarding a Brigade Support Medical Company in Iraq was a far cry from being an administrative assistant in Fayetteville, North Carolina, or being a teacher in Ocala, Florida; but it was where SGT Dolly wanted to be. She joined the military because she felt she wasn't being challenged by her civilian life and she was bored. While in class at EMT (emergency medical technician) training at Fort Lewis, Washington, SGT Dolly saw the towers go down on 9/11. "I couldn't believe it. I was just not willing to accept the fact that it happened, but felt proud that now all this training was good for something. I was ready to get it on."

Because of the potential danger when one was outside of the buildings in Iraq, each person was required to be fully equipped and wear their helmet and protective vest, and carry a weapon. CPT Maria understood and obeyed the rule, but others took it one step further: "Some people would go to sleep in their full battle rattle. I'd say to them, 'So you sleep like that every night? You are in a bed, in a building!' But they would sleep with their helmet on and their vest on. It weighed like forty-five pounds. Imagine that, every night."

MORTARS, ROUNDS, AND DWELLINGS

CPT Mark adhered to the protective covering rule when he moved between buildings. But, he soon learned that being inside was not a guarantee of safety: "In Balad, my first night working, you could hear mortars coming in. We didn't have this in Mosul where we felt pretty safe. Here I am my first night working, me and one of these Air Force docs, an anesthesiologist. I was helping him put a line [intravenous] in an Iraqi patient and you just start hearing, 'Boom, boom, boom!' louder and louder. I'm looking at him and I'm like, 'Does this happen a lot?' He just looked at me like this [pantomimed 'Duh! Of course']. They have this little PA system like an alarm or something that means we need to run and get our flak vests and our Kevlar and put it on and continue to take care of the patients. After we did that, some of the mortars got so close that you could hear the shrapnel on top of the tents. Me and the physician, the Air Force doc, we just looked at each other and he just finished up real quick and [then] we sat next to the patient underneath. It was scary. The mortar thing is what started to consume my mind. It was a daily thing. It wasn't always a daily shot close to us, but it was a daily thing that you never forget when you hear the sound."

Initially CPT Brenda didn't hear the mortars coming, but she saw the evidence of them where she lived and the precursors of trouble on the streets when she walked to work. "I moved three times while in Baghdad. The first place was right across the street from the hospital. It was like a little Iraqi apartment building. I stayed there for a couple of weeks and where my room was, faced the main street. There were bullet holes in the wall so you could look straight out and see the street. That's where my head was, so I moved.

"I worked night shift. So a typical day was walking to the hospital that was about a mile and a half [away] in full battle rattle. It was freaking hot. We walked down the main road of the green zone and you knew that you were going to be busy before you even stepped foot into that hospital because there would be Bradleys and Humvees parked on the street. Because you knew that they were coming to see a buddy."

That was her first clue, but there was more. "If the kids were out, trying to sell you DVDs, watches, and candy, you knew nothing was going to happen. But, if the kids weren't there, then you knew that you better walk with a doctor." These seemed like the same clues used by Vietnam nurses going out on a MECAP mission. If the children weren't around the helicopter landing zone, they usually pulled up and hightailed it back home.

LTC Ursula chuckled when she remembered her first experience with mortars. "When I first got there, the FOB itself did not get mortared very frequently at all. Towards the end, towards the last two months of my deployment, there was a great increase in frequency of mortars, specifically rocket-propelled grenades being fired at the FOB, from out in the desert, off of these trucks. For the most part we would laugh because they were such horrible aim. They never hit. They never came far enough to hit us."

Even if their aim was poor, any attempt was followed by full accountability of each staff member. "When we were being rocketed, even if it didn't hit the FOB at all, the entire FOB went on high alert and we heard what we called the big voice. There was this audio system with this big booming voice and they would call out, whatever the word of the day was that would tell us that we would all need to go to our unit. For us, it was the TMC [troop medical clinic]. We didn't have to go to the detention center. The troop medical clinic was closer to where we lived than the actual prison or the detention center. So we would go there for accountability because they never knew where all the grenades hit.

"So they had to get 100 percent accountability before we would be allowed to be released. This would disrupt quite a few evenings where you'd have to be in the TMC for three hours while they went to find everybody. Because if you slept through it, or you were doing something you shouldn't have been doing, you know like some of our, I hate to say it; but it happens on deployment, some of our junior enlisted might not be sleeping in their right bed. So until they had a 100 percent accountability, we could not go back and go back to sleep. And then you have to get up and work the next day. So it took its toll on us." The jokes about their poor aim stopped after LTC Ursula departed the area and learned that one of the mortars did hit and had killed a contractor.

LTC Ursula was grateful for the strict adherence to regulation and accountability while she was at Camp Bucca. "There were two or three nights when we were being mortared that they did announce overhead, there was a PA system that whatever the code was, I forget what it was, like code red or something. We all knew that we had to dawn all of our gear. You were sleeping in PT [physical training] uniforms so I would be in my PT shorts and my T-shirt. You would wake up and you would just put on the closest garments that you had, which were usually your sneakers, your flak vest, and your helmet. Then you get your pistol and you would walk as quickly as you could to the troop medical clinic, which was our rally point, basically for the whole CSH. It wasn't until 100 percent of the CSH was accounted for and they called the 'all clear' for the whole base that they would let us go back to our rooms to sleep. So there were some pretty long nights."

She was in the shower in a mobile trailer that had eight showers and sinks and it was her first Sunday in Tikrit; LTC Madeline recalled that first mortar attack: "I heard a boom and my roommate came running in there and she said, 'Madeline that was real!'" LTC Madeline wouldn't let me record her verbal response to the attack [I think it involved a lot of cussing.], but she did tell me what she did next. "We went back to the building that we were staying in because it was a cement building. We decided that it was probably safer than anything else we were around. . . I think they only hit once. After about twenty minutes or so we were given the all clear."

CPT Maria had no qualms about sharing her reaction to the mortars: "I was in the shower, shampooing my head and I hear a mortar and I'm thinking, 'Is it going to come through my wall?' So that's the end of my showering. I'm not showering anymore. I'm out of that shower and everybody would laugh at me because I would immediately go into the center hallway, and wait until we got the all clear. I had a group of friends that would come in the center hallway. They knew I was going to be there."

The mortars caught CPT Maria unaware in the shower and while walking to the dining facility for a hot meal. "It was just a short walk, but at times you'd still be ducking into the bunker because of mortars and car bombs and whatever. You didn't really feel too safe walking. I didn't feel safe walking. There were a lot of other people who didn't feel safe even walking to the cafeteria. You never knew when a mortar was going to come in."

One's perceptions of mortars and incoming rounds differed depending on your geographical location, the time of the year, and your deployment history. COL Umberto had already served in the blazing heat of Somalia and the frigid mountains in Bosnia when he was sent to Tallil and later to Mosul.

In both locations he was provided the same type of housing. "They moved us into these brand-new container types [houses], which were very nice, clean, and up off of the ground. They had heaters. They put cable TV in for you and the Internet. After being in Bosnia. . . even when they're firing at you or shooting mortars, it was a piece of cake."

With time in country, LTC Mary and her staff eventually began to judge the mortar sounds before reacting: "It was like, 'Oh, okay, yeah, that was far away. We're not going to worry about that one.' [Or you ask yourself] 'How close is that one?' You kind of listen to see what follows."

That reaction proved to be unsafe when it came to unexploded ordnances. LTC Mary recalled one that landed behind the dining facility. "You heard it coming. We heard it land [but] nothing followed it. There was no boom or anything, so we keep going and then you heard, 'Take cover!'" They wound up hunkered down and locked in the dining facility for two hours.

Another close call was when an insurgent drove a vehicle near the hospital with an IED (improvised explosive device) still inside. They weren't sure what was going to happen when they blew up the vehicle, so just to be safe they moved all of the patients away from the windows and tried to protect them as best they could.

CPT Tania said the thing that most challenged her while in Iraq was trying to care for critically ill patients on the medical evacuation flights from Baghdad to Balad as they were being attacked. "You would get shot at sometimes, but we were fortunate. We were never shot down on any of our flights. You're in such a confined space and you're taking care of critically ill patients and just trying to get them to their destination alive. And you are praying that the equipment doesn't die.

"The ventilator would stop and you have to start bagging your patient—and you cannot get a blood pressure on your patient." At that point there would be a mad scramble to push fluids (intravenously) to bring the patient's blood pressure back up. CPT Tania remembered a medic being on board the chopper, but she was the only nurse for the critically ill patient.

For those who worked in the "green zone" in Baghdad, traveling outside that protected area evoked fears of the IED that you could face at anytime. LTC Daina feared for her life. "When you go outside the wire when you're in a Humvee, I mean it's really pretty scary . . . and I don't think that's just me. I mean I think that's anybody who goes outside of the wire in a Humvee. You always have to be afraid of it . . . It's kind of nerve-wracking. I mean there are some people that did it five days a week and I imagine after a while it wasn't quite as scary for them as it was for people like me who didn't go out all that often."

When asked how she got through those trips, LTC Daina responded, "I prayed a lot, and I also had complete faith in the teams that I went out with. I had the utmost faith, admiration and just—they were like nothing I've ever in my whole life experienced, these young kids. I'm telling you, they are the heroes of this war."

PATIENTS BIG AND SMALL

"We used to play spades at night in the summertime. We were right on the path for the helicopters when they would fly to the hospital. I tell you, every time those helicopters flew over, there would be silence where we were, because you just knew. I mean you just knew. It was terrible." LTC Daina was talking about incoming casualties.

CPT Marissa described her first few days in country and being oriented to her ward duties by another nurse. "I saw things I'd never seen before. I'd seen amputees before but they were sixty-year-old men with diabetes. These were twenty-year-olds sometimes with double or triple amputations. I did so many dressing changes. That first day I was so scared.

"There was a young guy, he had to be twenty, around that age. He was probably a tough guy, a really tough guy usually. And we were doing a dressing change on the back of his thighs. You could fit a whole kerlex roll [cotton-mesh material about two inches in diameter and four inches in width] in his thigh without unrolling it. It would fit in his wound. I wasn't grossed out. I'd seen wounds before, but I'd not seen anything that big before. I was fine. But it was when we started doing the dressing change and he started crying. He was begging us to please, please stop. We had given him morphine. We just needed to do it and get it done."

CPT Marissa was awed by the steely determination coupled with ultimate compassion shown by the other nurse who "did what she had to do to take care of him" while his tears rolled down his cheeks. That nurse kept saying over and over, "I know it hurts. I'm sorry, but we have to do this."

After she was permanently assigned to the night shift, CPT Marissa was assisted by another Army nurse, two licensed practical nurses, and two to three medics to care for an average of twenty-two patients on an intermediate care ward. They were a busy crew as they prepared for six-to-eight patient air evacuations each night. Most American patients only stayed there twenty-four to forty-eight hours before going to a larger facility in Germany, then on to the United States. If they were critically ill, they would be stabilized and moved out as quickly as possible.

Periodically the number of evacuations jumped to fourteen in one night. "That's when you need to call in your day shift or have day shift stay over or call everybody to come help you because there's too many. You just can't do—sometimes it takes four people just to move a patient from the bed to the litter."

Because the actual air evacuation time was classified information, they never knew the departure hour until the last minute. This just-in-time notification meant rushing to medicate patients, to attach portable equipment, and to stabilize chest tubes for the bumpy ride in a rickshaw litter to the heliport staging area and onto the helicopter.

LTC Fay was there for the ground war in 2001. "The first day when the ground war started, they had injuries. We received a lot of injuries but there weren't that many American soldiers injured. It was the host nation soldiers that were injured. I've seen things on TV and thought, 'Oh, that's what they look like when they get blown up or they have a mortar sticking in them.' But then reality sunk in. This was a horror movie I'd never seen before flashing in front of my face. . . . The doctors were trying to get them in and take care of the Iraqi soldiers. . . . The shocking thing was seeing them. You could tell that they had been out there in the trenches all that time without food. They were very emaciated."

SGT Dolly also had been there early in the war and recalled her most vivid memory and the patient she will never forget: "They brought in a couple of guys from one of the units that happened to be stationed with us at that time. One had gotten crushed. He was hanging out the latch and when it rolled, it rolled on top of him and he got crushed. A couple guys inside had gotten thrown about inside. There wasn't much we could do.

"I was dealing with one of the soldiers and I couldn't figure out where he was bleeding from. I was trying to stop the bleeding and when I stuck my hand behind his head, I could feel his skull because he had a split in his scalp. So once we realized that, we stopped the bleeding; but at that point, there wasn't much we could do. I just closed his eyes. Both of those gentlemen died that day.

"That was probably the most vivid, hardest thing we ever had to deal with up to that point because they could have easily been your friend or someone you may have been acquainted with at one point or another. You could have just seen him earlier that day. I think that was kind of hard. I've seen dead bodies before but I never had to close anybody's eyes. That was hard."

One of LTC Ursula's memories has stayed with her: "I think one of the things is that even as a mental health provider, I can't make it go away. There was a British convoy that got hit and one of the guys lost a leg. In psychiatry, you're never that close to those kinds of wounds. True we go in and we do consults on people that have had losses, but to actually be in the ICU when they are taking down that dressing for the first time, to see the way that that amputation looks, one day after it happens, as opposed to six months after. It's unbelievable what it looks like. It looks something that hangs in the butcher shop.

"I remember standing in the ICU watching the orthopedic surgeon. He was a great friend of mine, so there's also that personal component. I'm worried about him [and know that] I'm going to have to talk to him tonight. He's there with the hospital commander, the OIC [officer-in-charge] of the hospital, watching. The guy is screaming bloody murder because it's obviously painful and the hospital commander is crying, the tears just rolling down [from] his eyes, and he's not making any attempt at all to hide the fact that he's crying. And him [my friend is] just trying to give some words of encouragement to this British soldier who lost his leg just yesterday. That is something that I don't think will ever leave me. It doesn't come in intrusively; I don't see it when I don't want to."

Most of CPT Frank's patient care was to the local Afghanistan residents. "When I got to Salerno we received casualties quite frequently, but it wasn't bad. A lot of the care that we provided was to the locals. This was part of, what do you call it? 'Winning the hearts and minds mission.' Yes.

"We heard so many stories about how some family that we took care of would go out there and actually report things to our soldiers. They would actually go out and get some of these guys that we were about to attack. So that's why that mission was so important. It was important for us to continue to take in these guys with the little resources that we had, so they could then help the 10th Mountain or whoever we were supporting, with their mission."

LTC George witnessed firsthand the turnaround of an insurgent who also happened to be a physician and patient in his hospital. As the chief nurse, LTC George made rounds daily and personally checked on each patient. He recalled his encounter with this young surgeon one morning during rounds. "He'd had his leg blown off and he had numerous infections. Finally, one day he broke down and he was crying. He was in the ICU and we asked him why he was crying and he said, "I've watched you over the past several weeks and I see that you give me and my people just as much care as you give your own soldiers and my people are Iraqi. He said, 'I am so ashamed of what I have done and those people that talked me into setting up the IED.' We had caught him when he was hit with a .50 caliber. He had been told that the Americans would torture him and cut his head off and he saw none of that. He saw nothing but goodness coming from everyone. At that point I had to turn away because he was starting to cry." The man died a few months later, but not before he saw over and over again that the staff treated each patient with an equal portion of respect, compassion, and dignity.

As a chief nurse LTC George was in a unique position to have "eyes" on the entire hospital, including patients, supplies, and staff in real time. He described it as being able to see the hospital "globally." His day began about 6 AM getting reports from the night supervisor on each patient's condition and their potential for movement out of the hospital. At any given time, 75 percent of their casualties were host nation: either Iraqi National Guard, Iraqi Special Forces, Iraqi Police, and Iraqi civilians, male, female, and children; most of the patients would remain with them. They were kept on one of two intermediate-care wards, a step-down unit, one of two intensive-care wards, or a six-bed unit reserved for prisoners (with two guards on duty at all times). "We thought it was best to separate them from our soldiers and Marines." They also had Brits and Australians as well as Polish soldiers and Bulgarian soldiers that were injured. The two eight-bed intensive care units (ICU) were restricted to those patients who needed assistance breathing so that it was not uncommon to have sixteen ventilated patients to care for at one time. LTC George was impressed with their portable and stationary medical equipment. "We had state-of-the-art ventilators. It was all touch screens and all paid for by, I'm sure, U.S. tax dollars. We also had the best cardiac monitors mounted on the walls. I can't remember exactly who manufactured them, but they were equivalent to the best ICU that we had back in any Army hospital or civilian hospital."

At 7 AM, LTC George joined other senior staff members for the Commander's status report on patients, equipment, and supplies. If they were short units of blood, LTC George had already anticipated the question and had the answer of how and when they were going to make up the shortfall. If their beds were filled with patients, the hospital commander needed to know how they were going to free up more beds. "He had to remind the doctors repeatedly in the early going, that once we stabilized them, we needed to get them out quickly because we knew that later that day we might receive another fifteen, twenty, or thirty more severely wounded patients and we would need to have beds for them.

"During our time in Iraq, it was a revolving door and our docs got to be very good at it. As soon as the patient arrived, they would start filling out the Patient Movement Request (PMR) form because that document was required to start the process of getting the patient moved out of the hospital. We then sent the PMR form up to the Air Force patient transportation office. Once they accepted the request, we could then coordinate transport by the Blackhawk helicopters with our critical care nurses and we could move the patients to Balad. That was a constant that went on all the time. During the commander's report we went through all our patients. If there were any questions we made sure to get answers from that report so we would know the plan of action. I would hear, maybe for the first time, 'Hey I'm moving this guy out today.' That would give me a heads up. I then had to make sure that the Patient Movement Request form was updated and the ICU staff alerted so that they could pre-position all of the equipment; so when the final word came, each patient was ready to go."

Each ventilated patient that was transported from their hospital in Baghdad to the Air Force hospital in Balad required a critical-care nurse escort to provide patient care during the thirty-five-minute flight. The difficulty came in trying to get that specialty trained nurse returned back to the hospital the same day. If transportation was not available, the nurse was required to stay overnight and then return the next day. As you could imagine, these unexpected delays wreaked havoc with the hospital's nursing schedule. Eventually LTC George devised a two-phased patient evacuation system in which he sent out his ventilated patients with their critical-care nurse escorts in the first phase. The nurses then had five minutes with the Air Force nurses at the Balad hospital bedside to hand off their patients, gather their equipment, and race to the Blackhawk flight line for the return trip back to Baghdad. The second phase included litter patients that did *not* require critical-care nurse escorts. The Balad Air Force hospital had at least four intensive care units to provide interim care until the patients were assigned a Critical Care Air Transport Team (CCATT), each with a nurse, a physician, and a respiratory therapist. This team then transported the ventilated, critically ill patient to the next stop on their way home to the United States.

LTC George had a critical piece of equipment that allowed him to do his job. "We called it the brick. It was a large Motorola® radio and it had a clip on it so I could wear it on my uniform. The emergency medical unit had one, each charge nurse had one, and the lab and the operating room each had one. All of the clinical units were on one channel so they could monitor everything such as when we were coordinating aero medical evacuations."

LTC George shared an example. "I could hear someone saying, 'We have two birds coming in to pick up your nine EVACs out.' They'd ask if you had a good copy. Then I would call the ICU and say, 'Did you copy that?' [They'd respond immediately] 'Right, we're good. I'm ready now; we're rolling down.' It was real time communication and I can't emphasize that enough. I would be standing in the emergency room when they were doing cardiac resuscitation on our soldiers. The ER doc always made eye contact with me when he was ready for the next step. He knew not to ask me to call the surgeons until he knew exactly what was wrong. Then they would ask me to call Dr. so-and-so, who was our vascular surgeon, or call our orthopedic surgeon. We were always looking out over the horizon. That kept me busy all day long. A lot of times, I would have to put my hands in it. I would be hanging blood or I would be pushing a patient down to the OR because the emergency room was so full."

How did he manage when the staff was overwhelmed with casualties? LTC George devised an A & B team system to supplement the emergency room staff. When he had a seven- to eight-minute warning of incoming casualties, LTC George had only to call in his Alpha team and he could have one registered nurse and one licensed practical nurse from each intensive-care unit report to the emergency room to help. If more casualties arrived he called upon the Bravo team (same staffing ratio) to assist. Having these pre-identified staff nurses report to the emergency room when needed allowed LTC George to care for a large number of unexpected casualties quickly and efficiently.

The only thing worse than a mass-casualty situation with a large number of adult patients was a mass-casualty situation with a large number of children. One day while stationed in Afghanistan, CPT Frank was teaching a class to his nursing colleagues about using a level-two intravenous administration system. The system is used for a trauma patients who need to get warm (body temperature) fluids into his or her body as fast as possible. Just as CPT Frank finished speaking, a Special Forces medic walked in with a five- or six-year-old female covered with blood. There had been a school bombing just a few kilometers away from their base. He received twenty-nine patients that day and it broke his heart. "They're so small, they can't always tell you how they are feeling, what's going on, so there's a guessing game."

A pediatric nurse practitioner, LTC Daina encountered some of the same problems with the Iraqi children she saw at a small clinic located just fifty meters from the red zone. The all-volunteer, part-time clinic staff came from the local Army and Air Force units. Those that could come during their off-duty time staffed the clinic a few times each week from noon until about 4 PM. Unlike the hospital situation where the Iraqi fathers stood vigil at the patient's bedside, this outpatient clinic was used mostly by Iraqi mothers and their children who braved checkpoints and personal searches before they were allowed in the door. The volunteers worked hard and on a typical afternoon, they could see between thirty to eighty patients. On previous assignments, LTC Daina had worked in similar medical clinics in Honduras, in Guatemala, and as she put it "all over the world." While in Iraq, she came to one conclusion: "People are the same all over the world. All they want is for their family to be safe, to have food to put on the table, to be healthy, and to be clothed."

LTC Daina also found that parents all over the world are pretty much the same. They love their children and when they are sick, the parents want them to get better as soon as possible. LTC Daina remembered several Iraqi mothers whose children had cerebral palsy. Through an interpreter, she had to explain to them that there was nothing she could do for their child and that the diagnosis had nothing to do with who they were or where they lived, and that there was no cure available anywhere in the world. Another Iraqi parent thought that LTC Daina could "fix" his little eight-year-old girl, who was in renal failure and on kidney dialysis. The child's father thought that this American nurse had some "magic something" more than the medical services offered in his country. Short of a kidney transplant, there was nothing more that could be done for his daughter.

Thanks to two important programs, many of the Iraqi children in need of surgery could be helped in other countries. LTC Daina worked closely with the National Iraqi Assistance Center, which is run by Iraqis and coalition forces. This center works with children in need of surgical procedures. They screen the children, find funding sponsors for the patient's travel and medical expenses (up to $10,000), and locate hospitals and physicians that could perform the necessary surgery. The second assistance program, Starfish, helped those in need of a surgical procedure. This program allows many of the children to have their congenital heart problems corrected.

Big or small, young or old, physical wounds are usually visible and most are amenable to some type of correction. Invisible wounds, those of the heart, mind, and soul, were not always so readily apparent, nor were they so amenable to nursing care.

WOUNDS INSIDE AND OUT

CPT Maria saw her psychiatric patients in her office, where she learned about their immediate problem, and their social, family, and educational background. Armed with this information, she presented her findings to the psychiatrist. Regardless of the preliminary diagnosis, CPT Maria's number-one concern was to ensure the safety of the patient and to ensure the safety of the hospital staff, military unit, and anyone else that might be near the patient. If necessary, a patient would be placed on a twenty-four-hour watch during which time they were never left alone, not permitted to take their own medications, and not permitted to carry a weapon. Under no circumstances was anyone allowed to bring weapons into her office and that included the soldiers who escorted the patient.

CPT Maria believes that every person has a breaking point. For the soldiers serving overseas, that point usually involved relationship problems at home, whether it was a "Dear John"/"Dear Jane" letter, or confessions of infidelity by the stateside spouse. She described her typical patient as somebody who was a good soldier, an "average" guy, who would completely lose his bearings once he realized that he was going to lose his spouse. Often, the realization triggered suicidal thoughts.

CPT Maria was especially vigilant when she scanned the faces of the soldiers who accompanied patients to the emergency room. She'd found that many times the escorts were in as much trouble as the patient. She remembered one soldier in particular and her instinctive reaction following the death of the soldier he had just escorted to the ER: "He just didn't look right. He was taller than me—and then I saw his eyes—they were scary. I thought he was going to kill himself so I ran after him. He reached the wall outside and tried to get his weapon out but I yelled, 'Don't touch that weapon!'" The soldier's wife had just broken up with him the day before after telling him that she was pregnant with another man's baby. The father of the baby was the suicidal soldier's best friend—the man who had just died in the emergency room as a casualty of war. He had just lost his wife and his best friend. His response was simply: 'I just want to die.' At that point, CPT Maria's job was to help him start the healing process.

When there was a traumatic event, the unit healing process usually started with a request by the commander of the victim. LTC Ursula, a psychiatric nurse practitioner, described some differences: "When it was an obvious trauma like a combat-related trauma, like a convoy, the commanders were much more certain of what they needed and when they needed it. 'We want a debriefing. We want group support. We want individual follow-up for those couple of people that fought.' But with a suicide, they didn't really know quite what to do so they were really looking to us for guidance. What we taught them was that nobody witnessed this so you're going to have to reach out to the people that were his roommates and also his friends that were closest to him. You're going to have to create an atmosphere of open-mindedness and welcome to these soldiers so that they are going to want some support from mental health."

LTC Ursula went on to describe how she reached out to other soldiers in the unit of a suicide victim: "We were not going to pursue people. We're not going to knock on doors. We're not going to intrude with people's privacy. But, if you can create an atmosphere where they can tell you we need help, they will come. And so we made sure that we went to things like the change of the guard at noon and midnight to put out information to all of them. In a situation like this of a soldier that had killed himself, we'd say, 'We just want you guys to know that this is our phone number; this is how you can find us; this is where we live or you can go to the Troop Medical Clinic anytime.' But we made sure that we didn't single people out because nobody wants to be approached like that, 'Oh, you must think I have a problem.' So we were very sensitive about stigma even over there."

CPT Maria never lost a patient to suicide but sometimes, as she listened to the soldiers, she was bowed low hearing about some of the personal burdens they carried, like horrible childhood memories of abuse, death, and murder. Many times she had to remind them of how far they had come as she spoke to their strengths: "I don't know how you made it this far . . . you must be a strong person . . . I see a strong person sitting here." Next, she would plant a seed of hope for the future: "If you can give them that one seed of hope, you have now started the process of healing."

CPT Maria, mental health medics, and the psychiatrist worked closely with the chaplains to help the surviving soldiers with the grief process. Given the circumstances of war, many times that grieving process began in the emergency room when one of their buddies died. CPT Maria would ask the soldiers to share something about their friend who had just died. She recalled some of their responses: "'Remember how funny he was?' 'Remember how kind?' 'Remember how he did this one day?' And then even through their tears, they might start laughing." She went on to counsel them to honor the memory of their friend by recalling the things that made their friend special, *not* "what he's like right now . . . the last picture of what you saw. He wants you to remember what just made you laugh, what just made you smile, what to you made him special."

That counsel was particularly difficult the night CPT Maria was called to the emergency room to see the husband of a female soldier who had just died. She found him crying out, "She was just a baby!" CPT Maria pulled the husband to the side and sat with him for awhile. Eventually she asked him how he planned to honor his wife's memory. She recalled how he suddenly sat up straighter and she could see that he was thinking of ways he was going to honor his wife.

"It's hard going through that grieving process because it has to be done so swiftly over there. Someone dies, we go to the chapel, we go to the morgue to say good-bye, and then we put them on a helicopter for the Angel Flight. The remaining soldiers are left with a pair of boots and a weapon to stick in the sand. Then they have to go back to work, have to go back out on the road. And then, they're more fearful because now they've seen what can happen and they know it could happen to them."

CPT Maria saw some patients once each week and other patients three to four times a week. With progress, she could increase the time between visits until finally she could remind them: "Remember the first time I saw you? And they would say, 'I was a mess.' And I'd say to them 'Well look at ya now! You're doing great.'" She recalled one memorable soldier: "I was called up for one soldier who awoke with both his legs gone. We got the consult to see him. He had to be the age of one of my sons, I think about twenty-something and the nurses didn't know what to do with him. Anyway, by the time I finished with him, I called him my 'bionic-man-to-be' and he was laughing. He was hugging me. He wanted fifty hugs."

CPT Frank was not a psychiatric nurse, but he witnessed and shared the inner strength of some of his warrior-patients. "We had received a couple of soldiers who'd been in an IED attack. One of them had cuts and bruises from fragment wounds. He was stable, but we had to recommend that he be sent back to the states to heal. I found him lying in bed crying so I asked, 'Are you in pain? What's wrong?' He said, 'I'm going home and my guys are still out there.' That's when I realized that the soldiers were not out there just to kill some bad guys. It's about the guy standing next to you. Your job is to get him home safely so when he [the patient] was sent home early, it's like he didn't do his job. His job was to take care of his boys—his comrades—and he feels like he failed them. You then just had to stand there to support him and let him know that he did the best that he could. He did his job and that going home is for him to get better. Later, if he wanted to get back, he could talk to his commander about returning."

Sure enough, CPT Frank witnessed just that with some other soldiers who were discharged back to duty and returned weeks later to say, "Hey thanks for everything you did." He also recalled one patient who'd been shot in the lung when another soldier dropped his weapon and it accidentally fired. They repaired the lung (thoracotomy) and the patient was sent back to the states. About two months later, CPT Frank looked up while teaching a review class on how to insert an intravenous line and saw that same soldier standing there attentively listening to the lecture. He'd returned to finish his tour of duty. CPT Frank said that he had a renewed respect for soldiers and it "made me want to stick it out. You can't get that from a civilian hospital or any other job—you just can't."

LTC Madeline expressed her concern about the number of rotations of duty some soldiers were experiencing and the length of their tours: "You have people that are on their second and third rotations over there and now they're extending them to fifteen months instead of twelve months. It's too much and the military medical treatment facilities back home are suffering."

CPT Olivia spoke to the reaction of having one's tour extended unexpectedly. "They told us in our eighth month, that they were going extend us to fifteen months. I really felt bad and I did the denial thing. For two months, I wouldn't change my calendar. I said to myself, 'I'm going to pretend that not one day has gone by.' (Laughs) That way I could pretend I'm not actually staying here fifteen months. Another nurse and I had this prayer thing going that God was going get us out of there in twelve months—but it didn't happen."

She went on to describe the reactions of others: "And then there was the anger and for some a breakdown with suicidal ideas and they had to be air-evaced out. There was a lot of depression with people saying, 'I haven't seen my kids in so long.' They're asking others, 'Why is my mommy lying to me?' 'Why is my daddy not telling me the truth? He said he'd be home on this date, and now it's this other date.' 'I don't know what to tell my family.' It took me three months before I could tell my kids that I would be extended. I waited until I came home on a two-week holiday leave to tell them, so I could cry with them and hug them. They were devastated—just devastated. But then they accepted it. They knew, 'Well, what can you do?'"

It turned out to be a big lesson learned for the Army surgeon general's staff back in the states. CPT Olivia explained: "The majority of the doctors and the surgeons stayed only six months anyway. So, with a fifteen-month tour for the nursing staff, you ended up with three different sets of doctors. Each group was fresh, coming in gung ho and wanting to change the rules and do things their own way. Things started to go downhill with the second group and it just continued further down by the time you got to the third group. Everyone was just worn out with injuries all the time: the same young faces, the missing limbs and the scarred faces. After seeing the effects on the nurses of one extended tour, the deputy surgeon general Major General Gale S. Pollock (the Chief of the Army Nurse Corps) was able to get permission to decrease all nurses' tours to a six-month rotation.

CAMARADERIE AND COMIC RELIEF

CPT Frank touched on a unique and precious element of being in the military: the camaraderie that is forged on the battlefield. For Army nurses deployed in Vietnam, Iraq, or Afghanistan, their battlefield was the bloody emergency room with its nonstop casualties and knowing that the staff member on your left and on your right will stay with you until the job is done and done to the gold standard. LTC Mary remembers thinking about her nursing staff after they'd just treated a number of Marines: "We could handle anything. We were great! Everybody was just so compassionate . . . it was kind of amazing. We took a deep breath after all that we had gone through and then kind of leaned on each other. We had the tears flowing; we had the hugs."

LTC Mary went on to describe the step-by-step review of all of their actions taken during that mass-casualty situation. "After any big event, we always did a walk-through and asked ourselves, 'How could we improve? What could we have done differently? How could we do a little better next time?' That's one thing I'm really proud of—that we were always looking for how we could serve our soldiers, our patients better."

LTC Ursula would have agreed about the pride they had for their work, but she also would have gone on to describe the special bonds formed under fire. "I just felt like I had girlfriends that I had known for twenty years but in six months, Sue (another Army nurse stationed with her) knew more about me than anybody else on this planet. When we were getting mortared and we had to put our flak vests and our helmets on and go get in the bunkers, we talked and shared. There is nothing like being with someone else when your life is being threatened."

Outside threat or not, just having enough staff to do the work was critical and the camaraderie was evident in each wanting to look after one another. When you are in a small forward unit, each staff member is vital to the operation of the unit. Think of an operating team with three nurses to cover two twelve-hour shifts with one day off each week—and oh, by the way, each nurse is entitled to a two-week leave of absence to go home after six months of working overseas. CPT Dalton explained how some felt when it was time to go home for their two weeks: "At the first opportunity that you get to go home, you kind of hesitate because you get this weird sense that you're leaving your buddies and you know that when you leave, you're creating a deficit to the manpower and that it's going to be hard on your peers. You don't want that and so you're kind of resistant to go."

It was difficult for them, to want to go and want to stay at the same time. The same axiom held true even when they were trying to relax on their one day off and have fun. Some wound up going back to work because of boredom and some because their help was still needed. Either way, it was contrary to good mental health and the need to balance the intensity of their work with some comic relief and quiet time.

LTC Mary's nurses had an active junior officer council that organized talent shows and dance parties. They even had monthly poetry slams where people shared their original poetry or they recited poems that they had enjoyed. Her husband taped their favorite shows and sent them over so that no one missed an episode of *American Idol* or *Oprah*. Promotion parties and holiday parties were CPT Marissa's specialty with the help of her family back home who sent party favors and specialty foods like refried beans for the Fiesta Party.

LTC Madeline eventually became the godmother for her head nurse's daughter. While in Iraq, they shared their "care packages" from home, including homemade fudge, specialty coffees from Denver, and bath and body products. Eventually, they each wound up taking two showers each day to try to get rid of all of the shower gels and lotions they kept behind "door number-three." Their off-duty times were filled with gym workouts, barbecues, watching movies, and surfing the Internet. Off-duty time activities for that precious one day with no work did not seem to depend on the year, nor the specific duty station. There were only so many things one would do. Hang out at the local swimming pool, watch the three-dollar, Blu-ray movies obtained from the nearby Iraqi shop, do some laundry, or when really bored, they went back to work and visited with the staff on duty.

LTC Daina said the people she was stationed with were "just so great. I mean we had such a good time and it really made me realize how important it was to be able to laugh with the people that you're working with. I mean you've got to be able to laugh in a situation like that."

LTC Daina went on to describe their Christmas Eve "mudding party" when it had rained all day and the mud was literally up to the top of their boots: "We got into one of these little John Deere Gators and we went driving all over the place covered in mud from head to toe." When she wasn't mudding, she was swimming every day of the week in a beautiful pool at the U.S. embassy complex and playing Spades at night.

Most of the nurses incorporated a two-mile run into their day to stay in shape for their grueling six-day, twelve-hour, workweek schedule, to help them sleep and to be sure they'd be ready to pass the requirements for their Physical Training (PT) test. LTC Ursula's workouts also included kickboxing lessons at least two to three times each week, taught by one of the nurses.

CPT Dalton agreed that humor helped to get them through the tough times. He recalled an April Fool's Day prank his staff played on him. He was a stickler for insisting that the staff respond quickly to any incoming telephone calls: "I made sure our phones were manned and answered within two rings. The staff covered the ear pieces with KY jelly and then called on a telephone nearby where I was standing. Of course I answered and got an ear canal filled with KY jelly. The staff thought that was hilarious." Their sense of humor carried over to the enthusiasm shown for every holiday. With the help of family and friends' care packages, they decorated for and celebrated each national holiday. CPT Frank remembered donning a wig and imitating a well-known singer for their Halloween Party.

LTC Vivian said that there were some really joyous, funny moments and some that were sadly humorous like the Iraqi detainee whose bomb was cell-phone activated and yet he still answered the call from his wife. Needless to say he lost both arms and earned himself a nickname to suit his actions: "dumb ass." She explained: "You have to have some outlet, some humor because you are working with people who want to kill you. The detainees would tell us that. They would say, 'We're grateful for your care but if we weren't here in this hospital, I would kill you.'

Imagine being the orthopod or the general surgeon who just took you to the OR to fix your hernia, or in some cases, fix your hemorrhoid because they did hemorrhoidectomies on these guys. They had to listen to them say, 'Thank you for the care. I feel a lot better, but I'd kill you if I wasn't here.'"

She went on to describe her relationship with the other staff members: "The camaraderie on that team was such that I just felt like I could trust, entrust my life to those people. My nurses, God I love them. I would go anywhere with them. Right now, if they called me and said I need you, I would drop what I was doing with my family to go figure out how I could help them. It just makes you that close."

LTC Vivian loved her staff and she meant it when she said, "We had to have ways to make ourselves laugh." The Morale, Welfare, and Recreation staff designed an activities day with an obstacle course. "We put the detainee suits on and we would go through an obstacle course like under barbed wire, and we'd have to push a Humvee, and then we had to carry a Humvee tire, and we'd climb up the berm, and then the camp's fire police would hose us down on the other side. It was just a way to really get filthy and laugh and just really let ourselves be ten years old again."

She provided lots of laughs on a previous deployment to Baghdad when she was traveling to various Forward Operating Bases with a backpack. "Now the backpack was pretty heavy. Being a female, I had some toiletries. Maybe I had two pairs of running shoes with me rather than one, probably a few books in there. I had a laptop as well. It was really, really heavy and I remember standing in Baghdad on a little flight pad, like right off to the side of the landing zone where the helicopter was going to come in and get us and the whole team was lined up. We were in a queue—the whole team. We had these big boxes of documents; big, heavy boxes of documents that nobody wanted to hold. So we had them sitting on the ground.

"We were all lined up in front of the document boxes and coming over the crest of the hill, in the summer, was this beautiful Blackhawk helicopter. It was just so beautiful. And we were all looking at that thinking, 'God, I wish I had my camera out. Wow, it's too late to dig for it. I'll just stand here and watch it.' As we're standing there watching it, I kind of felt a sense that my whole team had turned around. They were smart. You don't want to get hit with a helicopter blast, the prop blast. But I was so mesmerized by how beautiful it was that I didn't move. Well, the blast hit me so hard that I lost my balance. I didn't realize that all the document boxes were behind me and I still had that backpack on, so I went back and I was like a cockroach on my back. My feet were in the air, I could not get up. There was no way that I could move without somebody helping me. So the entire team was looking at me and they were cracking up with laughter. The only person that actually composed themselves quickly enough was the chaplain. The chaplain came over and he grabbed me and pulled me up with such force, I almost fell over on top of him so it was just a comedy of errors."

WE DIDN'T GET TO SAY GOOD-BYE:
DEATH ON THE BATTLEFIELD

A few moments of humor was sometimes all they had before tragedy snuck up and confronted them on their doorstep. LTC Teresa remembers going into the hospital one day and a young medic was sweeping the front steps. She thought to herself, "Uh, oh, somebody got into trouble yesterday." She joked with the medic who had been well liked at the hospital and went on to work. Later they had a really bad mortar attack: "I didn't think it was going to stop." When it was over she knew they had lots of casualties coming in, so she dropped what she was doing and raced to the trauma room: "… and I started getting everything ready. I had premade packets of medications and fluids we would need for casualties. They brought the first casualty in and hooked him up to the monitors.

"I started working on his intravenous medications, looked at the heart monitor and then said, 'Aww…he's dead.' Somehow at that moment, I turned to look at the internal identification board on the wall and saw the name of the patient lying there, turned away from me. Then I screamed. It was my friend who had been sweeping the steps that day. He and his friends ran for cover when they heard the mortars. Everyone ran into a building, but he didn't make it in time." She remembered how they all cried for him before the Angel Flight that night that took him on the first leg of his journey home. Unwittingly they started their healing process with remembrances of their lost colleague, "You remember when…? Oh yeah, the first time…?"

LTC Teresa will carry the memory of that medic for the rest of her life, as will CPT Frank of the medic he lost in Afghanistan. He was with a Forward Surgical Team (FST) mostly doing surgical cases and another medical unit was doing sick call. The medics in each of those units worked hand-in-hand depending on who had the heaviest workload. Both units were small and the staff became very close to each other. CPT Frank remembered many nights during their off-duty time when one of the female medics from the other unit, SGT Kate, would pick up her guitar and serenade the group with a song or he remembered how just her "bubbly personality lit up a room."

He later learned that SGT Kate had been sent out on a mission. "They had a rocket grenade attack their unit, hit their Humvee, and she died on the spot. She was just one of the really nicest … the easiest person to talk to. She was so friendly … knew everybody and talked to everybody on the Forward Operating Base. She was really good with the patients—even the locals, the interpreters—they all loved her. We had a great time when we all went out together. But, the point I'm trying to get to is, yeah, you can turn on the television and you hear that this soldier died and that soldier died. But to actually be there and to hear that it's someone that you got close to, someone that you know died. No matter how close you were to them, even just to work with them—and then all of a sudden you hear, 'Oh, they are dead.' That was really hard. That was really hard."

Our interview, more than two years after the incident, was the first time that CPT Frank had been able to talk about the pain of losing one of his coworkers and the responsibility he felt toward the enlisted medics and other staff members during her memorial service in the field: "I remember when we had the little memorial service. Everybody's crying and I'm just standing there, being tough. I did not cry." Whether it was because he thought he should be a tough critical care nurse, an in-control officer, or a strong a man, CPT Frank felt he could not cry. He had to hold it together and comfort her peers and the others in the unit. Today he knows that he might have been able to help more if he could have shown that it was okay to cry; to show his feelings of loss and mourning. He also regretted that he could not personally tell her parents what a wonderful person she was and how many lives she had touched. He hoped that her commander was able to convey his feelings of gratitude for the time she shared with him and the others in her unit.

In the time it took CPT Marissa to go to lunch and return, her head nurse had been critically wounded by a mortar attack. She recalled that the hospital had been mortared quite frequently during that time and ". . . maybe we got a little complacent. Even though they hit the hospital, we just kind of got used to it." That day she was to meet a fellow from the Blackwater camp and join him for lunch at the palace. Blackwater had over 500 contract civilian men stationed in the area and some dated the nurses. CPT Marissa had been detained during the mortar attack, but once they gave the "all clear" she joined her friend and they walked to the palace for their meal. On the way back to the hospital, after lunch, CPT Marissa was stopped by a military policeman. "He asked me, 'Ma'am, ma'am, do you work at the hospital?' and I said, 'Yes, I do.' He said, 'Can you check on some people for me?' I said, 'Okay.' He said, 'There was two of your own that we rushed in and we tried to get them to the hospital as quick as we could.' He said, 'Can you tell me if they're okay?' And I said, 'Okay.'" So now I am panicking and I'm walking faster. I get there and I say good-bye to him and I go into the hospital. And I walk up to the floor. It's my floor, and everybody looked very grave. Their faces were just gray. I said, 'Who was it? What happened? Who was it?' And they said it was CPT Ortiz who was a head nurse and my head nurse of the intermediate care ward. They'd been walking to the palace where I had just been—where I walked every day with this guy. They were walking to the palace when the mortar came in. And at that point, I think there were two bunkers between the hospital and the palace, far apart from each other. We were all wondering if they were okay. I mean they said they're in surgery right now. They're in surgery, they're in the OR both of them. So we're all holding our fingers crossed and waiting."

CPT Maria was also waiting along with the rest of the staff. I don't think she will ever forget that night as she described what happened. "I see the doctor coming and everybody's waiting to see how the surgery's going. It's probably about 6 PM, eighteen-hundred hours. I see the look on the doctor's face and she comes and puts her arms around me and everybody knew what that meant. She put her arms around me and said, 'She didn't make it.' She knew I was going to have to be there for them. The entire floor fell apart, all of her nurses. She was the head nurse on that floor and they had been with her since the beginning. I guess you could say their tears flooded the floor for sure—our tears—everyone's tears. I also saw anger—anger at the loss of such a wonderful person. We saw all the stages of death and dying there. The denial: 'This is not true. I can't believe this.' I saw the people falling to the floor, hugging each other. I saw the ones that just went blank and they let all their emotions just go. We had a visiting chaplain at that time and I figured it was just the right moment so I said, 'Can we have a word of prayer?' Then, all of a sudden there was more control and everyone came together. The general was there and the commander was there, everyone, and we all held hands in a big, big circle."

CPT Maria described how she personally reacted: "Later, I finally fell apart. I held myself together through the whole thing, but by midnight everybody was still crying, everybody had a long, long cry. Really, people were still crying for weeks. At midnight, I was sitting outside and finally I decided that 'Now I can cry.' I was sitting alone. I sat there on the corner, on the cement and watched everyone in the distance and just cried my eyes out. I was trying to hold everyone together with glue. I would be their support and I hugged them all. It's very, very sad. I thought, 'I wish the world could see all these wonderful people.' We were actually becoming like a family. We were like a family. Even when I see them today in the hospital, we hug each other. I hug all my staff, I don't care about Army regulations. I hug everyone. Some people would say, 'I can't hug you, ma'am. It's against Army regulations.' I'd say, 'I don't care. Hug me. Everybody needs a hug.'"

For some, a hug was okay, but for others they needed more to sustain themselves in the midst of such pain and agony. I'm also not surprised that CPT Maria asked for a word of prayer. Many of the nurses I interviewed frequently spoke of their strong faith in a higher power.

LIFT ME UP!

LTC Mary told me she believed in God and that she felt the experiences in Iraq made her faith even stronger. Her faith helped her, other nurses, and helped patients get through some of the tough times: "I used prayer for myself, with other nurses, and with patients. Sometimes patients asked for prayer and sometimes I offered it to them and they were very grateful for the offer." She also described various staff prayer groups—some for men, some for women, and some that were both men and women. They also had classes like the Purpose Driven Life and Financial Peace.

Although he called himself a Christian, CPT Dalton said that he did not go to the regularly scheduled Sunday church services very frequently while he was deployed. He found it ironic that while his unit took a Muslim chaplain to Iraq, they also had a large number of ordained ministers assigned to the hospital working as doctors, nurses, and medics. Amongst the large number of Catholics and Mormons assigned to his unit, CPT Dalton found a plethora of private church services at various times throughout the week and located all over the hospital.

Not all of the nurses believed in God and at least one nurse lost her faith while she was deployed. LTC Madeline said that one colleague referred to her as "my little agnostic friend." She did not lean on or believe in a Higher Power. When asked what gave her strength during her deployment, LTC Madeline said, "I had great friends and worked with great people. We found things to keep us out of trouble that were not illegal or immoral."

When CPT Nancy deployed to Iraq, she had just been divorced and struggled with her relationship with God. Initially, she was angry: "God, why did you let me marry this guy if you knew he would cheat on me? Why, why, why, why me? I know that is such a cliché, 'Why me?' but that's what I felt like."

She went on to explain: "So when I got to Iraq I was already in a bad way. Then when I saw everything I saw, it just killed me inside to see these innocent kids going home without limbs and everything else they were going through. And so I completely shut myself off from God while I was there—completely—no remorse over it. It was like, 'I don't want to deal with it anymore.' And I didn't find Him again until I came back home and I went home to see my family and my mom started to cry. She was concerned about me because I wasn't going to church but at the time I still didn't care. Then, it just hit me one day and I don't even know why. I can't remember, but I think it was in January and I said to myself, 'What am I doing?' So now I've been going back; I started going to church. I had stopped praying in Iraq. I think I said one prayer and that was when I went to see CPT

Ortiz in the morgue. I said a prayer for her family and I said a prayer for her. That's the only prayer I said in Iraq at all."

Back home in the United States at her new duty station, CPT Nancy now prays frequently, attends weekly services and a Bible-study class, and joined a singles group at her new church. She attributes her lapse in faith while in Iraq to "bad timing" given her divorce and then being deployed to a war zone. With a little more thought, she recalled that while she had been devoutly religious during her marriage, her husband had not been religious at all, and so they didn't have that important connection.

CPT Nichole was another nurse that did not attend religious services while deployed, but she prayed. "Oh, yes. Everyone prayed; prayer was like number one. I would say, 'Just keep praying. Pray for safety. Pray they never hit us.' Everyone prayed. I think prayer was everyone's number-one, big coping mechanism." LTC Daina said that she did not have a strong faith but "I found myself praying a lot more than I usually do. I was much more attuned to the clues that were going on around me. As far as I'm concerned there was divine intervention—things that could have gotten me into a lot of trouble but for some reason I didn't get into trouble."

LTC Teresa did not want people to blame God for their losses: "This is what we do so don't blame God if something happens. If a mortar comes in and I'm in the wrong place at the wrong time then it is your time. I know friends who said to me, 'My parents prayed real hard that I'd come back home and that's why I came back.' They just don't understand because everybody's parents prayed that they'd come back, and some did not. Your faith has to get you through. I think it's all about how you treat people, how you help each other through whatever."

CPT Frank remembers watching a sick child take his last breath. "It was tough. I think you've got to be strong spiritually and mentally to be able to handle stuff like that . . . if I wasn't getting down on my knees and praying everyday, I don't think I could have handled it very well."

When asked what was the most difficult aspect of being a nurse in Afghanistan, CPT Frank first paused to collect his thoughts and then responded: "I think it was just being honest with yourself. I think for us, especially ICU nurses, we try to play tough. When you get a really bad patient or you're getting attached to a patient and things go bad. You try to play tough—you don't want to cry—you don't want to express your emotions. You don't want to show any kind of feelings and I think that was the hardest part for me. But when you walk around holding on to stuff like that, it's not always good because sooner or later, you're going explode. So, for us, it was good that we had meetings after a bad case and for everybody to express their feelings. We're all very open with each other. For me, I had to actually go outside and if I had to cry, I would just go ahead and do it.

"And then I'd go back to my room and pray about it. Just having my own quiet moment with God made it okay. I'm learning that it's okay to be emotional and it's okay to express your feelings. It's okay to admit that you got attached to a patient and that you just want to let go. I think that that was the hardest part for me; just being honest with myself and being able to open up to people about my experience."

The nurses were lifted and supported by each other, their faith, their families, and their friends back home. LTC Mary described a recreation room used by most of the hospital staff. They called it "Baghdaddies" and it housed a pool table, television, game system, card table, and bookshelves with shared videos and books. Various groups sponsored different "game nights" and family-care packages were shared with the rest of the staff.

LTC Daina counted on letters, e-mails, and packages to keep her going. Her children were grown and her daughter worked the night shift in the states. Given the eight-hour time difference between Iraq and the U.S., LTC Daina's days were her daughter's nights and they were able to talk to each other three to four times each week. LTC Vivian counted on the support of her colleagues back in the states. "They never, ever let me believe that they had stopped thinking about me. When I tell you that there were times that I had five care packages on the floor of my pod that I hadn't even had a chance to open yet, I'd not be lying. I would almost get a care package everyday."

LTC Ursula's extended family and strangers lifted her spirits. Her in-laws, her children's schoolmates, and friends of friends all reached out to her. Her sister in-law's work staff at a bank and her coworkers all sent packages. She felt that the packages told them that what they were doing was important. She said, "There's just nothing better than to be remembered." And, she didn't mind if it was candy or deodorant. Her favorite was to get "fou fou stuff—like the creams and lotions." She and the other nurses would always divvy it up. "Oh, I got peppermint this time, you take the lilac and lavender."

LTC Vivian shared her thoughts on the toll a deployment could take on a marriage and the potential benefits for a couple being separated for one year. "I would share that it takes a very strong, very self-respecting marriage to survive these deployments. I consider my marriage to my husband the most important thing in my life. There are times in your life when you pay a lot of attention to certain things. There were times that I paid next to none, actually negative amounts of attention to him while I was deployed. But I knew that it never mattered; I knew that he still loved me. It didn't matter if I didn't talk to him for a week if I was really busy with my soldiers. But it was the kids that would draw me back. Now I would kind of forget about him but I would always call about the kids. You really have to have a degree of maturity and respect and just the knowledge that it doesn't matter. In the long run, I know you're there for me babe. These junior soldiers that have chaotic relationships to begin with, unfortunately they never survive these relationships. And I saw so many marriages fall apart because they weren't stable to begin with. It wasn't so much the deployment—those relationships just weren't going to survive anyway."

From their first glimpse of the combat zone until liftoff for their final ride home, these nurses experienced a special type of nursing unavailable to them stateside and unique living conditions like few others can even imagine. Their memories of Iraq and Afghanistan shed light on their typical and atypical work days; illuminated their reactions to incoming mortars and severely wounded patients; and identified the people and things that meant the most to them while overseas. Eventually for all, it was time to go back to the world that they had left behind.

WORLDWIDE...TEARS AND CHEERS IN THE REAR

FITTING BACK INTO THE WORLD AND READJUSTING YOUR STARTLE RESPONSE

CPT Maria got a preview of how she might react when she got home when she escorted a patient being air-evaced to Germany. She cried as she described an incident of how once she'd dropped the patient off at the hospital in Germany, she was sitting at a bus stop and suddenly, "I broke down. I never cried so hard in my life. After I left the patient, I fell apart. I was sitting there at the bus stop watching the whole world go by and then it hit me; everything here was normal. There were no mortars coming out of the sky. People were chit-chatting and cars were going by with families. That's when I said to myself, 'Nobody knows what's going on over there. Nobody knows all the pain that we have, all the sadness, all the loneliness, all the misery.' Oh, I have never cried so much in my life."

CPT Maria attributed some of her breakdown to sheer exhaustion: "One of the reasons why I was so upset is that I was tired. I had been up for thirty-three hours transporting the patient and I was so tired. I just wanted to rest. This liaison person from the transportation unit kept saying, 'I'll be there to pick you up in thirty minutes.' And one hour and thirty minutes went by and I was still sitting there. So she'd pop by again and say, 'I'll be back in ten minutes.' Well, another hour went by. I'm watching everything, I'm just sitting there and it was so cold outside. Everything just came together and I became mad about how I was being treated. Here they think we have some great life in Iraq. *Excuse me*, but *no!* We're living in sheer misery." This incident occurred in the middle of CPT Maria's tour and toward the end of her tour the feelings were still there and they frightened her—she was afraid that this would be her reaction to "normal" when she returned home.

"I already knew those feelings were there. I knew I was going back to the world where everything was normal again and I didn't want to forget the soldiers over there. The soldiers who are living in the same place, in that same room where I lived, walking down the same steps I did every morning to go to work. They will be there the same amount of time I was and I was sad thinking about leaving them there. I was glad about coming home. But when you come home, it's like the whole world doesn't see what's going on over there. It's like no one knew what was going on. So I kept worrying about that and I kept on doing my own pep talk, 'Okay, you know you're going to feel that way. It's going to bring you down because the world has forgotten. So get over it!'"

CPT Nancy described her feelings when it was time to rotate back home: "I remember writing in my journal, 'I just want to go home. I want to go home.' And then when it came to the time to go it was different. Most of the hospital personnel left and a few of us stayed back to orient the new combat-support hospital coming in. I was one of the ones who stayed and we were down to a skeleton crew. There was myself (a lieutenant), a sergeant, and an LPN. Only the three of us were left for night shift, so we had to work every night. Towards the end when everybody else had left for Kuwait, it hit me that we were really going to go home and then I started feeling bad. I felt wrong for wanting to go home."

She went on to explain: "I felt like I wanted to do more time. I felt like I didn't do enough during my time . . . there was so much more I had left to learn. When I first got there, I learned so much because of all those injured patients. . . . But then the patient load dropped off and I stopped seeing so many trauma patients and I wanted that—not that I want soldiers to come in hurt—I just wanted to work more. For my last few nights there, I was pulled to the emergency room, but by then I was so confused and too scatterbrained to help much. I wanted that time to learn a new skill but at the same time I just wanted to come home. Still, when I look back I know I'm ready to go back tomorrow." Even now that she is back in the United States, CPT Nancy still feels the pull to return to Iraq: "I saw something on TV and it stirred me up and then I wanted to go back even more. It made me want to go back and take care of the soldiers. The program wasn't about a hospital. It was just about soldiers and I wanted to go take care of them."

CPT Eli shared some of CPT Maria's concerns about public indifference now that he is back home: "I'm kind of disenchanted. It's kind of a double-edged coin. Life is going on and everything is continuing on here in the states. I think we're forgetting that there is a war going on over there—it's still there—it's still going on. I hope that the public support hasn't waned. Multiple organizations were supporting us through e-mail messages and sending us care packages. All of that was very patriotic. I hope those charitable organizations are still doing that. It's just weird to me sometimes to see the reactions of soldiers who have not been over there. I had my soldiers (here at a stateside hospital) watch that documentary *Baghdad ER*. I could see that some of my younger soldiers didn't get it. There was denial in their eyes as they were watching it—that this is a million miles away and it's not real to them."

LTC Ursula also watched *Baghdad ER* when she got home and expressed gratitude: "I've seen all of those shows that are really medically focused and talk about what I experienced and there's nothing about them that makes me angry. I feel grateful that there are cinematographers out there [who] are accurately capturing what we do as soldiers."

LTC Vivian described her flight home from Iraq and her first encounter with a readjusted startle response: "I came into Ronald Reagan Airport in Washington, D.C. There is something to be said for having to come back alone. It's a little different than when you come stampeding into a gymnasium with your whole unit, like at Fort Hood when my husband came back. I traveled in my uniform out of Fort Hood and I remember being in the coach section of the plane. We all had our seat belts on and I didn't notice that the hostess was slamming shut all of the bins. Well, when she slammed it near me, I hit the deck. I had just been back for five days. I was in uniform and I tried to get down on the ground, but I was still seat belted in. So the guy next to me said, 'Oh my God are you okay?' I'm like, 'I'm really embarrassed. I just got back from Iraq.' He said, 'Well, that explains it.'"

She continued: "I'm a normal person with normal mental health. That just shows you that when you're so in tune to doing what you are supposed to do, that when you hear a loud noise you get on the ground." Once she was home, LTC Vivian continued to respond to loud noises. "My startle response is much different than it was before I deployed. I'm much more sensitive to very loud noises. Even my husband commented this weekend, 'Boy you really jumped when that firecracker went off.' And I said, 'Because I didn't know that I was going to hear it.' Had I known, I would have been fine."

CPT Nick has been back for two years and he still can't bear the sound of a garbage truck emptying a dumpster and then slamming it back on the ground so that the lid bangs closed again. "I still get that feeling that comes over me—hit the deck—*right now!* In the beginning it was every loud noise that I didn't see coming."

CPT Dalton has attended a few reunions with his unit and related how these get-togethers provided an opportunity for them to share their experiences once they got home. "We discuss things that still affect us. In fact, I was talking to one of the doctors a couple of months ago and we were discussing how loud noises still bother you. We agreed that it took about six to eight months before you stop jumping at loud noises. We also noted that there was a tapering off effect before you could calm down and be fully integrated back into society."

It's been three years since LTC Mary deployed, yet she still reacts to the sound of helicopters landing on the base where she now lives. She could be watching television in her own living room, yet as soon as she hears the helicopter, her mind immediately goes on alert. Although she says this feeling is less intense than when she first came home, it still takes a moment or two before she can say to herself, "That helicopter is not for me; that's not what I do anymore."

Another Army nurse I'll call CPT Lucille was one year post-deployment when we first met. She was working on a military base that had helicopters flying overhead day and night on various missions. While in Iraq she'd flown with and cared for critically ill patients during many turbulent night flights. She described how, during the night flights, she would cover herself and her patient with a blanket to block out the light from the penlight that she held between her teeth so that she could check the patient's intravenous medication sites and vital signs: pulse, blood pressure, and respiratory rate. She prayed during every flight that her patient would live through the trip and make it to the next stop on his journey home.

Given the number of critically ill patients that CPT Lucille transported during that year, it is not surprising that several were severely burned patients. Imagine CPT Lucille under a blanket and in close proximity to a patient's decaying skin while she cared for him during the flight. She thought she would never forget the smell. The lingering effects affected her senses of smell and taste for up to one year after she returned home. CPT Lucille's resulting decreased appetite eventually left her with uniforms that were at least three sizes too large and had to be replaced. She said she didn't mind the weight loss so much, but found it hard to live with the nightmares that only allowed her to sleep two to three hours each night.

When asked if she'd told anyone about her post-deployment problems, she related that she'd made an appointment for an evaluation, but when the time came for the appointment, she drove to the clinic and just sat in her car. At that point, CPT Lucille had decided that she could "take care of herself." Being a very private person, she also disclosed that she had not discussed her tour of duty with anyone other than a few nurses that had been stationed with her and that none of them knew of her nightmares or her loss of smell and taste. Given that it was still months later when we finally met and she still was not eating very much, her sense of smell had not returned, and she was not sleeping more than three hours each night, CPT Lucille finally accepted that perhaps her "self-care plan" was not working and she agreed to talk to her primary care physician.

Today CPT Lucille has regained her sense of smell, her taste buds are functioning, she's back to her normal weight, she's sleeping through the night, and she is smiling. She doesn't want to remember the dark days of trying to handle things by herself, and now admits that perhaps she should have sought help sooner. When asked why she had not, she expressed a fear of being stigmatized by her peers and of being seen as "less than" by some superior officers. Despite CPT Lucille's admission that she had never seen any concrete evidence of either of those fears, she still harbors a concern that someone someday might learn of her previous difficulties.

CPT Simon also had a difficult time readjusting upon his return home from overseas. He'd lost twenty-nine pounds by the time he returned home from Iraq. Much of the weight lost was caused by gastrointestinal problems suffered in the weeks just prior to his departure from the combat zone. Perhaps more important, he shared that he hadn't sleep well while stationed in Iraq given his nightmares about incoming mortar rounds, worry about his critically wounded patients, and concern over numerous stateside family problems. "When you work night shift, you're not sleeping well and this goes on for days; I was falling asleep over my patients."

He kept his fears at bay and hid his sleep deprivation until about one week prior to his departure when he confided in a psychiatrist. The doctor prescribed Ativan and valium. The day he left, he described himself as "an emotional wreck. I had such good friends over there, I felt like I was deserting them because they had to stay. It crushed me and I would be crying, just crying for no reason."

After he arrived back in the states, CPT Simon's wife picked him up at the airport and they went to a nearby hotel where she had reservations. He described the scene: "When we got there, there was a Middle Eastern person who ran the hotel. We went into our room and I started taking stuff from my duffel bag. I was just happy to see my wife and all of a sudden I had extreme paranoia. I was looking out the window, looking for this Middle Eastern guy. He had family members there helping him run the hotel. Then I completely lost it. I told my wife I wanted out of there right now; we needed to pack our shit and leave. I left a bunch of stuff in the room. I thought someone was going to break the window and just start shooting me."

CPT Simon said that his wife tried to reassure him and remind him that they had already paid for three nights in the hotel. He said his response was: "I don't care about the money. I want to leave. I want a hotel on the fort right now. I'll sleep in the barracks if I have to." He went on to say, "I felt safe going back to the Army base, so we did that. I felt better, but I was still crying all the time. I was glued to the TV watching the news about Iraq, hearing how many soldiers got killed that day and then crying over it." CPT Simon and his wife wanted to go shopping at the

PX (post exchange, like a department store). He described the situation while in the store: "All of a sudden I said, 'I've got to get out of here.' I thought there was a suicide bomber [in the store]. I was looking everyone in the eye, like really strange. I ran out of the PX."

When asked if he told anyone about his symptoms or sought help CPT Simon said: "I did. You know everyone has to go through the post-deployment health thing. I did and I talked to a civilian PA or nurse practitioner. [First] there were these forms to fill out and on mine I put, 'Do you have nightmares? Yes. Did you see dead bodies? Yes. Do you feel anxious? Yes. Are you suicidal? No, I never was suicidal.' Everything pointed to [the fact that] I wanted some counseling. But the guy who interviewed me said, 'If you check that box right there (I think it said, Do you want a high level of psychological or psychiatric care at this time?), you'll be a patient and be here for weeks or months.' There was no way I was spending any more time there. I had to get my family and move to my next duty assignment. So he wrote me up as an acute stress reaction and he gave me more pills."

CPT Simon shared that he was able to hold things at bay during his leave and travel to his next assignment. But once he started working again, the symptoms returned. "I thought I was okay and then I started taking care of the guys with no legs and stuff and it all came back. It was like throwing gas on a fire. I started having nightmares again, flashbacks, emotional crying, and paranoia. The only thing I can attribute it to was I started taking care of my own Iraq patients again. This time they were here instead of in theater." CPT Simon could no longer hold it together and finally sought help.

CPT Simon was the second ANC officer I met who had been diagnosed with and received treatment for post-traumatic stress disorder (PTSD). Both nurses said that they initially felt shame that they "couldn't handle it alone." Both also admitted that they delayed seeking help because of fears that if anyone in their chain of command learned of their "emotional problems," that it would jeopardize their professional career. The female nurse was able to receive private, confidential care with her primary care physician without anyone in her chain of command being notified. Things turned out differently for CPT Simon.

Except for his initial post-deployment assessment request for help, CPT Simon did not seek care again until after he began self-medicating his physical and emotional pain with drugs. Eventually he received appropriate treatment for his underlying physical problems, PTSD, and subsequent substance abuse problems. He believes that at least five other nurses who deployed with him also sought and received "serious psychological counseling" to help them deal with their stress reactions post deployment. Personally CPT Simon is healing and thriving; however, professionally, he feels that he has been "shunned" by a few senior officers who didn't seem to be concerned about his health and welfare.

Had they been stationed in the same organization after being deployed, LTC Mary might have asked more about CPT Simon and CPT Lucille's experiences and given them each an opportunity to share what happened to them while overseas. LTC Mary also believed that there might be a perceived stigmatization associated with admitting that one might need mental-health counseling after an overseas deployment; however, she felt that the greatest gift that one could give a nurse who had been deployed was to ask about their service. "To listen to them and specifically ask questions about their tour. . . . I think that gives them the opportunity to really talk about their experiences and then to reflect on it."

LTC Mary feels that there has to be a more "nonthreatening" way to reach out to folks who are returning: "I think the main message we have to get out is that there is somebody there to talk to or meet them wherever and however they need to be met. And it's not the same for each and every person. Some might want something more formal and another might just need to hear, 'I'm here, if you want to talk.' Just reach out your hand to them."

As a psychiatric nurse, LTC Ursula believes that each receiving head nurse can make a big difference in smoothing a nurse's return back to work in the states. "I think it takes a certain type of head nurse to set the tone that it's okay . . . that you take a little bit of time emotionally to get back to where you need to be. I encourage all the head nurses to really take those soldiers who have deployed under their wing. Even if you know that they had what I would call a totally 'normal' deployment. They didn't see a lot of crazy stuff—their lives weren't at stake—it's still a transition—it's still a hard thing to get used to. And you don't realize it until you've been through that transition period."

When LTC Ursula first returned, she was offered an alternative job that was closer to her home and family. Surprised at the offer, she first declined it: "'Why, I don't need to do that.' The chief nurse responded to me and said, 'You may not realize that you need it, but it will be a nice transition.' And he was right, it was a nice transition to get back to being a soldier in the states again for a little while. So I say to all the leaders out there, the deputy commanders for nursing, head nurses, and section supervisors: 'Please be aware of your redeploying nurses and reach out to them. When you don't think you need to reach out to them, reach out to them. And show extra support and extra caring. Even just a phone call when they least expect it. Say, 'I'm just wondering how you're doing. It must be hard getting back to work.'"

Like their fellow nurses in Vietnam, the ambivalence about leaving the combat zone seemed to stem from various sources. Some did not want to be reassigned and separated from their battlefield colleagues. Some did not want to leave the most professionally rewarding and satisfying assignment they'd ever had, and some did not want to face the personal problems awaiting them when they returned home.

LTC Madeline was blown away by the welcome-home reception she and her colleagues received from civilians and retired military folks at the Dallas, Texas, airport. "You go through customs, through these frosted-glass, double doors, then through this gauntlet of people who are everywhere and you say to yourself: 'Oh my God!' It made me cry. I didn't know how much support we really had over there."

CPT Dalton was not as pleased with his ceremonial welcome home. "When we returned, we flew back into Fort Bliss and there was a large military reception there. We didn't know it was happening. When we came off the tarmac, the general was there along with a large contingency of state senators and representatives, an Army band, and our advance party. They held a welcome-home ceremony for us. But, we'd just finished a twenty-hour flight and we were exhausted. We had our gear on with our weapons and they were standing in formation with swollen feet. Some of us couldn't even get our boots back on. The welcome-home ceremony was very unwelcome at that time. We just wanted to go to bed and get horizontal and instead we had to listen to politicians welcome us home."

As a reserve component nurse thinking about going back to her civilian life after her deployment, LTC Daina's feelings vacillated as the departure time drew near: "As it got closer and closer, I kept thinking, 'Oh, this is no big deal. I'm just going to go home and I'm just going to reintegrate and it's all good.' But the closer it got to going home, the more I was thinking, 'I just don't know how I'm going to do when I get home. Am I going to be able to integrate back into my family? Am I going be able to integrate back with my friends? Is it just going be different?' [And guess what?] It really was.

"I mean I'm still adjusting to being home. But it's just different. I don't know. It was little things like when I got home and I went to change clothes—but I didn't know what to put on. Do you know what I mean? Over there I wore the same thing every day. For fourteen months, I had the exact same thing on every single day, and then I got home and I had to think about what I was going to wear. Finally I'd be able to put on a pair of scrubs and a T-shirt. Then I had to put something on my feet, but I just couldn't, so I just walked around barefoot. I just thought, 'I just can't make these kinds of decisions.'"

LTC Daina had only been back to the United States for three weeks when she shared her thoughts with me: "Driving, of course, has been really, really difficult because over there, everybody gets out of your way. If you see a car coming towards you and they don't get out of the way, you go through your rules of engagement. But if they keep coming at you, you shoot them if you have to. Then of course, over here, I'm driving down the street and people are passing me on the left and passing me on the right because I'm going about thirty in a sixty. That's been really different."

One nurse compared his time in Mosul, the second-largest city in Iraq, to a tour in Bosnia and declared Iraq a "piece of cake"—even when he was under mortar fire. COL Umberto said that it was pretty easy living when you considered that their workplace was right outside their living area and you didn't have to do a one-and-one-half-hour commute like some nurses do to get to Walter Reed Army Medical Center in Washington, D.C.

FAMILY REUNIONS AND SUPPORT

LTC Vivian's homecoming had to be one of the most endearing ones described by the nurses. She describes how the airline stewardess reacted upon learning that LTC Vivian had just returned from Iraq: "She made an overhead announcement to welcome me home and then she put me in first class. My family met me at the airport. Everybody had balloons and American flags. I'm in uniform and it was like that commercial on TV. Everybody stopped what they were doing and watched. People were crying. My kids jumped on me so hard I fell over. I'm lying on the ground at Ronald Reagan Airport. It's almost like a dream. I have never been more proud than that day coming back from Iraq. Really!"

Her homecoming was particularly sweet given the concern expressed by her four-and-a-half-year-old daughter when LTC Vivian and her husband decided to tell the children that she would be leaving: "So the next night we sat down and started to talk in general terms about the war . . . you see it on the news and the war is still going on and the soldiers are still going over there. Every night when we had dinner we say our prayers and we always pray for the soldiers in Iraq. I know that they know that Iraq is a place. I don't know in their little minds what they conceptualize as Iraq, except that Mom went there once and Dad went there for a year. So we told them that Mom was going to go back to Iraq in a few months. The boys just kind of brushed it off, 'Oh Mom, do you really have to go?' But the baby (the four-and-a-half-year-old) was silent. She kind of looked at me then spontaneously got up from where she was eating on the other side of the table, and came over to me and whispered in my ear, 'Iraq is bad.' This is my four-year-old whispering in my ear that Iraq is bad. Now who know what she thinks of as Iraq, but she just knew that it was going to take Mommy away for awhile again.'"

When asked how she responded to her daughter, LTC Vivian said, "I told her that it's a bad place, but there are good things that go on over there, and there are soldiers there. Then I asked her, 'What does Mommy do?' She said, 'You take care of soldiers.' 'And what does Daddy do?' She said, 'He takes care of soldiers.' So I said, 'So, Honey, wherever the soldiers are, they need people to take care of them, so I'm going to go over there and take care of soldiers.' The boys had some question about whether I was going to fight the war and I was very quick to say that as nurses in the Army, that's not what we do. We take care of soldiers and leaving it at that was good."

As it turned out, her boys and her little girl did just fine while LTC Vivian was away. But, a small problem started upon her return and continues to this day: "She was completely potty trained when we broke this news to them. And the whole time that I was gone, my husband had no trouble with her wetting the bed or having accidents at day care. The week that I got back from Iraq, she started having accidents at day care. I hadn't brought in extra changes of clothes and underwear for her in six months and the teachers said, 'You need to start bringing in underwear and pants and stuff. We think she's having some trouble with you being back.' I'm like, with me being back? She should be relieved. But I think there is this underlying anxiety with her about Mommy having to leave again. She's the baby. There's always that special connection with your youngest."

Some of the nurses returned home to little ones or grown children still living at home and some to adult children, married and living with their own children. Regardless, Mom or Dad was back safe and they were grateful. COL Umberto was met at the airport by his adult daughters. LTC Daina was welcomed home by her thirty-six-year-old son and thirty-three-year-old daughter.

LTC Daina downplayed her work in the combat zone and instead focused on what still needs to be done for the soldiers: "Everybody should just verbally tell the troops how you support them over there. Another huge thing that we can do is to take care of their families back here. I'm convinced that if their families are not being taken care of at home, they cannot focus on what they're doing over there. It makes it so hard, because all they want is what everybody wants: they want their families to be safe and they want them to be cared for. They want them to have the medical care that they need. I also think that they [the public] can get out and vote. I think that's really important. I think that they can volunteer their time. I think they can try to assist with the families of the younger service members whose families are here, who are floundering. Many times what happens is that the young families, especially the active duty people, all get transferred and then the family is left behind. Like if their families are in California and they're transferred to Fort Bragg and then three months later, the husband or the wife is deployed, that means that the other spouse is left there with nobody to help them."

LTC Charles came from a military family and he could [not] say enough about the support given to him by his wife and two children: a ten-year-old son and an eight-year-old daughter. "We talked about it. We were very up-front with our family and kids. My family was very supportive. My mother was able to write and call. I was very blessed with a great family support. The mail system was very good where we were stationed. I think there were days when the convoys got blown up but as you know, mail is a combat multiplier. Whoever doesn't think mail is important, hasn't been to war. A letter from home is huge. E-mail and phones are depending [on] where you're at, they are huge multipliers too. But for me, a handwritten letter or package or just anything from my wife and kids was huge. I was the typical father, had the kids' school work up on my walls in my room and pictures. Those were the things that really made a lot of difference."

SLICK-SLEEVES

Part of the military family who greeted the returning Army nurse in the workplace were fellow nurses who had not yet deployed sometimes called "slick sleeves." I first heard this term at Walter Reed Army Medical Center in 2008 when an Army Nurse Corps officer pointed to her camouflaged BDU (battledress uniform) sleeve and said, "See, no combat patch—they call me slick sleeves." She went on to explain: "Once you tell someone that you are an Army nurse, the next question is always, 'Oh, and were you stationed in ____?' You can fill in the blank with the combat area depending on your age and whatever was going on at the time; whether it was Vietnam, Iraq, or Afghanistan. If your answer is no, then you see the visible deflation, the disappointment that 'Oh, then you can't know my hurt, my pain, my personal horror stories, my nightmares. You just can't understand.'"

She went on to explain: "But what they don't understand is that even though we didn't deploy overseas to a combat zone, we still see the same patients, the same wounds when we serve on the wards at Walter Reed." I understood and remembered the trauma patients that were treated after tank accidents in Fulda, Germany, or on the Burn Unit in San Antonio Texas. Maybe these nurses weren't there with the soldier within the first twenty-four hours of them being hit or injured, but they are there for the next few days, weeks, and months of their recovery in the emergency rooms, the operating rooms, the intensive-care units, and the rehabilitation wards. Our reserve component nurses and second-career, retired nurses also serve as civilian nurses caring for our soldiers in Army medical centers, Veterans Administration hospitals, veteran homes, local hospitals, and public-health centers across this country. Some of them don't have a patch either, but they also serve our wounded warriors.

Indeed I did understand what she was talking about when I thought about my best friend LTC Tina (a hospital computer system expert) whose idea of a field deployment was a soft bed at the nearest Holiday Inn, a bubble bath, stereo music, and a few good books. Given her lack of experience in a combat zone, some folks used to tease her and today they might call her slick-sleeved. But, what they could not know was that before she was a computer expert, LTC Tina was the senior nurse in charge of an emergency room, a recovery room, and an intensive-care unit in military facilities around the world. She didn't hear the snipers in Vietnam directly, but she saw the results of their work when she was stationed at Walter Reed. She didn't hear the mortar rounds of Iraq, but she saw the destructive effects of the Kobar Tower bombings as she greeted the shattered and maimed troops at the US Army Medical Center emergency room in Frankfurt, Germany. She didn't hear the roar of the tanks during the first ground war, but she was there to close the eyes of those soldiers who had flipped their tanks in Fulda, Germany, and comfort their buddies. Slick-sleeved Army nurses everywhere must hear the message loud and clear that they are valued for the work they do for wounded warriors regardless of where they are assigned.

PATRIOTISM AND FOREVER FRIENDSHIPS

The Army nurses interviewed seemed to share and live by the core values of patriotism and service to others. Each nurse told stories of how these values shaped their professional and personal lives, affected their immediate family members, and identified them as leaders in their civilian and military communities.

Well established in her civilian nursing career, LTC Daina joined the Army as a reserve component nurse at age forty-one. When asked why she joined so late in her career, she said: "Do you know how many times I've been asked that question over the past fifteen years? It was right after Desert Storm. I think it takes somebody like you who would probably understand that I just had this wave of patriotism that came over me. I think people who are in the military understand that, but I think the general person walking down the street has no idea of what that means. And so for them, I just tell them that I had a midlife crisis and joined the Army."

Another epiphany hit LTC Daina: "It was in 2005 and I had taken command of a minimal-care detachment [unit here in the U.S.]. I had been with the Army for about fourteen years and I was thinking to myself, 'If I can't have at least one deployment under my belt in my military career, I will really feel incomplete.' I know you understand. See, you try to tell that to a civilian and they think you've grown a set of antennae or something. They don't get it—they don't understand it. So I talked to my husband about it in-depth. I mean I might be gone for eighteen months, so I really wanted him to understand what this would mean. It didn't matter. His response was: 'You just do what you have to do.'" With her family's green light, LTC Daina set out to find a unit that was going to Iraq.

She found a unit in October 2005 that was set to deploy in February 2006. How ironic it is that a pediatric nurse practitioner actively searched for and found a position as a preventative medicine officer so that she could serve the troops in Iraq. Even more ironic is that before she even arrived in Iraq, LTC Daina was selected for, trained as, and assigned to be a civil affairs officer. Never underestimate the tenacity of an Army nurse!

LTC Daina spent her first six months in Iraq working with the Baghdad Provincial Reconstruction Team (PRT) focused on enhancing their educational services. Her second six months in country allowed her to work in her clinical specialty and care for the local Iraqi children. Her return home just three weeks before our interview was joyous. "Everybody was just so really glad to see me and they just kept saying, 'Oh my gosh, you look so good. You look so good.' So I guess I didn't fall apart over there."

It was more than just surviving the fourteen months in Iraq; this fifty-seven-year-old Army nurse thrived in an environment where she could serve her soldiers, her patients, and her country. LTC Daina's daughter listened in on our interview and when asked if she had any words for her mom, she replied, "You gave your children something to be proud of."

As a reserve component nurse, LTC Daina returned to her civilian community and relishes her monthly contact with her military family. Many of the active duty nurses returned from Iraq and went on to new individual assignments; some also went on with their careers with new extended family members. LTC Madeline witnessed the promotion of her head nurse to Lieutenant Colonel while in Iraq; the same day they both participated in a MASCAL that was called so they could care for twenty-eight Iraqi citizens who had been burned in an explosion. In 2007 the two nurses celebrated fifteen years of friendship and they still talk to each other at least two to three times each week.

CPT Brenda and CPT Sara served together in Iraq. You can see the sisterly love and joy they have for each other in their homecoming photo that sits on my desk; BDU uniformed arms slung over each other's shoulder, both grinning to beat the band. Although miles apart now with one still on active duty on the East Coast and the other in the Midwest working as a civilian now thinking about joining the reserves, both still talk weekly and each has saved their Iraq reminiscences *only* for each other.

Most of the nurses admitted that other than their interview with me, they had not shared their Iraq experiences with anyone else. CPT Brenda explained: "I can't watch the news. Not so much because it brings back memories—it brings up the feeling that I want to be there to help. You start to feel useless, like 'Why am I not there? Why am I not there to help?' I mean there is still a pull back."

CPT Brenda has volunteered to return to Iraq. She went on to explain her feelings: "Remember the presentation you did about Vietnam nurses saying that they felt so useful over there? Well it was the same for me. In Iraq you felt like you were accomplishing something over there because you are in the middle of the fight. We had the same sentiments as those Vietnam nurses, so that night I went home and called Sara. We couldn't believe you understood what we were feeling."

CPT Sara had returned home to the Midwest to marry her sweetheart and begin to raise a family, but she still struggled with missing her Army family and Army nursing. She was surprised by the depth of her longing and eventually took CPT Brenda's suggestion and joined the local reserve unit to maintain her connection with the military. Preparing to retire from the Army Nurse Corps, LTC Ursula also understood that yearning to somehow remain connected to the military and she wanted to share her thoughts with others who might be planning to leave military service: "When you retire, consider taking a job as a GS (government civilian) or a contractor so you can still continue to take care of soldiers. That's what I plan to do. I'm going to do exactly what I do now but just in a different outfit like you're wearing now; in a business suit because I just can't stop taking care of soldiers. There's nothing more important to me than a soldier in a uniform. That's what gets me up in the morning."

The shared love of soldiers and love for your Army colleagues makes for forever friends as they share your life's joys and sorrows. A former chief of the Army Nurse Corps, Brigadier General Hazel Johnson once remarked that, "Over the years, Army Nurse Corps colleagues and friends become our second family and we cherish our time spent together." General Hazel was reminiscing about her career and the Army Nurse Corps family she still holds dear in her heart many years after she has retired.

Given a twenty- to thirty-year career in the Army Nurse Corps, ANC colleagues have the opportunity to lift and hold each other many times during life's ups and downs. CPT Brenda flew across the country to be a bridesmaid in CPT Sara's wedding. CPT Brenda's wedding gift, to her forever friend CPT Sara, was a framed copy of their Iraq deployment story and photo as published in an ANCA newsletter. But for some, their personal experiences were not always joyous.

Of all the nurses interviewed, a few went to or returned from Iraq to face some of life's most difficult personal challenges such as infidelity by their spouse, financial problems, pending divorce, loss of their spiritual roots, seriously ill children, and/or the death of a parent. CPT Nilda had been in Iraq only one month when she was notified that her mother had passed away in Central America. The hospital staff in Iraq encircled her with support and smoothed the way for her transportation so that she would make it home in time for her mother's funeral. CPT Nilda was able to stay in Central America for twenty-two days to help organize her mother's affairs and comfort her family. Then it was time to go back to work, to return to Iraq.

CPT Nilda admits now that she buried her grief "like a good soldier" so that she could return to duty and care for her patients in Iraq. The last leg of her trip back to Iraq showed her just how fragile she was emotionally. CPT Nilda reported that while she was a passenger in a helicopter, the gunner began firing his weapon out of the side of the chopper as it crossed the border into Balad. CPT Nilda said that she just bowed her head and prayed that God would take her quickly. When the helicopter pilot saw what she was doing, he apologized and explained that they were *not* under attack, just test firing their weapons. She shared that although the terror of those moments remained with her, they were somewhat relieved by the overwhelming support provided to her by her ANC colleagues when she returned "home in Iraq."

After the completion of her Iraq tour and her return to the United States, CPT Nilda said that she received a call from a former chief nurse "just to check on me." CPT Nilda admitted that she tried to hide her feelings, but her chief nurse kept nudging and prodding until finally she admitted to periodic painful feelings of grief, depression, and sadness. She said that her chief nurse told her that this was normal given the number of losses that she had experienced in the past year with her mother passing, the death of a dear friend, and then leaving her job and friends in Iraq. With follow-on periodic calls to check on CPT Nilda, her former chief nurse provided the support she needed as she worked through her grief and helped her to move on. CPT Nilda also noted that her firm spiritual foundation and local chaplain support also helped to give her more peace, inner strength, and support to be able to "march on."

CPT Nilda's chief nurse served as an unofficial "godmother" in her life; one who reaches out to help in the midst of a great loss with its pain and inner turmoil. The role of "godmother" within the ranks of the ANC seems to be an unwritten and unspoken position freely filled by many senior and retired ANC officers. Each nurse I interviewed shared a story of at least one superior officer who believed in them, stayed in touch with them over the years, and held the high watch for them when they were troubled. For a few, the position of godparent was filled by a godfather. Regardless of gender, godparent support seemed to permeate an entire career, went up and down the chain of command, and moved into the civilian community as their relationships eventually became "forever friendships."

MG Gale S. Pollock, former Chief of the ANC, first nurse to serve as the Deputy Surgeon General of the Army, and now retired from active duty, frequently shares the story of a senior noncommissioned officer stationed at Fort Dix who would come to her parent's home every Sunday for dinner. That senior Sergeant told nine-year-old Gale that he had faith in her and he knew that she could be anything she wanted to be. He also told her that he had survived his Vietnam War wounds because of the outstanding care that he had received from Army nurses, and he would forever be grateful to them.

Young Gale took that faith in her abilities to heart and knew then that one day she would become an Army nurse. What she didn't know then was that she would eventually become a nurse anesthetist, a hospital commander, and the person who would establish specialty pay for Army nurses, decrease the Army nurse deployment time from one year to six months, and drive proactive efforts to support all deployed nurses. That Vietnam Wounded Warrior served as General Gale's first godparent in a long and distinguished career and gave her the encouragement and support to believe in herself while living in the midst of family chaos. The ripple effects of his long-ago actions impact the nurses who serve in the combat zone today. Sometimes you receive support from a godparent and sometimes you *are* the godparent and you get to pass along some of the love and support that you received, thereby creating more forever friendships.

Another role that seemed to emerge in the highly charged emotional atmosphere of a combat zone and endure beyond distance and time with assignment changes and even retirement is that of being a brother or sister to your teammates. LTC Terri's experiences as a family nurse practitioner, embedded with various Special Forces (SF) teams in Afghanistan, clearly demonstrated and epitomized the combined concepts of being a gold standard caregiver, a loving godparent, and a respected sister for not one, but several soldiers and one critically wounded warrior. The objective of her Afghanistan job assignment was for LTC Terri (the senior ANC officer, one of four nurses assigned to the Battalion) and her one Army medic to be attached to various SF Units as needed, so they could offer medical assistance (MEDCAP) visits to targeted Afghan villages. Flown into each area with their SF team, the health care visits enabled LTC Terri and her medic to provide modest health care much like what might be available in a neighborhood outpatient clinic.

Their supplies were flown into Kandahar where they would resupply themselves just before each mission with the following: over the counter pain medication like Tylenol and Motrin; bandages and sutures for deep cuts; intravenous fluids for dehydration; baby formula; eye ointments; and steroid creams for dermatitis; as well as personal hygiene items such as combs, lotion, powder, toothpaste, and tooth brushes. This valued service made the Special Forces' visits very popular in the villages and helped to gain the trust of the Afghan women and to garner critical information about the Taliban. Eventually their team learned to put semipermanent ink markings on the hand of each Afghan woman served so they could readily identify the women who had already been seen. Before they devised this accountability system, they found that the women would get their medical care and then get back in line for another visit to get more supplies. Their health care team usually stayed for just one day, but periodically they had to stay overnight in a remote area.

LTC Terri explained that just a few months into her seven-month tour, she, her female medic, a female interpreter from the U.S., and their Special Forces team (riding in five Humvees) were ambushed by about fifty Taliban soldiers. They had spent the night before secured in an orchard because a critical piece of equipment had malfunctioned (a bucket loader tipped over) and they had to wait for permission to destroy it so that they could move on. That permission came the next morning. It was noon the next day by the time they had destroyed the bucket loader, packed up their supplies, left the orchard, and emerged into a clearing.

By the time that LTC Terri's Humvee (#4) emerged from the orchard into the clearing, she said that she heard over the radio, "'Man down! Man down! The chief is down!'" The second in command of the SF team was Warrant Officer 2 Romulo Camargo, better known as "Chief Romy." He had switched seats in his Humvee to allow LTC Terri's female interpreter to ride shotgun and he sat in the more vulnerable rear seat in the second Humvee. The chief was critically wounded in the back of the neck. LTC Terri said that when the alarm went out over the radio, she was sitting in the rear seat of the fourth Humvee in the convoy and was told to "man the 240" (M240 machine gun) while the SF troops in her vehicle ran forward to protect their perimeter and guard their wounded leader. LTC Terri said that she immediately responded, jumped up and into the rear-facing Humvee seat, and fired the M240 into the hillside.

When asked how she knew what to do with the M240 (machine gun), LTC Terri said that whenever she had had "down time" back at their Forward Operating Base, the SF troops would help her to practice on the firing range with all of their weapons. Once she was in place and firing the weapon, she remembered thinking to herself, "My place is with the Chief." She called for relief of her firing position and then ran to assist the combat medic who had already gotten the Chief on a litter and lowered to the ground. They could not detect any breath sounds so the medic performed a "field cricoid" (made a small incision in his neck, to allow air to flow through and into his lungs) and LTC Terri "bagged" him (manually forced air into his lungs) and applied pressure to the exit wound by his right clavicle.

LTC Terri then shared that the team leader, a Special Forces Captain, called for a "9Line" (a Chinook helicopter used for medical evacuations) and close air support from the Air Force. An F16 fighter jet arrived to secure the general area and a landing zone for the Chinook. LTC Terri reported that within thirty minutes of being hit, the Chief and his combat medic were on their way to the next level of medical support at a large forward operational base. From there they went to Kandahar for an overnight stay and a CAT scan, which revealed that the Chief's C2 (upper part of his spine) was shattered. They next spent six hours in Bagram Air Base, moved on to Landstuhl Regional Medical Center in Germany, and finally arrived at Walter Reed Army Medical Center (WRAMC) in Washington, D.C., within three days of him being shot. The Chief then spent a few weeks at WRAMC being stabilized before being moved to what he now calls his "temporary home," the Spinal Cord Injury (SCI) unit at the James A. Haley Veterans Administration Hospital in Tampa, Florida.

One year and two days after that ambush, I met the Chief, his Army nurse LTC Terri; his combat medic, SFC Steven S. Hill; the Special Forces team; and their former 7th Special Forces Group Commander, COL Sean P. Mulholland, at a community luncheon with 250-plus family members, friends, and local veteran leaders. Everyone gathered that day to welcome the Chief back to his hometown in Citrus County, Florida, and to honor him for his service and sacrifice. Ensconced in a motorized wheelchair and accompanied by his VA nurse, the Chief was on a temporary pass so that he could share in the celebration. A large contingent of Rolling Thunder members on their motorcycles escorted Chief Romy, his wife Gabriella, daughter, and son to the Black Diamond Golf and Country Club driving range where they witnessed the U.S. Southern Command Parachute Team jump from 2,000 feet with red smoke billowing from the heels of their boots and the American flag waving from the commander's back. Listening to the accolades of the speakers at the luncheon, Chief Romy was clearly loved by all and wished only the best in his ongoing recovery. His laughing but serious response was that he plans to walk again, join up with his unit, and return to Afghanistan to finish his tour of duty. He looked at his former commander and said, "You still owe me 120 days." The Chief received a standing ovation as everyone applauded his goals.

There was a unique military/civilian community that saluted the Chief that day in Citrus County, Florida. It is part of Congressional District 5, which represents the largest Congressional district of veterans (116,000) in the United States. The veterans and civilian citizens of Citrus County are proud to demonstrate their patriotism. Their annual Veterans' Appreciation Week Program includes a military ball, social, fair, political forums, luncheons, musical tributes, a memorial service, a Massing of the Colors ceremony, a parade with ninety-nine-plus entries, and two weeks of volunteering for their award-winning "Veterans in the Classroom Program" that is available to every primary, middle, and high school. Members of their major veteran service organizations work together all year on community projects that help to educate the public about patriotism, feed hungry families, provide financial assistance to needy veterans, and welcome home returning Iraq and Afghanistan patriots with community gift baskets.

The camaraderie and "forever friendships" that I witnessed that day with the Army nurse, the SF team, and Chief Romy had been nourished by get well cards, weekly telephone calls of encouragement, twice monthly visits by someone from the team (when they were in the country), and frequent e-mails. LTC Terri flew into town for the luncheon and admits that these soldiers are now and probably always will be part of her extended family, her brothers. She calls them to check on their health, family affairs, and state of mind. Even though she is no longer on the battlefield with them, this combat nurse and her ANC colleagues around the world will continue to look after all of their military brothers and sisters wherever they might be serving our nation.

HOME...HOLDING, HELPING, AND HEALING

CARING FOR ARMY NURSES AND WARRIORS: SURVIVING THE STRESS OF WAR

Recently I was meeting with one of my soon-to-be-graduated nursing students; I asked her about her plans after graduation. To my surprise, she was an ROTC student headed to San Antonio, Texas, for AMEDD (Army Medical Department) basic training specifically designed for nurses and doctors. Following basic training, she was going to be deployed to Landstuhl Regional Medical Center, the U.S. military hospital in Germany that receives the wounded warriors direct from the battlefield. She told me she hoped to deploy as a combat nurse to a war zone after her service in Germany. I have known her for two years and have been working on this book for a year of that time. Having heard the voices of the nurses whom Dr. Sharon interviewed, I thought I was more sensitive to the stresses combat nurses experienced and the urgent need for special training and preparation for such wartime deployment. However, I realized that my fellow teachers and I were sending this student and other ROTC nursing graduates to a potential deployment without any special preparation from us. This revelation renewed my conviction that we needed a section of this book that provided compelling and useful information to assist four groups.

The first group is the combat nurses and warriors; the second group is the families and friends of nurses and combat troops; the third, the personal and professional communities they return to; and fourth, the civilian and military caregivers who provide their pre- and post-deployment health care. It is our hope that this book will help these four groups of readers to armor up against wartime stress; to understand stress reactions in order to help themselves and know when to seek help from others; and to inform civilian and military caregivers how to identify and treat the effects of wartime stress and stress reactions in nurses and warriors. The strategies for combating wartime stress are divided into three sections: first, what can be done before deployment; second, what can be done during deployment; and third, what can be done after deployment.

We have included a fact sheet about the prevalence of PTSD and depression (see Appendix A) in current and previous wartime nurses and warriors. As you will see, the large numbers of warriors who are experiencing postwar stress reactions is alarming; these escalating numbers have captured the attention of the nation.

WHAT CAN WE LEARN FROM PREVIOUS WARS?

Post-traumatic stress disorder and depression are the most common wartime stress reactions for warriors, but in previous wars, stress reactions have been called *combat fatigue, battle fatigue, exhaustion, railway spine* or *railway hysteria, shell shock,* and *soldier's heart.* After Vietnam, PTSD (post-traumatic stress disorder) became the term used for the most severe stress reaction.

In addition to the stories Dr. Sharon has shared from her interviews with combat nurses, I would like to provide some background about wartime stress in warriors and caregivers in previous wars so that we can learn from their experiences. One of the first images to come to mind is the film and television series *M*A*S*H**, associated with the Korean War. However, wartime stress reactions and depression are far older than the second half of the twentieth century; they are not new warrior and healer experiences. Certainly the Civil War and World Wars I and II were traumatic for many participants. They were multiyear wars and troops and nurses were deployed for long periods of time, often enduring dreadful living conditions. After World War II, soldiers and support staff —like nurses—had to say good-bye to people they had come to know and love. Many wartime romances and friendships were continued; some were terminated. Nurses often experienced feelings of loss of knowing that they were important and needed, and that what they were doing was invaluable—in contrast to the combat field, the stateside jobs seemed meaningless and left them feeling unimportant. Also, veterans returned to communities and families that were totally unprepared for the change in their returning loved one—what had happened to them was a complete mystery to those who stayed behind. Most of us viewed the wartime stress experienced by actor Brad Pitt in the movie *Troy* but didn't think about the relation to stress reactions in current warriors. Shay (1994) compared the ancient battles of Troy with Vietnam in the handling of the wounded and dead and the rituals surrounding death in battle. In both Troy and Vietnam, the dead were brought out with the wounded during or after the battle. In Troy, rituals of death were performed by fellow soldiers and commanders, whereas in Vietnam the wounded and dead were evacuated to other areas to be treated or dealt with by strangers. (When there was time, a symbolic field funeral was held using the boots, rifle, and helmet of the lost soldier.) This meant that grief work was interrupted and strangers handled and returned the corpse to the U.S. We can't overstress the importance of the chance to see and take care of the dead body as a healing process for the nurses and warriors.

At the same time, caring for a stranger's body is often traumatic; yet this is most often the process used in wartime. Also, in recent wars, nurses often care for the wounded and dead in the civilian and enemy soldier population, which further complicates the grief reactions over the death of our warriors. However, even more distressing, in Vietnam as is the case in Iraq and Afghanistan, there was often not even time to mourn in safety so mourning was and is often delayed or never facilitated. When time and the rate of incoming casualties permitted, the emergency treatment teams gathered for after-action reviews to identify treatment, review lessons learned, and to share their feelings of frustration, anger, helplessness, grief, and sadness.

Similar to the experiences described in our interviews, the feelings described by the caregivers and warriors while they are in the war zone include feelings of helplessness; constant threats to their own safety; and overwhelming sensations such as sights, sounds, and smells. They also spoke of the impact of seeing and handling wounded and dead bodies—especially those severely wounded by modern warfare who might have died in previous wars; and observing the devastation to the lives and well-being of civilians caught in war situations. These stress reactions are most common and severe when troops are deployed more than once; are deployed for longer periods of time; have previous experience with war; are in areas where the fighting is especially intense; or are wounded themselves. All of these factors are very true in Iraq and Afghanistan as combat stress is experienced at all times, even in supposed relaxed situations, and the length of deployment is significantly longer and more frequent than in recent wars. All of this makes the stress reactions especially devastating.

The reactions of combat vets in general are described above but there are reactions that are unique to certain populations. These populations include nurses, women, warriors and nurses of color, and Reservists and National Guard troops. We are especially interested in nurses at war.

NURSES

As the nurses in Dr. Sharon's interviews expressed, nurses experience stress reactions with differences and similarities to the reactions of combat troops. Let's look at those reactions to the current wars by studying nurses' reactions to their experiences in past wars. While we can learn lessons from all wars, the nurse experience in the Vietnam War has been the most researched.

Repeatedly experiencing patient death and serious injury can lead to PTSD in the wartime or civilian world. Just as Dr. Sharon has described in the earlier sections of this book, in Vietnam and in Iraq and Afghanistan, nurses are volunteers but still arrive in the war zone to find themselves shocked by the living conditions, the constant danger, the lack of privacy, the fatigue from long hours and an extremely heavy patient load, the very severely injured warriors, and the different social life. Some of the traumatic and stressful experiences of the nurses were seeing these young warriors so destroyed by the war; sending young troops back to combat once their physical wounds healed; treating so many casualties at one time, sometimes without enough supplies; adhering to the "triage-out" policy of leaving soldiers wounded too severely to be saved to die without treatment; saving soldiers with enormously compromised quality of life who in former wars would have died on the battlefield; being too inexperienced to handle the severity of injuries; the morality of saving patients with very serious, permanent injuries that severely impacted the quality of life of the warrior vet; and not fully understanding the politics of the war.

One of the common reactions to service in wartime is the desire to simply adjust to and survive the war and go home; innovation and creativity were important in that effort to survive. Also important in that survival strategy were friendships— with colleagues, patients, sometimes even civilians in country. Friendships between nurses and patients helped them adjust to living and working under conditions for which they had little life experience and little preparation.

The trauma that nurses experience that comes from watching the suffering and death of others is especially severe in nurses who have served in a war before. Previous war experience adds to the wartime exposure and seems to have a multiplier effect to that experienced in only one deployment. In Iraq and Afghanistan, the Army nurse experience is more like the combat veteran experience in that there is no front line. The nurse is never completely safe from injury and can experience the war firsthand with incoming rounds or IEDs while traveling.

Most nurses say they wish they could know what happened to the soldiers they cared for after they were airlifted out of the war zone. There was no closure for the nurses and we know that this interfered with normal grieving. Again, just as with the nurses interviewed by Dr. Sharon, supportive social networks while deployed were very helpful in preventing stress disorders. However, Dr. Sharon found that few active duty nurses she interviewed shared their experiences with each other when they returned home and went on to their next duty assignment. The Army

Nurse Corps identified this problem and conducted a pilot program called "Veterans Resiliency Program" in 2009 to facilitate sharing of their combat experiences. They invited five Vietnam nurses (all retired) and fifteen OIF/OEF nurses (all active-duty) to an off-site location for one weekend, with the help of two facilitators. The nurses shared stories, tears, and laughter and declared their experience a rousing success. How poignant that this weekend program was so similar in format and success as that described by LTC Elaine after her tour in Vietnam. Nurses are encouraged by the camaraderie among warriors and caregivers.

It is clear that the Vietnam nurse veterans were emotionally attached to the warriors they served. Even though the Vietnam War experience was difficult but rewarding, as mentioned above, these nurses bemoaned the fact that they did not have follow-up information on the patients they treated (Ravella 1995). In most studies, the nurses had connected emotionally to the warriors they treated and were anxious to know if their efforts resulted in survival or recovery. Such information was not available and the fact that they did not know what happened to their patients limited the ability of the nurses to find meaning in their efforts.

After serving in Vietnam, because of the hardships in living, most of these nurses described coming back to the United States as a happy experience. However, because they felt they were doing important work in Vietnam, while they watched the disrespect from the anti-war protesters, they felt dissonance and disconnected.

WOMEN

Since the majority of nurses in the U.S. are women, (about one-third of ANC officers are male nurses), the specific experience of women in the military is also of interest. Until recent times, females only served in such support roles as nursing and not in direct combat roles. However, in these current conflicts, and given there is no clear front line, women are more exposed to combat than in previous wars. As with all troops, having been in a combat situation before increased the stress symptoms of female Vietnam veterans after another deployment to a war zone. It seems that the reawakening of the previous wartime reactions puts the newly redeployed warrior into the stress reaction spectrum at a more serious level than a newly deployed person in a first deployment. Among nurses, older, more experienced nurses fared better than young, inexperienced nurses.

The Vietnam women veterans experienced the same negative reactions from the public as did Vietnam vets in general, but they also had the added burden of dealing with discrimination against women in a uniform. They often felt rejected and that they were not appreciated. So they often tried not to be identified as

Vietnam vets and resisted treatment for many of the same reasons male vets did. In addition, they often believed that they had had it easy compared to the combat troops and, therefore, should not be having problems or were not worthy of treatment. The survivor guilt described above is also experienced by nurses and warriors who were not on the front lines or in the immediate vicinity of the trauma. This survivor guilt kept them from seeking therapy, at least until their symptoms overwhelmed them. Years later, as these women underwent therapy, they often did not connect their current problems with their Vietnam experiences until the therapist helped them make the connection.

MILITARY SEXUAL TRAUMA (MST)

Even though women vets may avoid treatment, it is clear that some do experience stress reactions and depression after current wartime experiences. They also experience an issue not experienced in the alarmingly high rates by men—military sexual trauma. Department of Veteran Affairs researchers reported that one in seven female service members who had deployed to Iraq or Afghanistan and later sought VA health care anytime from October 2001 until October 2007 had been sexually harassed or assaulted during their service (Maugh 2008). These rates were in contrast to only 0.7 percent of male troops who had similar experiences. Additionally, of those females who reported harassment or assault, they also were 2.3 times as likely to suffer from PTSD and more likely to suffer from depression or substance abuse disorders. The researchers also noted that this was the first study that found a correlation between sexual abuse and mental health problems associated with deployments (Walsh 2008).

Some recent estimates are as high as 20 percent of military women report experiencing sexual assaults or severe, threatening harassment (Walsh 2008). Just as in civilian situations, these women are often further victimized by the system that treats them as if they somehow encouraged or participated willingly in the sexual behavior. Or the system may not take appropriate or any action, further alienating the female soldier. Because of the under reaction and under protection of female warriors, they then are reluctant to seek treatment in the system, all of which may result in a severe stress reaction (*Minority Nurse* 2009; Walsh 2008; McVickers 1985).

Given that none of the nurses interviewed spoke of any incidents of MST, I asked Dr. Sharon if she had encountered it during her military career. Her response proved to be the most painful discussion we had in writing this book. I asked her to write an account of her experiences and share some of her personal feelings at the time and how she is dealing with her feelings now.

The first incident happened when I was deployed in 1985 for six weeks to an area outside of Fort Bliss, Texas, with the 8th EVAC Hospital. Although at the time I was permanently stationed at Letterman Army Medical Center in San Francisco, my simultaneous temporary assignment for proficiency training was as the chief nurse of the 8th EVAC Hospital. A temporary assignment, called PROFIS, becomes activated when that unit is deployed to a combat zone or elsewhere to support warriors during their training exercises. There was a small core group of administrative staff members permanently assigned to the 8th EVAC in Monterey, California; but most of the clinical staff came from Army hospitals across the country. Shortly after we set up the hospital in a large open field, in Temper Tents [temperature-controlled modular units] and opened for business, I received a midnight visit from a small group of enlisted women who had been permanently assigned to the 8th EVAC. They asked to speak to me confidentially and privately so I invited them into my sleeping room [a large supply box used to transport equipment]. A spokesperson for this group of Hispanic women explained that they were being harassed by a senior sergeant [also Hispanic] in their unit and they wanted my help to make him stop. I was the senior ranking female in the hospital during the training exercise. They also told me that previously they had reported the problem up their chain of command at their base, but nothing happened. When asked to give me examples of what he had done, they reported the following allegations: 1) The sergeant made frequent unannounced room inspections at 2 AM so that they had to jump out of bed in their night clothes and stand at attention by their bed, as soon as he turned on the lights and shouted, "Room inspection!" 2) Whenever he walked past one of them outdoors, he always shook their hand and leaned in appearing like he was saying something complimentary. But he was simultaneously saying what he wanted to do with them sexually (in Spanish) and rubbing his middle finger across the palm of the enlisted woman's hand he was shaking. 3) Earlier that day the women had been off-loading supplies from railroad cars. Some of the women had been standing on top of a boxcar when the sergeant yelled up to them in Spanish and said that he wished that they would take off their pants and jump on his face so that he could lick and kiss them.

By the time they finished talking that night, we were all in tears. I first told them that they were right to come forward and report his unacceptable behavior and that I was especially proud of them for reaching out again after they had been ignored the first time they reported the problem. I promised them that I would take it from there to ensure that he was held accountable and that they need not fear any type of retaliation from him or anyone in their command group. At that point I was stepping out on faith because this was my first encounter with sexual *harassment in my career (fourteen years by then). Given that they had already tried their own chain of command unsuccessfully, I reported their complaints to an Inspector General [also known as the IG] office outside of their command chain. I was impressed with the swift response of an immediate investigation and when their allegations were upheld, appropriate action was taken against each person involved in the incidents and the cover-up. Even though my heart hurt for these women who experienced such blatant disrespect and abuse by their unit leaders, I did not take the situation personally.*

That was not the case with the second incident which occurred almost ten years later while I was the Chief of the Department of Nursing at Eisenhower Army Medical Center, Fort Gordon, Georgia. One evening while working late in my office, I looked up from my desk and saw one of my female, senior noncommissioned officers passing by. I called out a greeting and asked how she was doing. She responded so clearly I can still hear the snarl in her voice today, "What do you care?" I immediately jumped up from my desk and called her into my office. This was not the straight, by-the-book, confident, senior leader that I knew entering my office with tears in her eyes and rage emanating from her body.

When I asked what was wrong, she kept responding that I already knew about her problem. I assured her that I did not know about her problem and I would appreciate it if she would explain it to me. She then shared that a more senior, male, noncommissioned officer in my department had been making untoward advances like locking her in an elevator between floors and touching her against her will; refusing to accept a required document from her unless she came close enough so that he could touch her inappropriately; and pinning her against an office countertop so that he could grope her body. She said that the incidents had started over a month ago and she had reported each incident up the noncommissioned officer chain of command. She had been told that they were investigating her allegations but no action had been taken. She thought that I knew about the incidents because she had discussed the problem with the most senior noncommissioned officer in my department.

I was speechless, horrified, and so ashamed that she had been made to suffer like that "on my watch." I calmly told her that I would meet with the commanding general the next morning and brief him on everything that she told me, including the lack of response from the company command staff. For the first time in my military career, I went home and I wept most of the night. I felt like I had failed her and wondered if there were others in my department who also had been assaulted. [I stayed up most of that night typing up everything that she told me.] I knocked on the commanding general's door the next morning one hour before he was to get the hospital patient report. At that point I was still so choked up I could hardly talk; I just handed him the detailed report of what she had said. When he finished reading the report, this calm, quiet, restrained general jumped up, flung his chair across the room, and yelled for his secretary to get the IG [inspector general] in his office immediately. The general then ordered a complete and thorough investigation that was to be completed within forty-eight hours. He also called the female noncommissioned officer to his office and told her the timeline for the investigation and requested that she be in his office to hear the results.

Within forty-eight hours we all joined him again in his office to listen to the report of the investigation. Each of her allegations about the senior noncommissioned officer had been substantiated and each person culpable of negligence in the cover-up identified. Further, the Inspector General found that many of the enlisted [lower-ranking] staff knew of the allegations and were waiting to see how it would be handled. The general rendered the most severe military punishment for each person at fault and then ordered the development and implementation of mandatory sexual harassment training for each person who worked at the medical center. He wanted everyone to know that what happened was reprehensible and would not be tolerated.

As I shared these two incidents with Dr. Diane on the telephone and now as I write my recollections of the second incident, I must admit that I wept again remembering her abuse, her pain, and her feelings of helplessness. I also wept remembering my own journey, a long buried assault and much delayed diagnosis and treatment of PTSD. That treatment [Rapid Trauma Resolution with Dr. Jon Connelly] taught me how to clearly separate my present-day feelings from the memory of my assault and frame the assault within the context of old and therefore irrelevant objective data that does not have the power to hurt me today. Today I am grateful for my treatment, which occurred many years after my assault and wish that that same type of treatment had been available for my senior noncommissioned officer.

Even with my newfound skills, I still shed tears today because I see the assaults and the abuse of power continue with new perpetrators and new victims. I read about sexual assaults and the abuse of power in our school systems with trusted teachers and still in some of our military units around the world. Each time another incident occurs without repercussions, the unspoken message is that this is acceptable behavior. When some of my military brothers today ask me how to draw the line between what is abusive and what is not, and are truly puzzled by a situation, I give them two clear ways to test the appropriateness of their words or actions. Please note that I give them two tests because I have learned that a *few seem to have a high tolerance for inappropriate behavior and fail the first test by responding with comments like: "Oh, it was really not a big deal; surely not enough to fire someone or to impart severe military punishment."*

For the first test I would say, "Ask yourself if whatever you are about to say or do becomes a headline in your local newspaper tomorrow, would you be shamed by it?" Even if they fail this first test, most seem to finally get it with the second test in identifying the line between what is appropriate and what is not. I say to them: "Ask yourself, if someone else said those same words or did those same things to your mother, sister, wife, or daughter (regardless of age), would that be okay with you or would you have to hurt them?" The bottom line is that if they are not appropriate words or actions for your loved ones, they are not appropriate actions for anyone else's loved one. Granted, a very few might still miss the mark with both tests thereby making it even more imperative for fellow leaders to be proactive advocates in protecting subordinates regardless of their gender.

It is important to understand the effect of such sexual assault and harassment on women serving in combat, especially in the current wars in primarily Muslim countries. There, our female soldiers face the same usual attitudes male soldiers experience plus those attitudes that are about the seeming subservient role of women in Middle Eastern society. In addition, women veterans have battled negative attitudes about women in combat and have received fewer services for the stresses of war in general and, for military sexual trauma, have even fewer choices since they may not trust services provided by the military or by men. It is even more painful when experienced by female soldiers (*not* nurses) who volunteered to accompany such units.

Former VA Secretary James B. Peake, M.D. (also former U.S. Army Surgeon General) heard the voice of the female veteran and on August 28, 2008, charged his senior VA leaders with providing a single portal of entry "for these women, so they don't have to feel like they are fighting their way through that old boys', largely men's network, and they have access to mental health, primary care, and gynecologic care in a single portal, with appropriate privacy and waiting rooms, and sensitivity to the needs that our women veterans deserve." By November of that year, a VA Women's Health Workgroup responded to his call and presented their findings on an assessment of the current state of care and their recommended solutions for improvement (Department of Veterans Affairs Under Secretary for Health Workgroup 2008).

In March 2009 the newspaper *AUSA NEWS* (2009) reported that the Secretary of the Army, Pete Geren, was initiating a new campaign of education, investigation, and prosecution of those accused of sexual harassment and sexual assault within the ranks. The secretary stated that there had been 1,800 convictions for sexual assault since 9/11 and that their actions were "a crime against core values" and "a crime that destroys unit cohesion" (*AUSA News* 2009, p. 3). The program received $44 million for the campaign, which included training and workshops, interactive Web sessions for soldiers, and a commander's resource Web site. The training was to involve leaders at all levels and include metrics to measure success for each part of the campaign and strategy. The Army's senior personnel chief is LTG Michael Rochelle, characterized sexual assault as "the most under-reported crime in the world" (*AUSA News* 2009).

THE COMBAT FEMALE

The literature also cited an additional stressor for some women when they left military service and sought health care, specifically problems encountered in obtaining services from the U.S. Department of Veterans Affairs (VA). In the past this organization has had various policies that seemed to prohibit the treatment of and limit the monetary compensation for female veterans because they were not considered to be "combat" veterans, and were therefore not eligible for full veterans' benefits. This was a particularly hurtful organizational response when experienced by female nurses who had been considered to be "Battlefield Angels" by the soldiers they had helped during the war. Given the expanding roles of women in combat and the blurring of battlefield lines in Iraq and Afghanistan, we are seeing more female casualties and a subsequent need for more equitable care at VA facilities.

A change in the VA leadership in April 2009 seemed to highlight the contributions of the female combat veteran when President Barack Obama nominated L. Tammy Duckworth as the Assistant Secretary for Public and Intergovernmental Affairs for the VA. A Black Hawk helicopter pilot with the Illinois National Guard, Duckworth flew combat missions in Iraq until she was shot down in 2004 and lost both legs and the partial use of one arm. She refused a medical retirement, continues her service in the National Guard, and recently served as the Director of the Illinois Department of Veteran Affairs. During her tenure there from 2006 to 2009, she initiated unique veteran programs that targeted joblessness, homelessness, long-term medical care, and post-traumatic stress disorder. This powerful advocate for all disabled veterans was confirmed by the U.S. Senate on April 22, 2009, and sworn into office two days later by the new VA Secretary, Eric K. Shinseki.

The Honorable Eric K. Shinseki (2009), a retired general officer and the former Chief of Staff for the Army, has been very clear in his overarching goal to transform the VA into a twenty-first-century organization that works for the veteran who is seeking services. Specifically he wants a seamless transition for the wounded warrior between their active duty medical care and their VA care (to include an electronic record); timely and equitable access to appointments, care, and disability determinations; and two-year advanced funding in the budget cycle. Secretary Shinseki also has signaled for a more "welcoming attitude" and "can do" spirit by VA staff members in administrative offices and health care facilities across the country. Assistant Secretary Duckworth (2009) noted that some new services have been established that address the specific needs of the female veteran such as on-site child care. She also shared an admonition from Secretary Shinseki: "What is good for a female veteran, is good for all veterans."

These two new senior VA leaders are staunchly backed by the Military Officer's Association of America (MOAA) as noted in their May 20, 2009, statement on "The Growing Needs of Women Veterans: Is the VA Ready?" That statement to the House Committee on Veterans' Affairs 1st Session, 111th Congress was prepared and read by CDR René Campos U.S. Navy, Retired in her role as MOAA's Deputy Director for Government Relations and as a legislative warrior and advocate for all military members, veterans, retirees, their families, and survivors. Her short answer to the question was, "Not yet!"

The full statement provides a comprehensive description of the current population of women service members and women veterans; pending legislation related to women veterans; and piercing descriptions of the difficulty experienced by some women in the military and with their treatment at the VA. CDR (R) Campos acknowledged that with the Committee's push for oversight, funding, and legislation, the "VA is now making significant progress in a number of areas" and she hoped to see that progress continue. She concluded with specific recommendations for the passage of key legislation; implementation of a comprehensive women's health care model; funding of the training and evaluation of the VA's Women Veterans Program Managers; and identification of best practice models to achieve gender equity/parity in compensation and health care. Other recommendations spoke to global goals such as sustaining VA funding increases that had been achieved in recent years and the implementation of a seamless transition program for separating, retired, and disabled veterans.

For those who still question the veracity of women participating in combat, they are encouraged to view the documentary film *Lioness* (lionessthefilm.com). This film tells the story of five female soldiers sent into direct ground combat, but without the same training as their male counterparts because of the combat exclusion policy that prohibits women from participating in direct combat. These women, three enlisted soldiers (two mechanics and a supply clerk) and two officers (one signal corps and the other a West Point graduate and company commander) were known as "Team Lioness." Each volunteered to be attached to a Marine combat unit to help defuse tensions with local civilians while they conducted house to house searches in Ramadi, Iraq. The initial intent of their assignment was for the female soldiers to assist with the search of women and children, but instead resulted in them fighting in some of the bloodiest counterinsurgency battles of the Iraq War right alongside the combat warriors. Because there was no paper trail for these temporary, "attached" assignments, these women returned home with no official documentation of their experiences that they needed to obtain benefits for combat related trauma. Filmed one year after they returned to the U.S., the women candidly share their diaries and memories of their harrowing year and the subsequent emotional and psychological problems encountered since their tour in Iraq (*Lioness* 2009).

THE YOUNG WARRIOR AND RESERVISTS

I started my section of the book with a story about my early twenty-something student and here I want to talk about the young warrior. Many of the volunteers serving in Iraq and Afghanistan are young, having had very few life experiences before their military service. Although studies have mentioned that the cumulative effect of wartime stress can increase stress in further deployments, previous military experience (presumably without the stress) appears to have an "immunizing" effect on veterans, thereby making the young warriors at special risk for stress disorders. In addition, the treatment systems, especially the VA, are not accustomed to treating young vets. They haven't really seen young vets since the Vietnam and Korean wars except for some from the Gulf wars. These young vets are not seeking services from the government systems right now but are likely to seek services in large numbers when the full effect of their wartime service hits them.

NATIONAL GUARD POPULATIONS

Another complication for the VA system is that the combat warriors in OEF/OIF are often Reservists and National Guard troops; these troops are in flux between the veterans, active duty, and civilian health care systems and are seen and treated by both the military and civilian health care systems. They are treated by the VA system after deployment but then can be redeployed into active duty. They are in a category all their own.

Reservists and National Guard troops are rapidly deployed and some feel they have too little time to prepare; when they joined the military they never expected to go to a war zone; and their family life and careers are severely disrupted. As a result, the Reserve and National Guard troops have a higher suicide rate than regular troops partly because they are less prepared for combat and partly because they get less help transitioning back to the civilian world (Korn 2008). They also suffer more PTSD and depression than regular troops (Friedman 2006). It is important to remember that Guardsmen and Reservists have the legal right to return to their preservice jobs at the rank they held before deployment. While this is generally viewed as a positive benefit, this may be a disadvantage in that they are separated from and not in contact with the people they served with in combat, who would be best equipped to understand their stress reactions.

VETERANS OF COLOR

Just as women and nurses have unique stress experiences in wartime, people of color also have issues that differ from the mainstream post-combat population. The U.S. Department of Veterans Affairs (VA) says that about 20 percent of its 23.5 million veterans are people of color. In order to more appropriately serve this population, the VA's Center for Minority Veterans (CMV) has assisted in the move to have each VA health care facility hire a Minority Veterans Program Coordinator (MVPC) who serves as an advocate and liaison for minority veterans. The liaisons also serve women as a minority (*Minority Nurse* 2009).

Minority veterans have additional challenges such as lack of access to VA services, "...disparities in health care centered on diseases and illnesses that disproportionately affect minorities, homelessness, unemployment, lack of clear understanding of VA claims processing and benefit programs, limited medical research, and limited statistical data relating to minority veterans" (*Minority Nurse* 2009). One minority group of veterans who deserve special treatment is the Middle Eastern veterans who have special stressors serving in Iraq and Afghanistan because of their own heritages (*Minority Nurse* 2009). They often find themselves discriminated against by their fellow servicemen and by the people of the countries in which the conflict is occurring. Even as wartime veterans, their loyalty may be unfairly questioned as terrorist groups dominate the current wartime scenes. These discriminatory practices are especially destructive not just at the individual level but at the system level at a time when the recruitment of native foreign language speakers is crucial to the military and intelligence communities.

Another group of minority veterans singled out for special program support are Native American veterans. Although Native Americans traditionally volunteer in wartime in high percentages, Native Americans typically do not utilize VA services to the extent other groups do (Hernandez 2009). The Native American vet population is very heterogeneous based on the fact that there are 562 federally recognized tribes in the U.S., each with its own culture and with many different languages. But, as most of us recognize, we must take into account the common traditional viewpoints about health and healing within Native American populations (*Minority Nurse* 2009). For example, Kafer (2009) commented, "In traditional Native American culture, health and healing begin first in the spirit, then the mind, then in the body. . . . In the Western model of health care, it's an opposite paradigm—health and disease begin first in the body, then in the mind, last in the spirit" (p. 1). There are some special programs for Native American veterans but not nearly a sufficient number of such programs. The Gathering of the Healers at the Southern Arizona VA Health Care System in Tucson, Arizona, is an example of a program especially for the Native veteran population.

The VA system is also concerned about the lack of diversity in the health care workforce. One program designed to expose nurses to culturally diverse populations and to recruit nurses of varied backgrounds to areas with mostly white nurses is the VA Travel Nurse Corps (TNC). While this program meets the needs of nurses who prefer short-term commitments, it also is desirable to a diverse nursing population and, therefore, provides to the VA system a group of more diverse nurses just as the veteran population is increasing in diversity.

HOW DO YOU KNOW IF YOU OR SOMEONE YOU LOVE HAS A STRESS REACTION?

While we can learn much from previous war experiences, there are also significant differences with the current wars. These differences include being in the war zone at all times, so there is a need to be constantly vigilant; the fact that the new technologies allow many extremely wounded soldiers to survive but with gruesome wounds; and the redeployments and lengthening deployments that increase the stress exposure and the chances of stress reactions.

Just as the stress reactions can vary from mild to severe, the symptoms vary in severity. If you or someone you love is experiencing some of these symptoms, seek help from someone experienced in working with postwar warriors and nurses. The most common symptoms are hypervigilance or hyperarousal, reexperiencing traumatic events, unusual and dangerous risk taking, constant wariness and a feeling of danger, avoidance of certain situations or emotions, serious startle responses, numbness, confusion, and suicide ideas or attempts. Many of these symptoms arise from the need to continue the adrenaline-stimulating experiences of war and a desire to avoid the wartime reactions of guilt, anger, and fear.

Just as with the nurses interviewed by Dr. Sharon, there is a continuum of stress reactions following major trauma such as wartime service. Some warriors and nurses experience severe stress reactions and others mild reactions. Some have a reaction to a single event and some to several or numerous events. Some experience symptoms for only a few days and others for a lifetime. Some experience stress or depression only and others have several mental health issues. The more severe the physical injuries, especially if there are long-term disabilities and disfigurement, the more likely that a serious stress reaction will be experienced.

Most authors who have written about postwar reactions of vets consider these reactions to indicate that the vet has a mental health problem; however, some authors believe it is really a normal reaction to a horrible trauma, and that it would be highly unusual for a vet to survive it without some severe lasting effects such as strong emotional and physical reactions. These reactions are then considered "normal" for the circumstances. While we agree that all warriors and caregivers will experience stress, the degree of the stress reaction determines whether this is a normal or abnormal, short-term or long-lasting, reaction.

There are numerous triggers for postwar stress reactions, including sights, smells, and sounds that are reminiscent of the war experience and reactions to the anniversaries of events such as the date of deployment or of traumatic experiences. Other triggers are situations with even remote similarities to one of the wartime traumatic events. Even positive experiences linked in memory to stressful events can trigger a stress response. While drugs and alcohol are often used to try to blank out the feelings and memories, in the long run they can loosen the warriors' hold on reality and bring memories flooding back. The book *Down Range: To Iraq and Back* provides a detailed description of behaviors once the soldier returns home.

CAN YOU ARMOR UP AGAINST STRESS REACTIONS IN PREPARING FOR DEPLOYMENT?

The U.S. military has learned from the stress reactions in previous wars and now tries to prepare troops and the medical teams with survival skills to use during deployment. The Navy has a program called Operational Stress Control Training (OSCT). The U.S. Army has *A Guide to Coping with Deployment and Combat Stress*, which is a detailed guide with sections on combat and operational stress, coping with stress, providing support to your "Battle Buddy," leader guidance, coping with deployment separation from loved ones, and dealing with the injured and dead.

The Army recently started a pre-deployment training program to teach emotional resiliency. The Real Warrior Web site (DCoE 2009) has an excellent section on preparing for deployment that suggests the following strategies: be patient, be prepared, be flexible, be open, and be healthy.

Before deployment, the military may screen to determine who may have the most resiliency and who may be the most susceptible to wartime stress reactions. Sometimes this begins in the recruitment process using approved assessment tools. The military can help them learn to cope with the stress of wartime using two different strategies. One is to work with the soldiers before they are deployed to help them cope with the stress without having a stress reaction or depression. The military can also screen out those soldiers or nurses who are too vulnerable to such stress reactions to be deployed. There are several different tools that can be used for the pre- and post-deployment screening. But there is controversy over whether these screenings should be done. If the soldiers or nurses are career military, to be "screened out" for combat could be devastating for their careers. Others say the tool is useful to evaluate stress reactions of a group and to predict what services are needed for the group, but should not be used to predict or evaluate individual reactions. There are commonsense predictors of difficulties in a war zone; for example, if the soldier or nurse has had traumas in childhood or displays neurotic and anxiety behaviors as an adult, they are more likely to have stress reactions.

Whether screening tools are used or not, nurses and warriors need help with learning coping strategies before deployment that will help them "armor up" against stress reactions. Some coping strategies relate to the unit team spirit and the quality of the team members and, therefore, the respect they have for one another. As Dr. Sharon found in the interviews, nurses also can cope using their spiritual beliefs and their supportive network. In the Scannell-Desch (2005) interviews of twenty-four Vietnam War nurse vets, the nurses offered advice to future military nurses. They recommended journaling, training for deployment, caring for yourself, finding and using support systems, talking about your experiences as a catharsis, understanding the mission, and being well prepared and having self-knowledge about their own abilities. The nurses felt that the journaling was about thoughts and feelings that the nurses were experiencing and that the intensive, focused training should be about dealing with trauma and being realistic to prepare them before deployment. They believed that through journaling and talking about their experiences, they could help nurses who were coming behind them. If nurses had less nursing experience, they had more risk for negative outcomes during deployment, especially in developing and using a support network and coping with the stress of war. Nurses who are redeploying to a war zone need special attention because the number of redeployments increases the risk of stress reactions. The length of each deployment also increases the risk of stress reactions. For this group, the Department of Defense Deployment Health Clinical Center at Walter Reed Army Medical Center produced a *Redeployment Health Guide: A Guide for Service Members and Their Families*. The advice in this publication is applicable for both nurses and warriors who are redeploying.

CAN YOU MINIMIZE THE STRESS WHILE IN COMBAT?

To deal with the constant danger in current war zones, the soldiers and nurses are trained to be combat-ready and vigilant at all times. These constant adrenaline-driven fight or flight stress reactions cause serious changes in the brain as well as emotional changes and can be experienced by caregivers as well as soldiers. As Dr. Sharon discovered in her interviews, everyone in the current war zones must be extra cautious in order to survive.

Warriors and nurses should mourn as the trauma happens, not delay those reactions. Sometimes the crisis situation requires action and not emotions but once the situation is as quiet as can be expected, nurses and the teams should discuss their emotions and debrief the traumatic situation. Military and nurse leaders need to encourage warriors and nurses to react and cry if they feel like it. Because these deaths and serious wounds occur during ongoing combat situations in which survival and saving the wounded is the first priority, it is essential that warriors and health care teams be deliberately brought together after the intense combat to debrief and grieve together.

As noted earlier, the Vietnam nurse veterans were emotionally attached to the warriors they served and one of the most difficult aspects of the war experience was not knowing what happened to the warriors they served. The nurses had connected emotionally to the warriors they treated and were anxious to know if their efforts resulted in survival or recovery. The Iraq nurses experienced the same yearning… to know what happened to their patients. Dr. Sharon shared that several nurses checked the obituaries in the *Army Times* newspaper to see if they could identify one of their patients.

Most nurses relied on personally proven and familiar strategies to reduce or buffer the effects of emotional hardships, whereas some discovered and used new strategies. In relating this service to the stress reactions of nurses, experiencing death and serious injury in patients can lead to PTSD during wartime or in the civilian world. Just as Dr. Sharon has described in the earlier sections of this book, nurses described similar experiences in Vietnam, including stressful living and working conditions, constant personal danger, extremely heavy workloads, severely injured patients, and long hours of work.

In addition to the professional coping strategies described earlier, nurses employed personal coping strategies as well. These included reminding themselves that certain things are inevitable in any war, relying on usual and unusual support systems, calling on an inner strength or spirituality, diverting themselves with hobbies and exercise, using humor to relieve stress, and talking or writing about their experiences. Also, maturity and the ability to relax are important attributes. While it is not a healthy strategy, many Vietnam War nurses describe using alcohol and drugs to relieve stress. Given the cultural restrictions and military regulations, alcohol was severely restricted on most bases in Iraq. The same coping strategies described above were used by nurses after that war as well.

Ironically, in spite of these devastating war experiences described by nurse vets, most nurses found their wartime service to be the most rewarding time of their careers and that they had experienced the most personal growth through that work. Dr. Sharon found that almost all of them look forward to returning to the war zone.

CAN OTHERS HELP WITH REINTEGRATION?

Even with the most creative and thoughtful preparation for war and effective coping strategies during deployment, the reintegration adjustment needs to be strategically planned and implemented. In addition to the combat stress and mental illness, other factors affect reintegration adjustment. For example, throughout history returning veterans sometimes were feared even when revered and were often shunned because of the nature of their wartime experiences and the level of violence involved in those wars. Most people in the United States remember the shunning of Vietnam veterans when they returned home, as if the war was their responsibility, even though most were drafted against their wishes.

The homecoming reunion with loved ones is a very important time for returning vets and their families. Both the families and the vets are different from what they were before deployment and life for the family will probably never be the same again. For this reason, there are programs to help with this stage of wartime service. The U.S. Army *Guide to Coping with Deployment and Combat Stress* has a section on reunion with loved ones. There are numerous suggestions about such things as dealing with unrealistic expectations, going slowly in the reintegration, taking family time, and talking through the division of labor in the family since the spouse is accustomed to making all the decisions alone.

For the warriors, there are many programs to help with the reintegration after deployment. One of the most important is the leader and platoon training both before and after deployment. The Battlemind-After Actions Review (B-AAR) involves leisure team-building activities, then the After Actions Review helps warriors recognize and adjust to fear in combat, to the constant combat situation, and to reintegration after deployment. It deals with redeployment and its special dangers. The Warrior Adventure Quest (WAQ) program is designed to break down barriers to communication among fellow platoon members. Another program for soldiers is RESET in which there is a program for the first forty to ninety days after returning that includes a period of seven to ten days of decompression and thirty days of block leave. The program "Tools to Assist Your Troops" encourages peer interaction and debriefing for officers and leaders and involves group debriefings and support. The program, which is voluntary, sets ground rules such as confidentiality, being on time, that one person speaks at a time, that there will be no grandstanding, that there will be a commitment to self-improvement, that there will be no alcohol or substance use before the meeting, that members will notify the group if the person will be absent, and that there will be no violence (people learn how to deal with anger in the group). This program also provides help for vets before reuniting with family and friends, encourages them to "confess" experiences to get rid of the emotions, and provides help dealing with conflicts.

Postwar adjustment is affected by many factors, including a general resilience and survival mentality. Those warriors who view the combat adjustment challenge as a need to maintain control and commitment fare better after combat. Personal competency strengthens resilience to combat stress.

After the wars, there were no institutionalized programs to help Army nurses adjust; they coped in various ways. Most kept their silence, like the Vietnam nurse vets, who found it most useful. Some experienced symptoms and delayed their reactions for years. Some coped by changing their clinical focus and writing about their experiences in journals not shared with others. Almost all wanted to replicate somehow the experience of being needed and making a difference.

Studies specific to nurses in Vietnam shed light on postwar adjustment. After returning from deployment, nurses wanted the chance to save lives and serve in meaningful ways. They were less sympathetic to patients who were less wounded or ill than their wartime patients, although some didn't want to work with suffering or dying patients. Other nurses decided that psychiatric patients provided more rewards than physically ill patients.

COMPASSION FATIGUE

Just as civilians who have experienced a loss, there are some similarities with the losses experienced in war. The stress reactions of nurses after wartime is similar to the vicarious trauma found in civilian nurses in highly stressful environments. This phenomenon is often called compassion fatigue and sheds some light on the stress reactions experienced in war. Basically it is the constant exposure to severely traumatized patients that leads to an indescribable exhaustion affecting all aspects of the caregiver's life. The pain is severe and acute. Nurses in potentially vulnerable positions are encouraged to take care of themselves. Just as with combat stress reactions, those most likely to get compassion fatigue are those exposed to trauma before, are inexperienced nurses, can easily feel inadequate, are frightened by what they are experiencing, and are in physical danger themselves. A civilian example is what happens to nurses responding to a major disaster like a hurricane.

What can be done to help with compassion fatigue? First, take a self-assessment test to determine if you have compassion fatigue or burnout. Dr. John-Henry Pfifferling and Kay Gilley (2000) offer their own quick "state of mind" assessment with nine questions that could help you determine if you need a more formal, validated measure such as the Maslach Burnout Inventory (MBI). For the past ten years, the MBI has been recognized as a leading measure of burnout in human service, education, business, and government professionals.

If you realize that you are at risk for compassion fatigue, there are several steps that you can take to prevent or recover from its drain of your physical, emotional, and spiritual energies. First, find people who will listen without judging and share your thoughts with them. Then, maintain a healthy lifestyle with a balanced diet and enough exercise, and generally take good care of yourself. Do things that are fun. Learn to be alone. Get in touch with your own feelings. Help organize a support group with other people who are experiencing stress. Don't make major decisions while you are feeling stressed. Try to defuse your anger and stop showing it to others. Follow your seriously injured patients through rehabilitation so you can see their progress. Seek your own brand of spirituality to help make sense of what you have experienced. Anticipate anniversary reactions; these anniversary dates can trigger a level of arousal that has a chemical effect on the brain and the warrior or nurse will have a difficult time for up to three days. Stay positive, reduce the amount of time spent complaining, have patience, and know that peace of mind will come. Remember that this is not a mental illness but a normal reaction to the stresses you have experienced.

My coauthor, Dr. Sharon, has developed a course on compassion fatigue for military nurses called Armor Up to Fight Compassion Fatigue. This course is equally applicable to civilian caregivers who are suffering from compassion fatigue or burnout. She uses Kathy Freston's (2008) eight pillars of quantum wellness to help caregivers build their own personalized, protective suit of armor with daily meditation; detailed visualization of your goals; planned fun activities; conscious eating at each meal; daily exercise; self-work such as journaling or individual/group therapy; spiritual practice, and service to others.

SCREENING FOR STRESS REACTIONS, PTSD, AND DEPRESSION

As described earlier, a certain and growing number of nurses and warriors will develop normal or severe stress reactions. We also need to address the treatment of warriors and nurses with severe stress reactions, PTSD, and depression. The first step in treating traumatized vets is to screen for severe trauma. Programs are needed to teach warriors, their families, and military nurses to recognize the symptoms of war stress reactions and encourage warriors and nurses to seek help. However, the screening for stress and depressive reactions usually falls to military or civilian primary care staff.

Primary care providers need to screen vets for severe traumatic stress reactions and be trained to recognize and manage these reactions. The National Center for PTSD uses a quick checklist of trauma symptoms with returning warriors and nurses. There are some other screening tools that lay people and health care providers can use, including screening tests that need to be culturally and socially acceptable, valid, and easy to use, such as the Primary Care PTSD screen, Structured Clinical Interview, the PTSD—Interview by Watson, and the Clinician Administered PTSD Scale. The Real Warrior Web site (DCoE 2009) links various screening tools through the Military Pathways™ Web site. It is very important to protect the confidentiality of the soldier and prevent job discrimination against those with stress reactions and depression.

There are some controversies about PTSD screening. Because of the existence of delayed-onset PTSD, which can occur months or years after the war experience, screening on return is not always accurate in identifying the true prevalence of PTSD. Also, the screening tools and process may not be valid and confidential, which may harm the vets rather than helping them.

SEEKING CARE

For many reasons, although there are many effective treatment strategies, vets with stress reactions and/or mental illness often don't seek care for these illnesses. Reasons for not seeking help include fear that seeking treatment will hurt their career in the military; concern that taking medications may affect their performance; concern about the potential side effects of medications; fear that peers will view this as a sign of weakness; worry that treatment won't provide immediate relief; fear that the treatment will not be kept confidential; and distrust of the system. Even though many soldiers don't seek care, the numbers who do seek care are still very high and many leave the military because of their symptoms.

The military and the VA are ill prepared to meet the need for treatment because of the length and the complexity of the treatment needed and the fact that the military needs more mental health professionals to adequately treat the numbers of returning vets with stress reactions and depression.

PTSD TREATMENT APPROACHES

As Dr. Sharon found in her interviews, in addition to the stress disorder, some Iraqi and Afghanistan soldiers have been found to have other mental health disorders. While depression, with thoughts of suicide and homicide, is the most common other mental disorder that is triggered by the wartime experience, other mental illnesses are either triggered or made worse by the war experience.

Sadly, if the nurses and warriors seek help for their stress reactions, they may get only minimal care for various reasons, including the fact that there is a shortage of experienced and knowledgeable providers, and that some of these soldiers will need long-term and complex care. Those who do seek and receive treatment for PTSD find that there are many different approaches used. Sometimes the choices can add to the confusion and vets aren't sure which treatments are most appropriate for them. Hopefully we can help sort through the options and describe those that have been studied and proven effective. In any case, the treatment plan has to be individualized for each particular vet and his or her unique symptoms.

Different treatment approaches fit best with different stress reactions. Normally, a complete recovery is possible from a stress reaction resulting from a single event. From an acute catastrophic stress reaction, which is very debilitating, complete recovery may not be possible but significant improvement is. According to Raj (2006), the five post-traumatic stress disorders require different treatment approaches and often have different results.

The five post-traumatic stress disorders are:
1. Normal stress reaction
2. Acute catastrophic stress reaction
3. Uncomplicated PTSD
4. PTSD
5. Severe stress reaction

The normal stress reaction to a single event is best treated by individual and group debriefing; complete recovery is possible. The acute catastrophic stress reaction, which is very debilitating, requires that the warriors and nurses be taken out of the situation and receive treatment immediately, especially medication that can help them get some sleep and relief from the anxiety, with psychotherapy for the long-term; complete recovery is not ensured. Uncomplicated PTSD is best treated with cognitive-behavioral therapy, group therapy, medications, psychotherapy, or a combination of all of these. Most often PTSD exists with another disorder such as depression, substance abuse, or panic and anxiety disorders; both diagnoses must be treated. Post-traumatic personality results from long exposure to such situations as wartime service and requires inpatient treatment that includes the family and rehabilitation services.

For severe stress reactions, patients need more than one type of treatment at once and still may not have a full recovery. Estimates of having a complete recovery from PTSD range from one-third to one-half of patients who are treated; some improvement is possible with most patients. For most vets, the reintegration phase lasts a lifetime.

Do combat nurses have similar recovery chances? Nurses tend to ignore, control, or minimize their stress symptoms. Many times it is not until much later, when they are being seen for seemingly unrelated symptoms, that the history taking unearths the link to stress reactions. They may know that their postwar coping is not as effective as their prewar coping but they underestimate the amount of influence the war experience has had on their mental health. Just as with the warriors, once the symptoms are severe enough that the nurse seeks treatment, the nurse needs quick relief from the symptoms, then longer-term therapy. The survivor guilt must be confronted directly and the belief that they should be "superhuman" addressed. Individual and group therapy work is usually recommended and, just as with the warrior vets, the closeness of individual therapy may be too threatening at first.

The training and characteristics of treatment providers are crucial to the success of treatment. These providers should be well trained and carefully selected. This is difficult because there is a dearth of mental health professionals in the system. In fact, it has been estimated that there is a vacancy rate of 40 percent for some active duty roles. In fact, the military has issued a call for more mental health professionals. Psychiatric nurse–practitioners have been a valuable addition to the treatment team in the combat zone and in stateside fixed facilities.

Other therapies are described for victims of PTSD or severe trauma reactions in wartime. Many of them are cognitive therapies that try to change the way the patient thinks about the experiences or traumatic events. Just as the emotions can control the way the mind works, the mind can control how emotions work, so cognitive therapies change thoughts in the hope of changing emotional reactions.

One cognitive therapy is cognitive processing therapy, in which the goal is to help the vets stop blaming themselves for events that were out of their control. The goal is to help the vets see that bad things just happen sometimes and can't be prevented. A similar therapy called cognitive-behavioral therapy (CBT) is recommended by the U.S. Army in their guide for military personnel and includes exposing vets to reliving the stressful events under controlled and supported circumstances. CBT includes exposure therapy, cognitive restructuring, and stress inoculation training. Hypnotherapy is also used to help the vet remember stressful events that may not be easily recalled because of the stress associated with them. The Real Warrior Web site (DCoE 2009) links to the online courses for stress inoculation therapy (SIT) and other CBT strategies offered by *www.essentiallearning. net.* Cognitive memory therapies should be used after other therapies have calmed the acute crisis reaction. These memory strategies include the rewind technique, which is like watching a film of the trauma, then experiencing it running backward; prolonged exposure; traumatic incident reduction that involves reexperiencing the traumatic incident with a therapist; healing rituals or rituals of atonement such as are used in many indigenous cultures to provide forgiveness to the vet; thought field therapy, a technique of recall and physical body tapping; grief and mourning therapy; healing imagery; the counting method, where the therapist counts to 100 in two minutes while the vet remembers a traumatic experience; dream management and processing; cognitive rehearsal; life review; and art therapies. In all of these cognitive therapies, the goal is to change the distorted thoughts in order to change the disturbed emotions.

Another treatment method is the Rapid Resolution Therapy™ (RRT), developed by Dr. Jon Connelly to treat past traumas including rape and sexual abuse and wartime stress reactions. The treatment goal is to prevent the past traumatic experience from blocking desired change. The treatment is conducted in either a single full day or two or three sessions in a row rather than in long-term weekly sessions. Proponents say the effects are long lasting, that the therapy is painless, and that the therapy works with both emotions and the intellect.

A similar strategy is called flooding, or direct exposure therapy, which is carefully planned and executed in a safe environment and is followed by cognitive techniques such as thought stopping, guided self-dialogue, cognitive restructuring of the vet's worldview, and skills training such as relaxation techniques, anger management, and assertion training. Another cognitive therapy is called Learned Optimism, or the ability to see the good things in each day.

Group therapy is often recommended so that vets from the same war will be placed in groups together, and women vets will be in women-only groups. The vets can then discuss feelings about their similar traumatic experiences and begin to think differently about these events. Groups generally meet once a week for up to fifteen or sixteen weeks.

Wartime traumas often raise serious spiritual questions that need to be grappled with openly and with supportive counselors. As Dr. Sharon found in her interviews and in her research on the Vietnam War and the wars in Iraq and Afghanistan, spirituality is often used as a coping strategy and military chaplains played a key role in supporting patients and staff. Drug therapy is often recommended when symptoms are preventing normal functioning and to help the vet withstand the stress of reliving the traumatic events. The goal is to help the vet through the crisis and use other therapies in conjunction with the medications to improve long-term functioning.

Many other therapies have proven to be successful with stress reactions. Psychotherapy is sometimes recommended for PTSD sufferers, especially when symptoms persist; when used, the therapy needs to be long-term. The hope is that the vet will experience the full range of emotions and grief surrounding the traumatic events in a protected environment with a knowledgeable and skillful therapist. Another group of therapies helps vets to control or overcome their anxiety; these include relaxation techniques, breathing exercises, and positive thinking. Many vets have both stress reactions and drug and alcohol addiction; the substance abuse issues should be addressed first or treated together with the mental health issues. Vets often have other physical issues as symptoms of their stress reactions such as sleep disorders and nightmares. Specific therapies are necessary for such symptoms.

DEPRESSION AND SUICIDE

As was described earlier, severe stress reactions and depression are the two most common disorders for Iraq and Afghanistan vets and they often are experienced together. Of course, suicide is an extreme form of depression and it is on the rise in the military. It is much higher than in civilian populations. The PTSD and depression result in personal, work, and financial difficulties that then increase the depression and can lead to thoughts or acts of suicide. This is among people on active duty, including Reservists and National Guard troops who have been called up. Because of this serious problem, the military and the VA have developed initiatives to identify and treat potential suicide risks and prevent actual suicides. Spouses and friends and military buddies are being taught to recognize the signs of depression and suicidal thoughts. They also teach soldiers to "Ask your buddy. Care for your buddy. Escort your buddy."

ALTERNATIVE AND COMPLEMENTARY THERAPIES

Many alternative therapies have been recommended for PTSD and compassion fatigue. In 2008 the Army began a program of research to study, through rigorous clinical trials, the use of new therapies to treat the post-traumatic stress of veterans, including such possibilities as herbal medicines, spiritual practices, meditation, massage, movement therapies such as yoga, acupuncture, storytelling, art, pet therapy, deep breathing, Outward Bound-type programs, biofeedback therapies, and twelve-step programs.

TREATMENT SETTINGS

Many combat warriors and nurses return to their primary care providers in these settings for their health care. These settings can assess and diagnose the trauma reactions, evaluate the need for treatment, prescribe medications, and refer the vet for hospitalization if it is necessary to prevent harm to the vet or others.

Family support needs to be built into the treatment plan and they should be helped to talk with the vet about the traumatic experiences. The warrior or nurse has constructed walls around their emotions and thoughts about the wartime stress and will need to be helped to tear down the barriers for loved ones and friends. Communities also need help and can provide help to the vets and their families. Communities have "adopted" warriors and sent packages and cards and then are helped to welcome back the warriors into their communities. Advocacy efforts by health care providers to educate communities on how to respond to the needs of returning warriors and combat nurses is especially important with discharged warriors and National Guard troops and Reservists.

SELF-HELP RESOURCES

There are some excellent resources for self-help for vets with war trauma. Williams (2002) in the updated workbook for self-help encouraged writing about the trauma, drawing/picturing the fear, using positive self-talk, and other techniques to overcome the PTSD symptoms. Rosenbloom (1999) also authored a self-help workbook to help heal people who have experienced trauma by identifying their normal ways of coping and learning new strategies; the workbook includes cognitive strategies that help the sufferer learn how he or she thinks about the trauma and its aftereffects, ways to feel and be safe, how to trust after trauma, how to regain control, how to value himself or herself and others, and how to feel close to people again.

Other authors have offered self-help advice. Matsakis (1996) described the biochemistry of PTSD and exercises to deal with self-blame, exercises to distinguish between grief and anger, ways to review triggers, and exercises to examine suicidal thoughts and feelings. Cantrell (2005) offered advice to vets on self-help techniques. To manage anger, Cantrell recommended the use of physical exercise appropriate to physical limitations; using less caffeine, alcohol, and drugs; utilizing relaxation/ study/meditation techniques; and exercise and an appropriate diet. Cantrell further offered "First Aid for PTSD" such as talking about the stress experiences, writing about the experiences, avoiding self-medication, and relaxation techniques. Cantrell stresses the importance of evaluating the expectations that self and partner/spouse have of the nurse or warrior being home again, and learning how to trust again.

WHERE CAN YOU GET HELP FROM THE GOVERNMENT?

Many organizations provide help to troops, nurses, and their families before, during, and after deployment; some of these are private and volunteer-run and others are government-run. The government resources that provide support for troops and families during deployment are primarily run by the individual services (Army, Navy, and Air Force). Additional resources can be found under the umbrella of the Department of Defense (DoD), which has the Deployment Health Clinical Center, DoD Force Health Protection and Readiness Programs, the Defense Centers of Excellence for Psychological Health and Traumatic Brain Injury (DCoE), and Military OneSource, among other programs.

The VA, with more than 200 facilities around the country, is the primary service organization for veterans who have left active duty. Unfortunately, the VA has many detractors who say the facilities have long waiting lists; overloaded staff; scant and inaccessible specialized services such as mental health; little experience with National Guard troops and Reservists; barriers to accessing services; inexperience with young veterans of current wars; violations of confidentiality, and no mandate to treat families or active duty personnel. The VA would respond to their critics that they are woefully underfunded and understaffed. As noted earlier, that response may be valid but it is no longer acceptable to Secretary of the Department of Veterans Affairs, the Honorable Eric K. Shinseki.

The Veterans Outreach Centers (or Vet Centers) of the VA work with vets or can make referral to outside sources. Partnered with the U.S. Surgeon General, the U.S. Army has the Proponency Office of Rehabilitation and Reintegration, which provides policy and guidance for the rehabilitation and reintegration of returning troops. The National Women's Trauma Recovery Program is a civilian residential treatment program for women vets with PTSD.

The Military Health System Web site is a new online communications tool for active duty troops. My HealtheVet provides help finding and accessing VA services. The VA Seamless Transition program helps returning vets get benefits information. The VA Vet Center Readjustment Counseling Services and the America's Heroes at Work are U.S. Department of Labor and Defense projects designed to help veterans with PTSD get work after deployment. Other government supports such as the Department of Labor Local Veterans Employment and Training Program are also designed to help vets find work in their home communities. There is also the Disabled Veterans' Outreach Program. There are efforts to establish and fund a program for National Guard and Reservists to provide a 90- to 120-day transition back to civilian life.

The National Institute of Mental Health provides research funding and information about effective treatments for PTSD. The U.S. Substance Abuse and Mental Health Administration provides information about PTSD and resources. The military has other publications for returning vets. For example, the Department of Defense publishes *Coming Home*, a guide to the warrior after deployment for the reintegration phase. The topics are reuniting with your spouse, reuniting with your children, reuniting with parents, extended family members and friends, and taking time for yourself. These are listed in the Resources section. The National Center for PTSD has two useful publications called *Returning from the War Zone: A Guide for Families of Military Members* and *Returning from the War Zone: A Guide for Military Personnel*. The guides are intended to offer suggestions for troops and families to use in understanding the transition back to civilian life or military noncombat life. The guides are especially useful for the families of members with PTSD and other stress reactions and provides information on where to go for help.

Also, the Department of Defense pamphlets mentioned above for returning vets have a companion pamphlet for spouses of returning vets and includes what to expect, the importance of communication, and the need to take time for themselves. Both pamphlets suggest going slowly. Other publications include those from the Military Family Resource Center that provide information for families of deployed service members.

The Rand Corporation, when it released its report entitled *Invisible Wounds of War* (2008) also released two pamphlets: "Post-deployment Stress: What You Should Know, What You Can Do," and "Post-deployment Stress: What Families Should Know, What Families Can Do." Both pamphlets can be downloaded from the Rand Web site as PDFs.

Concern for the mental health of nurse veterans goes back to at least World War II when the *American Journal of Nursing* (1945) recommended personal counseling for veterans. In 2005, the Chief of the Army Nurse Corps, MG Gale S. Pollock, declared her determination to ensure that the Iraq nurse and warrior veterans not suffer from PTSD. She recommended various strategies for nurses, including debriefings, counseling sessions, and small group meetings to talk about combat stress. The goal was to help nurses and physicians maintain a warrior mentality and develop the skills needed for survival in the hostile wartime situation. She was also trying to reduce the length of nurse deployments from one year to six months, and improve nurse retention.

HOW CAN OTHERS HELP?

Many of the programs for vets and their families use volunteers (see the Resources section for programs such as Deployment LINK). Operation Home Front supports the troops and their families back home during deployment and following deployment. They provide emergency assistance, help with daily living issues, housing, and finances. They offer a community for the families. Soldiers' Angels and Brothers at War have numerous teams and projects in which volunteers can get involved. This includes supporting/adopting an individual soldier, baking for the deployed men and women, making blankets for wounded soldiers, cards and letters for families and troops, support for chaplains, care packages, remembrance for those who have died, help for veterans' facilities, travel for vets who are injured, telephone calling cards for families and vets, and gifts for families and kids. The USO continues to provide support and entertainment for troops and their families.

Other organizations make specific recommendations for helping combat nurses, especially during deployment. Cardillo (2007) suggested ways that volunteers and civilian nurses can help military nurses. First, she suggested visiting them (when this is feasible in country and in the U.S.) since volunteers often visit the troops but rarely visit the nursing staff. Also pictures and notes of appreciation and support for the job they are doing are important. She recommended the sharing of resources and best practices; providing updates on issues and people and a connection to the civilian nursing world; encouraging them to participate online with conferences and in-service programs to keep them connected and up-to-date; and acknowledging them at such events.

WHO ELSE IS HELPING AND HOW CAN YOU JOIN THEM?

Dr. Sharon shared descriptions of four military associations she felt were vital to the health and support of active duty Army nurses throughout their careers: The Army Nurse Corps Association (ANCA); the Military Officers Association of America (MOAA), The Reserve Officers Association (ROA), and The ROCKS, INC. Each organization nourishes a different aspect of the thriving Army nurse corps officer from second lieutenant to general officer and, beyond, to civilian service in our local communities.

ANCA serves as a lynchpin for cementing the nurses' "forever friendships" initially formed on active duty. It is a voluntary organization dedicated to connecting current, former, and retired U.S. Army Nurse Corps officers for support, communication, social sharing, preserving their history, and enhancing the goals of the ANC. Generous donations allow ANCA to award annual scholarships to students attending established baccalaureate nursing school programs.

Most of the ANCA Web site (*https://e-anca.org*) is open to the public and provides information about their scholarship program, membership criteria, and its history. It also provides links specific to active duty Army nurses such as the Army Nurse Corps home page with its motto "Embrace the Past, Engage the Present and Envision the Future," mission, and vision. This site also has the Chief of the ANC's blog where individual officers can comment about issues spotlighted that month. Other related links include ANC Recruiting, ANC History, ROTC nurse programs, Women in Military Service (WIMSA), the Vietnam Women's Memorial Project, the Army Medical Department (AMEDD) and AMEDD school, the Army Surgeon General's office, other AMEDD Corps home pages, and Walter Reed and MEDCOM newsletters.

ANCA's quarterly publication *The Connection* is a vehicle for organizational updates and messages from the Chief of the Army Nurse Corps and the association's president. This publication also includes features on regional activities; a research, literature, and arts column; and requests for help locating individuals who served with a unit at a particular time. *The Connection* also has an ANC history column, a section to identify members who have been in the news; and highlights of the ANCA mentor and coaches program. Another column, "Lean on Me," highlights the unique career paths, varied backgrounds, and various deployment experiences of nurses who have served in Iraq or Afghanistan.

The Connection is aptly named because it serves as a vehicle to stay in touch with friends across the country. Volunteer regional directors pull together individual member news updates so that regardless of where you live, you can keep up with all the news of your "forever friends," whether it is their recent vacation, new grandbaby, or new job. Separate features allow you to identify and congratulate newly promoted officers, update your address book with those who have moved, and welcome "home" those who have retired. The Parade Rest section tells us of members, nonmembers, and family members who have made their final transition. Once every two years, ANCA members gather together for a biennial convention or as some like to call it, the family reunion.

Given that all Army nurses are commissioned officers, the second organization pivotal to a nurse's career is the Military Officers Association of America (MOAA). This independent, incorporated, nonprofit, politically nonpartisan organization of 370,000 members is open to all active duty, National Guard, Reserve, retired, and former commissioned officers and warrant officers from all uniformed services: Army, Marine Corps, Navy, Air Force, Coast Guard, Public Health Service, and National Oceanic and Atmospheric Administration. Auxiliary memberships are also available for the surviving spouse of a deceased officer. MOAA is this country's largest and most influential association of officers that is dedicated to a strong national defense and representing the interests of officers at every stage in their career and beyond. It plays a proactive role in military personnel matters, especially proposed legislation that affects the career force, the retired community, and veterans of the uniformed services. A sampling of MOAA's legislative gains from 2000 to 20008 is provided in Appendix F so that you can see the significant depth and wide-ranging breadth of critical issues surrounding the active duty and reserve force; health care, retirement, and survivor issues for the veteran and military family.

In 2009, *The Hill,* an influential newspaper that covers Capitol Hill, named the Military Officers Association of America (MOAA) as one of the top lobbying organizations in Washington, D.C. for the third consecutive year and is the only military- or veteran-related association on the newspaper's recognition list. MOAA is the leading voice on compensation and benefit matters for all members of the military community including enlisted members. Every two years the membership votes on specific resolutions that address their overarching goals. This participatory form of organization and functioning is made possible by having members who are highly educated, informed, and proactive, coupled with an automated legislative response system that is targeted and timely. If a key legislative issue comes up for a vote, individual MOAA members are immediately alerted with an informational/action e-mail that allows them to immediately generate and send a personalized letter to their congressional representative and/or senator. The thousands of MOAA messages that can be generated and sent within a short period of time make for one very loud, powerful, and influential voice on Capital Hill.

MOAA is governed by a board of directors with thirty-six officers from the seven uniformed services. The daily business of the organization is conducted by paid staff at their headquarters in Alexandria, Virginia, under the auspices of its president. MOAA's full-time headquarters staff is dedicated to serving, assisting, and educating each MOAA member. Staff members use a variety of tools such as offering an up-to-the minute, open, and very comprehensive Web site (*www.moaa.org*), most of which is open to the public. It also has an extremely responsive customer service center (800) 234-6622 prepared to answer member questions on the spot or at least within twenty-four hours.

Another MOAA benefit is their robust program of interest free loans, grants, and scholarships for students going to college. These school assistance programs are open to the children of any military person who died while in service to our country; currently serving and retired enlisted personnel; former, active duty, and retired officers. The application form, deadline, and more information can be found at the Web site.

MOAA hosts an annual business meeting (the site is rotated around the country) to update members on pending legislation, to review the financial health of the organization, to recognize excellence in service to members, and to provide educational seminars.

MOAA also cosponsors professional symposiums on homeland security, wounded warrior care, and more. MOAA joins with the U.S. Naval Institute to host high level forums for policy makers, civilian partners, and military and political leaders. The title of the 2009 forum was "Coping with Unseen Injuries: From Battlefield to Homefront." More than 600 participants heard progress reports from the Chairman of the Joint Chiefs of Staff, warrior commanders, clinical leaders, VA staff members, and family members of those diagnosed with PTSD and Traumatic Brain Injury (TBI). Their educational program is further distinguished by hosting the first-ever MOAA Spouse Symposium in Virginia Beach, Virginia.

Another benefit for the Army nurse and other Army officers is the option to receive many informative publications (see Appendix G) that are free for members and are made available to the public for a nominal fee. Responsive to the needs of its younger members, MOAA has placed many of its publications online and offers special interest group blogs such as one concerned about the future of health care for its members, family members, and the returning service member. The blogs allow participants an opportunity to comment on an issue or to raise new issues.

The MOAA headquarters staff offers three career fairs each year for those preparing to depart from their military service. The MOAA Web site has posted more than 35,000 job opportunities and initiated a State Networking Program to provide better job opportunities for MOAA members and MOAA spouses. The Benefits Information Department (BID) and The Officer Placement Service (TOPS) stand ready to assist each MOAA member and their spouse.

The backbone of MOAA's organizational strength is a voluntary grassroots system of affiliate organizations that choose to partner with the national MOAA organization to attain their mutual goals. Affiliates, whether they be chapters (local organizations) or councils (a coalition of chapters within a state) are self-governing and supporting. Today in 2009 there are 35 state councils and 416 chapters that span this country. Depending on the location, most chapters have some type of program dedicated to supporting wounded warriors and their family members, as well as active duty officers, deployed units, and family members left behind.

Most MOAA chapters hold monthly meetings and serve as a hub of fellowship, community service, educational programs, and traditional social events such as picnics, dances, dinner shows, and parties. Many chapters also have TOPS (The Officer Placement Service) liaisons to assist officers separating and retiring from active duty in finding rewarding civilian employment. As respected and proactive community leaders, most MOAA chapter members also oversee their local annual veteran tributes and parades; Veterans in the Classroom's educational programs; and local college scholarship award programs. The welcome letter posted at a MOAA chapter's Web site *www.CitrusCountyMOAA.org* ends with a paragraph that seems to illustrate the bonds of a "forever friendship" initially forged in foxholes, field tents, and deployed hospitals: "We are a family and if you choose to join our chapter, you can count on us to be with you on every step of your life journey; to celebrate your joys and to support you during life's challenges. We are indeed 'Leaders . . . Proud to Care and Ready to Share!'"

A sister organization to MOAA is the Reserve Officers Association (ROA). The Nurse Corps is augmented by many Reserve and National Guard members, and the ROA strikes a unique balance between an individual's civilian career, Reserve career, and their family. This independent, nonprofit, politically nonpartisan organization of 63,000 members is open to all commissioned and warrant officers from all branches of the uniformed service including the Army, Marine Corps, Navy, Air Force, Coast Guard, Public Health Service, and National Oceanic and Atmospheric Administration.

Chartered by Congress since 1950 and founded in 1922, ROA is one of the oldest military advocacy organizations in existence. They advise and educate Congress, the president, and the American people on issues of national security, with unique expertise on Reserve issues. ROA advocates for adequate funding of equipment and training requirements, recruiting and retention incentives, and employment rights for all members of the Reserve.

Here is a sampling of some of its most notable and recent successes:
- Established Tricare Reserve Select, and got gray-area retiree access to Tricare
- Increased the threshold of active duty days a Reserve member is allowed to accrue over a year three times over the course of decades
- Obtained travel reimbursements for monthly training
- Helped implement a GI Bill for the twenty-first century
- Helped improve the Montgomery GI Bill for Selected Reservists
- Protected Tricare Reserve Select premiums
- Ensured Citizen Warriors are treated fairly by the Veterans Benefits Administration
- Doubled basic allowance for housing to Reserve Component members who are called up in support of a contingency operation
- Substantially affected the outcome of The Commission on the National Guard and Reserve final report recommendations, most of which were adopted
- Ensured proper funding for equipment and training for Guard and Reserve forces
- Protected the establishment of a National Guard and Reserve Equipment Appropriation
- Highlighted health-care delivery gaps in coverage and continuity of care by DoD and Veterans Affairs
- Protected the future of the Reserve Forces Policy Board
- Helped improve the partnerships between the Reserve Components and troops' civilian employers

- Established the definitive resource on the Uniformed Services Employment and Reemployment Rights Act and the Servicemembers' Civil Relief Act
- Protected the military member's right to vote

ROA sponsors the Servicemembers Law Center, the definitive resource in employment rights, military voting, and the Servicemembers Civil Relief Act. This law center provides free legal assistance to anyone in need as well as advocates for legislative improvements in its areas of expertise.

The association is member driven and it gathers for a national convention annually in Washington, D.C. There, the members vote on specific resolutions to further their legislative agenda and participate in educational programs. One agenda item of note is the annual medical seminar hosted by ROA's elected national surgeon (who is currently the Commander of the Army Reserve Medical Command), offering inexpensive Continuing Medical Education credit. Their participatory form of organization and functioning is made possible by having members who are highly educated, informed, and proactive; coupled with an automated legislative response system that is targeted and timely. If a key legislative issue comes up for a vote, individual ROA members are immediately alerted with an informational/action e-mail that allows them to immediately generate and send a personalized letter to their congressional representative and/or senator. The thousands of ROA messages that can be generated and sent within a short period of time make for one very loud, powerful, and influential voice on Capitol Hill.

ROA is governed by a board of directors with twenty-seven officers from the seven uniformed services. The daily business of the organization is conducted by paid staff at their headquarters on Capitol Hill, with the prestigious address of One Constitution Avenue. Their Minuteman Memorial Building Headquarters is directly across the street from the Capitol Building and neighbors the Supreme Court and Senate office buildings. ROA's full-time headquarters staff is dedicated to serving, assisting, and educating each ROA member. Staff members use a variety of tools such as offering an up-to-the-minute, open, and very comprehensive Web site (*www.ROA.org*), most of which is open to the public. It also maintains a blog and is very active on all the social media sites with a robust outreach program. Their customer service center at (800) 809-9448 is prepared to answer member questions on the spot.

While most members join ROA to support its mission, there are a considerable number of member benefits that come with an ROA membership. They maintain a career center offering transition assistance, resources for Reservists to find active duty tours, and other job postings. They have an education resource center with scholarships, a law review library, and connections to schools knowledgeable of the unique needs of a Reserve member. They also offer various travel and leisure programs, insurance and financial benefits, and an online marketplace.

One of the signature elements of ROA is its advocacy through education. Under the umbrella of ROA's Defense Education Forum, they issue reports and studies, and host seminars on various topics of interest to national security. These range from climate change and energy policy to mental health care delivery. The symposiums always incorporate the Reserve Components' idiosyncrasies, but usually appeal to the broader national security community. Many of these programs are cosponsored by leaders in academia such as the Foreign Policy Research Institute, George Mason University, and other notable entities. In 2008 and 2009, a heavy focus was placed on a series of events on post-traumatic stress disorder (PTSD) and traumatic brain injury (TBI), culminating in an extensive report that can be found on ROA's Web site. Because of ROA's location on Capitol Hill, its seminars and educational forums draw heavy audiences from legislators having a real effect on policy. Many of the suggestions, recommendations, and conclusions that result from a DEF event are subsequently incorporated into law or policy.

Much of ROA's education is also done through its professionally produced magazine, *The Officer*. ROA's magazine has modified its model to be more of a journal format, educating audiences on various interest items to Reservists.

Another point of interest for nurses is that ROA is affiliated with the Confederation of International Medical Reserve Officers, headquartered at NATO. More information on this organization can be found through ROA's Web site.

The backbone of ROA's organizational strength is a voluntary grassroots system of departments and chapters throughout the world to attain their mutual goals. Today in 2009 there are 55 state departments and over 372 chapters that span the globe.

The final organization that can nourish a thriving Army nurse corps officer both during and after active duty service is The ROCKS, INC. (*www.rocksinc.org*). This organization started with a few minority officers who wanted to support each other through the tough Command and General Staff College (CGSC) experience at Fort Leavenworth, Kansas, and graduate. These Army officers then moved on to assignments at the Pentagon and other places in the Washington, D.C. area and realized they wanted to continue to support each other. They formalized their relationship at their first official meeting on October 9, 1974. That small band of U.S. Army field grade (major and above) brothers eventually grew to be totally diverse with female officers; company grade officers (lieutenant to captain);

commissioned officers from all uniformed services whether they were active duty, reserve, retired, or ROTC cadets; and widowers of its members. Now 1,300 strong, ROCK members are in fourteen chapters across the country and two interest groups in Iraq and Afghanistan. Originally called the "No Name Club," they later changed their name to The ROCKS, INC. The new name was chosen to honor one of their founding members, Brigadier General R. C. "Rocky" Cartwright, who was killed in a plane crash on the way to a meeting.

The ROCKS, INC. demonstrates its core values of "Concern, Dedication and Professionalism" with officer programs that enhance professional development throughout one's career regardless of one's corps. This means that as a lieutenant or captain in the Army Nurse Corps, you could attend one of their monthly meetings or speaker programs and be seated next to an Armor or Infantry or Signal Corps Officer of any rank. It also means that you can call upon any other ROCK member for advice and guidance about your career, a personal problem, or a difficult work situation. Another key aspect of the monthly meetings is the fellowship time and the social interactions that over time become the foundation of more "forever friendships."

Their "Leadership Outreach" program schedules volunteer ROCK member team visits to Historically Black Colleges and Universities (HBCUs) to provide professional, social, and career guidance to ROTC students. This outreach program also speaks to the personal side of entering the military as an officer. Team members try to address a potential social chasm that may be experienced by some students as they leave home for the first time and enter a structured, formal, professional system. ROCK team members share their lessons learned as to how they successfully adjusted to being a professional leader in a 24/7 military world. The organizational objective is to help ensure a smooth transition for each student from the college campus to basic training and active duty. The mentorship that begins during the team visit continues at chapter meetings and during their annual national leadership conferences.

The ROCKS, INC.'s annual three-day National Leadership and Training Conferences provide speakers from the most senior levels of the active duty Army, the Chief of Army Reserve and the Director, Army National Guard, as well as the leaders of major military commands such as Training and Development Command (TRADOC), Cadet Command, Human Resources Command, and Recruiting Command. The national conference themes are approved by their National Board of Directors and usually speak to enhancing a broad range of leadership skills such as "Making a Difference: Mentoring and Inspiring the Next Generation of World Class Leaders." National Leadership and Training Conferences are approved by the

Department of Defense and allow local commanders to give permission for their officers to attend the program.

How fitting that The ROCKS, INC. National Chairperson received a congratulatory message October 26, 2009, from the Commander of Fort Leavenworth, Kansas, and Commandant of the Command and General Staff College congratulating the organization on its thirty-fifth anniversary. The message sent by LTG William B. Caldwell, IV reads in part: "The ROCKS have come a long way since the early days here at Fort Leavenworth. Those foundations of service and camaraderie are alive and well . . . Your organization's core values of Concern, Dedication, and Professionalism are as important now as ever while we continue to move forward as a Nation at war. We wish you another thirty-five years of success in shaping and mentoring our young men and women in uniform."

Many organizations help Iraqi and Afghanistan veterans (see the Resources section). Some of these are the Coalition to Salute America's Heroes, the Coming Home Project, the Wounded Warrior Project, the PTSD Alliance, the National Veterans Foundation, the National Suicide Prevention Lifeline, Employer Support of the Guard and Reserve (ESGR), Hearts toward Home International, ONE Freedom, Inc., Operation Comfort, Soldier's Heart, the Returning Veterans Project NW, the Soldiers Project, Strategic Outreach to Families of All Reservists, Valley Forge Return to Honor Workshops, and Veteran Love.

The publication *Resources for Concerned Citizens* is a blueprint for getting involved in helping veterans and their families. In this publication, it is recommended that people begin by renting videos, reading books, and watching documentaries to become acquainted with war. There are tips to help communicate with returning veterans, including welcoming them home, not pressuring them to talk about their experiences, offering support, and being gentle with them. The publication also explains how to get involved politically, and how to insist on good treatment for vets by governmental veterans' agencies by making very personal appeals. There are also sample volunteer activities such as writing articles, arranging entertainment, helping build or repair veterans' homes, counseling veterans and their families, arranging fund-raising and support events, teaching therapeutic creative arts classes, and donating frequent flyer miles to vets and their families.

Other organizations are dedicated to helping vets and their families. The Nurses Organization of Veterans Affairs (NOVA) is dedicated to helping improve the quality of care provided. The Give an Hour program is a not-for-profit organization that enlists volunteer therapists to give an hour of their time to treat troops and their family members. Many social service and mental health provider organizations are affiliated with Give an Hour. If you are a therapist, volunteer time to treat vets. Even one hour per therapist in a community is a great help. You can also volunteer for Operation Comfort. Point Man International Ministries offers support, spiritual healing, and information to vets.

Numerous sources exist for VA claims filing help. One informative Web site is ptsdhelp2000.com with its Humane Guide to VA Benefits.

There are also military/vet-related projects and programs such as the Veterans for America (VFA) with the motto "addressing the causes, conduct and consequences of war." VFA has programs for National Guard members and families, for wounded veterans and their caregivers, and for PTSD claims assistance.

Some mental health organizations work with veterans and their families including the National Alliance for the Mentally Ill, the National Mental Health Association, Screening for Mental Health, Sidran Institute, and the National Association of Social Workers.

Sending care packages to troops in Iraq and Afghanistan can be done through such organizations as the freerepublic.com, Marine Parents, and The Care Package Project. These organizations give addresses to use, advice on how to get through customs, how to send nonperishable items, and identifies items that are forbidden in Muslim countries. Operation Crayon teaches you how to send packages for local kids and families. There are prayer-chain projects, sites like Operation PAL to help you send cards and letters, and sites like Team Marine Parents that teach you how to hold fund-raisers for vets and their families.

There are also many associations specifically for subgroups or populations of active duty, retired and former military members and their family members identified by their service, war or conflict, profession, gender, or ethnicity, including the Women Marines Association, National Military Family Association, Vets 4 Vets, Iraq and Afghanistan Veterans of America (IAVA), Disabled American Veterans, the American Legion, Veteran's Outreach Program, Army Nurse Corps Association (ANCA), Women in Military Service for America Memorial Foundation, Inc., and the Military Officers Association of America (MOAA). There are unit associations that provide peer counseling and, through the Veterans Improvement Program (VIP), visit the Vietnam Memorial together. Any of these service organizations can help locate survivor support groups for veterans.

There are advocacy groups such as the Women's Research and Education Institute, the Alliance for National Defense, National Organization of Veterans Advocates (NOVA), Women Organizing Women (WOW), Group—Veteran Advocacy, Military Families Speak Out (MFSO), and Veterans for Peace.

Many organizations have Web sites to provide information about the history of wars and warriors, caregivers, and the military. This includes the Military Officers Association of America, the Minerva Center, Illyria.com, WomenVets.com, Women in Aviation, Native American Women of the Military, Military OneSource, the National Archives, the Army Nurse Corps historian, and the U.S. Army Center of Military History.

CALL TO ACTION: SPEAK UP AND STEP OUT IN SUPPORT

Those of us in civilian life owe a debt of gratitude to those who fight the wars for us—those who volunteer to serve in wartime knowing all the risks they face. In these times when service to one's country is not adequately appreciated because of the politics of war, these men and women volunteer to protect and serve their country so we can live in freedom. Whether we agree with the wars we are fighting or not, we must honor those who risk their lives for us.

There are many ways that we can support these warriors and their health care providers. As a start, we can ask the Army nurses who have deployed to continue talking with and supporting each other. We offer some sample questions in Appendix C that they can use to initiate some discussions. For those who have not yet deployed, we also offer sample questions for their discussion. For friends, family members, and supporters we ask that you also become educated about their experiences. We then want you to speak up for the legislative, financial, and community support that they need. Finally we want you to take action; step out in support of the nurses and our wounded warriors who will need us even more when they come home.

We can send letters, packages, or e-mails. We can provide cell phone minutes and cell phones so they can stay in touch with their loved ones. If we are therapists or clergy, we can give of our time to help with the wartime stress and their readjustment. If we are other kinds of caregivers, we can learn about evidence-based practices so that, when we work with the warriors and families, we are providing the most effective care possible. If we are members of a community from which a warrior has deployed, we can welcome them home with celebrations and quiet support that goes the distance and is not just a single event of celebration and respect. If we are an employer, we can hire vets and support them through the difficult readjustment period. If we are researchers, we can study the most practical and effective ways to help these troops and publish the results of these evidence-based studies so others can learn from our research. If we are faculty members in colleges and universities, we can help prepare students who are going to war or provide special care and support to those who have returned from war. For those of us educating ROTC nursing students, we can learn from the studies and implement best practices on how to help these nurses armor up before deployment. If we work for the government with veterans or active duty personnel, we can research and implement ways to help these troops and veterans. We can volunteer in homeless shelters that help homeless vets get care, find permanent housing, and stay on their medications and other treatments designed to help them cope with the residual damage of wartime service.

When we were conducting research for this book, we ordered many used books online. In one of the self-help workbooks, there was a handwritten note in the front of the book, obviously written by a previous owner of the book. We quote the note here to provide inspiration to those who are struggling with stress disorders:

> *The past is over and done. It has gone back to nothingness from whence it came. I am free. I have a sense of pride and self-worth. I am confident in my abilities to love and support myself. I have learned that I am capable of positive growth and change. I am strong. I am united with all of life. I am one with the universal power and intelligence. Divine wisdom leads me and guides me every step of the way. I am safe and secure as I move forward to my highest good. I do this with ease and with joy. I am a new person, living in a world of my choosing. I am deeply grateful for all that I have and for all that I am. I am blessed and prosperous in every way. All is well in my world.*
>
> > *This too shall pass!*
> > *I am willing to change!*
>
> —Unknown author

We have quoted this anonymous note here to provide inspiration to all: those who are struggling with stress disorders and those who are not struggling, both of whom want to thrive and grow as military professionals.

APPENDIX A:
PTSD AND DEPRESSION FACT SHEET

ALL POPULATIONS

About 1.64 million U.S. troops have served since 2001 in Operation Enduring Freedom (OEF) in Afghanistan and Operation Iraqi Freedom (OIF) in Iraq (Tanielian and Jaycox 2008).

In the current U.S. wars in Iraq and Afghanistan, a recent RAND (2008) study stated that although almost 20 percent of the more than 300,000 Iraq and Afghanistan vets report symptoms of post-traumatic stress disorder or major depression, only a bare majority have sought treatment (p. 1).

The National Center for PTSD (2005) reported that the vast majority of Iraq combat veterans experienced "being attacked or ambushed, receiving incoming fire, being shot at, seeing dead bodies or remains, and knowing someone seriously injured or killed" (p. 2).

The National Center for PTSD (2009) describes "four types of symptoms: reliving the event, avoidance, numbing, and feeling keyed up" (p. 2).

Seal et al. (2007) found that "of 103,788 OEF/OIF veterans seen at VA health care facilities, 25,658 (25 percent) received one or more mental health diagnoses" (p. 476).

King et al. (1998) studied a national sample of 1,632 Vietnam veterans, 26 percent women and 74 percent men, and found factors that influenced postwar adjustment, which were the presence of hardiness and social support as resilience-recovery factors. Those with hardiness dispositions, control, commitment, and change as challenge had fewer PTSD symptoms. King et al. stated that there are several factors that may influence the hardiness of the nurse or warrior; these include personal strengths and general competency.

De Luca (2009) states that "studies on identical twins indicate there is a heredity factor involved in the development of PTSD" (p. 1).

De Luca (2009) states that "people who feel partly responsible for the traumatic event have higher rates of PTSD than those who do not feel guilty" (p. 1).

The RAND study (2008) found that about the same number of Iraqi and Afghanistan vets are affected by depression as are affected by PTSD and that these two often go hand in hand.

Raj (2006) found that most often PTSD exists with another disorder such as depression, substance abuse, panic and anxiety disorders and both diagnoses must be treated.

The Associated Press (2009) states that last year—2008—the suicide rate among soldiers was the highest in decades and is much higher than that of the civilian rate of suicide. The AP article said further that "the most common factors for suicides were soldiers suffering problems with their personal relationships, legal or financial issues and problems on the job."

The RAND study (2008) noted that many who are experiencing mental health issues don't seek treatment because they think it will hurt their military career or they worry about medication side effects or the stigma associated with seeking services. Even those who seek treatment get what RAND called "minimally adequate" care, not the full array of services needed to treat these complex problems.

Even with the fact that vets often don't seek care, a study of 303,905 Army soldiers and Marines found that Iraqi vets had a high use of mental health services and often left the service after Iraqi deployment (Hoge 2006).

The RAND study estimated that "the societal costs of PTSD and major depression for two years after deployment range from about $6,000 to more than $25,000 per case. Depending whether the economic cost of suicide is included, "the total societal costs of the conditions for two years range from $4 billion to $6.2 billion" (p. 3).

The Web site *ptsdsupport.net* (2009) described those most likely to get compassion fatigue—"those who have a history of trauma are more vulnerable to compassion fatigue; those care givers who are inexperienced, and fear not being able to do their jobs, who are afraid of what they might see; care givers who are in danger themselves" (p. 1).

Friedman (2006) also cited research with Vietnam vets that showed that PTSD is more likely in wounded vets than vets who are not wounded.

The National Center for Homeless Veterans (2009) states that 23 percent of the homeless in the U.S. are veterans (p. 3).

Hart (2000) found that vets are more likely to suffer stress reactions and depression the longer they were exposed to war service and the more intense the combat.

Friedman (2006) cited studies showing that 80 percent of PTSD sufferers have another psychiatric disorder.

Grieger (2006) followed 613 soldiers who were hospitalized after serious combat injury and found that "high levels of physical problems at 1 month were significantly predictive of PTSD and depression at 7 months..." (p. 1777).

SPECIAL POPULATIONS: NURSES

The Rand report (2008) *Invisible Wounds of War* identified some groups at greater risk of stress reactions, including women, Hispanics, those with longer deployments, those with the most combat trauma, and reservists and National Guard troops (Tanielian and Jaycox 2008, p. 435).

Boivin (2005) found that about 65 percent of Army nurses are in the Army Reserve, with about 29 percent being active duty nurses and 6 percent belonging to the National Guard.

Norman (1988) interviewed 50 nurses who served in Vietnam and found that "two variables: the intensity of the wartime experience, and supportive social networks after the war, influenced the level of post-traumatic stress disorder" (p. 238). Norman also found the "the nurses' experience was not better or worse than that of combatants" (p. 242).

Stanton (1996) interviewed nurses from WWII, Korea, Vietnam, and Operation Desert Storm, discovering five common themes including:
- the personal reactions to the wartime service,
- life in the military,
- being a nurse in the military,
- providing a social context for the war, and
- living with the wartime images and sensations

Other adjustment mechanisms were creative endeavors. Stanton also discovered that there was one theme that threaded throughout the reactions—surviving by adjusting to the wartime situation—and that the most important means of adjusting and coping were improvising and innovating.

La Salle (2000) interviewed three Vietnam nurse vets and found that they had certain feelings in common—respect for the quality of the medical teams, the sense of camaraderie, and the willingness of the team members to help one another.

La Salle (2000) said that the Vietnam nurses coped by their belief in God and the support of peers, and that spirituality and peer support were the two most common factors in coping with the stress of wartime service.

Rogers and Nickolaus (1987) studied Vietnam vet nurses and found that many nurse vets controlled their symptoms through suppression but would discover the connection to symptoms later in life. "Most have a vague awareness that the Vietnam experience has created a coping style that impairs their readjustment to civilian life" (p. 12).

In the Scannell-Desch interviews of 24 Vietnam War nurse vets (2005), "nurses described seven areas of advice they would give to future military nurses: advice about journaling, training, caring for yourself, support systems, talking about your experiences, understanding the mission, and lack of preparation" (p. 603).

Baker (1989) used data from two studies of military nurses assigned to Vietnam and found that "Army nurses with less than two years RN experience prior to their assignment were found to be more at risk for such negative outcomes as having trouble maintaining close relationships during deployment and coping with the stress of war."

King and King (2009) studied women Vietnam veterans, most of whom were nurses, and found that about 27 percent of them had PTSD sometime after their war experience (p. 1).

Scannell-Desch (2000) found that most nurses relied on personally proven and familiar strategies to reduce or buffer the effects of emotional hardships, whereas some discovered and used new strategies.

Stanton (1996) found that, with Vietnam nurse veterans, friendships between nurses and patients helped them adjust to living and working under conditions for which they had little life experience and little preparation.

Stanton (1996) found that, after the wars, some Vietnam nurse veterans adjusted by being silent and repressing the experiences and that adjustment took years in many cases.

Stanton (1996) found that the feeling of not being appreciated sufficiently was held by most of the nurse veterans regardless of which war they were involved in.

Raj (2006), in describing Vietnam nurse veterans, found that younger, more inexperienced women with significant experiences with death and dying combat troops had a poorer postwar outcome.

Baker (1989) found that service in the war influenced the professional choices of nurses after the war, saying that nurses tended to be dissatisfied with their post-Vietnam War assignments, especially in the first two years after deployment. Baker also found that the nurses missed the opportunity to save lives.

Norman (1992) studied 50 Vietnam nurse veterans and found that "their experiences in the war directly affected the way 43 [of the] nurse veterans approached their choice of clinical work. Women changed their focus for four reasons: they disliked working with patients; they found it difficult to be sympathetic to average patients after working with war-wounded soldiers; they had seen enough suffering and death; they wanted to work with psychiatric rather than physical ailments" (p. 111).

SPECIAL POPULATIONS: WOMEN

Walsh (2008) reported that from 2001 to 2008 about 190,000 military women were deployed in Iraq and Afghanistan and that about 20 percent of those servicewomen have PTSD symptoms. She further noted that women have twice the rate of PTSD as men and that sexual assault and severe sexual harassment is a much too common occurrence, with 20 percent of servicewomen reporting military sexual trauma.

De Luca (2009) states that "women are two to three times more susceptible than men" (p. 1) to having stress reactions.

In the article "When Mommy Comes Marching Home," Walsh (2008) comments that women in the military develop PTSD at a rate of 20 percent compared to 8 percent of men.

Leveque (2008) reported that 253,000 women veterans (of the 1.7 million total women veterans) were seeking care in veterans' facilities.

As with all troops, Wolfe (1992) observed that having been in a combat situation before increases the stress symptoms of female Vietnam veterans after another deployment to a war zone.

McVicker (1985) studied women Vietnam veterans and found they often believed that they had had it easy compared to the combat troops and, therefore, should not be having problems or were not worthy of treatment. Years later, as these women underwent therapy, they often did not connect their current problems with the Vietnam experiences until the therapist helped them make the connection.

McVickers (1985) writes about the delayed awareness of stress reactions, saying that Vietnam women veterans apparently didn't experience the violent or aggressive stress reactions that male vets did until they were in therapy and began expressing their emotions.

The *Minority Nurse* journal (2009) states that women vets from Iraq and Afghanistan have a special set of issues including the mental health issues and stress disorders described in all vets, and the additional issue of sexual trauma.

Vogt (2009) found that "women may take longer to recover from PTSD and are four times more likely than men to have long-lasting PTSD" (p. 2).

Walsh (2008) cited another alarming statistic: 20 percent of the women in the military report suffering sexual assaults or severe, threatening harassment compared to 1 percent of men.

McVickers (1985) noted that many Vietnam women veterans had "bitter memories" of sexual assault or harassment and the subsequent lack of appropriate action by the military; women vets may then not seek services from military or VA related sources.

Bender (2009) states that "female veterans are now between two and four times more likely to end up homeless that their civilian counterparts" (p. 1).

SPECIAL POPULATIONS: YOUNG WARRIORS

Seal et al (2007) found in their study of Operation Enduring Freedom (OEF) in Afghanistan and Operation Iraqi Freedom (OIF) veterans seen in VA health care facilities that "the youngest group of OEF/OIF veterans (age 18 to 24 years) were at greatest risk for receiving mental health or post-traumatic stress disorder diagnoses compared with veterans 40 years or older" (p. 476).

According to *Minority Nurse* journal (2009), the young veteran can be viewed as a new "minority group" because the VA has not had many young veterans since the Vietnam War. While the percentage of OEF/OIF veterans in the VA system right now is less than 5 percent, the number of young veterans/warriors who need help is most likely much higher but VA hospitals have not treated young veterans since the Korean War.

SPECIAL POPULATIONS: PEOPLE OF COLOR

The U.S. Department of Veterans Affairs (VA) says that about 20 percent of its 23.5 million veterans are people of color.

Native Americans typically do not utilize VA services to the extent other groups do (Hernandez 2009).

SPECIAL POPULATIONS: RESERVISTS & NATIONAL GUARD TROOPS

The Reserve and National Guard troops have a higher suicide rate than regular troops partly because they are less prepared for combat and partly because they get less help transitioning back to the civilian world (Korn 2008).

Friedman (2006) found that National Guard and reservists in the Persian Gulf War had more PTSD and depression than regular troops.

TREATMENT AND PROGNOSIS

Hart (2000) noted that combat veterans often experience anniversary reactions; these anniversary dates can trigger a level of arousal that has a chemical effect on the brain. The warrior or nurse will have a difficult time for up to three days.

Friedman notes that "if evidence-based practices are utilized, complete remission can be achieved in 30 percent to 50 percent of cases with PTSD, and partial improvement can be expected with most patients" (p. 592).

APPENDIX B:
BASIC INTERVIEW QUESTIONS

1. Thank you for sharing your background, career path, and experiences during your deployment to _____ (Vietnam, Iraq, or Afghanistan).
2. Please state your name, rank, and clinical specialty.
3. Where and when did you attend nursing school?
4. How did you learn about opportunities for the Army Nurse Corps?
5. Please share your ANC career path until now? When you attended basic training and your assignments since then?
6. When and where were you stationed overseas?
7. Please tell me more about the time when you were notified that you would be going to Iraq:
    a. How did you receive the news?
    b. How did you prepare?
    c. What were your professional concerns about being deployed?
    d. What were your personal concerns about being deployed?
8. When you arrived in the country, where did your actually land and did you immediately go to your assigned unit?
9. Tell me about your processing experience and your first few days in country.
10. What was going on in country military-wise when you arrived? Up tempo or pretty quiet?
11. Tell me about your living situation. Where did you sleep, eat?
12. Describe a typical work day for you.
13. What is your most vivid memory of your year in _____ (Vietnam, Iraq, or Afghanistan).
14. What did you find most difficult about being a nurse/doctor/medic in Iraq/ Afghanistan?
15. How did you spend your off-duty time?
16. What was the most demanding situation you experienced during that year?

17. Is there one particular patient that you remember? Tell me about him/her.
18. Do you have a strong faith? How did that play a role in sustaining you during the year?
19. How about prayer? Use of a chaplain? Attending weekly or daily services?
20. What is the funniest thing that happened to you?
21. What are you most proud of from that year?
22. What did your family, friends, and colleagues from back home do to support you while you were overseas?
23. Can you describe your feelings when it was time for you to rotate back home?
24. How were you received when you returned to the States?
25. Since your return home from being deployed:
    a. Have you ever visited the Vietname Wall?
    b. Since you have returned, have you experienced any response with yourself, patients, or staff to the TV documentary *Baghdad ER* or the Big & Rich CW song "8th of November," which is about soldiers in Vietnam? (Only asked of OEF/OIF nurses.)
26. What can retired Army nurses and the public do to support nurses that are now deployed?
27. What can retired Army nurses do to support the active duty stateside nurse?
28. What can the public do to support you and our soldiers?
29. Thank you for your time today to enlighten us about your experiences and thank you for your service to our country.

APPENDIX C:
POST-DEPLOYMENT GROUP INTERVIEW QUESTIONS

Discussion questions for dyads, triads, or small groups of Army nurses <u>if you have deployed</u> to a combat zone:

1. Do you identify with any particular nurse or situation in *Angel Walk*?
2. How were your experiences similar to those described?
3. How were your experiences different from those described?
4. How were your experiences different from the Army nurses who served during a different time and in a different theater?
5. How did you react to treating enemy soldiers?
6. Did you ever ration medication? If so, why and how did you feel about it?
7. Did you ever treat expectant patients? How did you feel at the time? How did you feel later?
8. Is there anything that you wish had been included in your school curriculum or military field preparation courses to better prepare you for combat nursing?
9. What gave you strength while deployed?
10. Did you experience ambivalence when you returned home and if so, how?
11. How would you describe your emotional response to serving in combat?
12. Did you have any difficulties adjusting when you came home and if so, how?

Discussion questions for Army nurses who have <u>never</u> deployed to a combat zone:

1. Did you identify with any particular nurse or situation described in *Angel Walk*?
2. Do you feel prepared to be deployed to a combat zone and if not, what else do you need to learn or do?
3. How do you think you would react to treating enemy soldiers just after they'd injured our troops?

4. How do you think you would react to the need to ration medication due to time or availability?
5. How do you think you would react to treating expectant patients?
6. What do you think that you can do in your current role to support your returning colleagues?

Discussion questions for friends, family members, supporters, and nursing professors:

1. What surprised you most about the experiences of the Army nurses and warriors deployed to a combat zone?
2. What can you do now to support a nurse or warrior stationed in a combat zone?
3. What can you do to support Army nurses and warriors when they return home?
4. What do you wish that you knew before your loved one or colleague deployed and how will you get that information?
5. What can you do now to support our wounded warriors and their nurses in your community?

APPENDIX D:
GLOSSARY OF TERMS

Abu Ghrahaib *(or spelled Grahaib)*: site of a prison in Iraq, also known as Baghdad Correctional Facility

ACLS: advanced cardio life support

AK 47: Russian machine gun

AMEDD: Army Medical Department

ANCA: Army Nurse Corps Association; open to active, retired, and former ANCs

Angel: a soldier killed in combat, Operation Iraqi Freedom slang

Angel walk: the procession (with soldiers lining the path and offering their last salute) of transporting a soldier's body on a litter from the hospital/morgue to the helicopter that is waiting to carry them on the first leg of their journey home.

Ar Ramadi: A city in central Iraq 110 kilometers west of Baghdad on the Euphrates River

Article 15: Article 15 gives a commanding officer power to punish individuals for minor offenses.

AUSA: Association of the Unites States Army

B-AAR: the Battelemind-After Action Review program helps them prepare to experience fear during combat and then readjust when they come home

Bagged: manually force air into a patient's lungs with a face mask and inflatable bag

Baghdad: the capital of Iraq; 7 hours ahead of EST

Bagram: a major air base in Afghanistan; located about 60 kilometers north of Kabul and currently occupied by each service and their coalition partner units having sizable tenant populations.

Balad Air base: 68 kilometers north of Baghdad; one of largest in the country

Battle rattle: full battle rattle is close to 50 pounds worth of gear including flak vest *(with ceramic plates in the front and back pockets to protect the heart and lungs)*, Kevlar helmet, gas mask, ammunition, weapons, and other basic military equipment

BCLS: basic cardiac life support

BDU: Battle dress uniform, camouflaged (patterned to help them blend into the environment) tan for desert wear or green for jungle wear

Berm: In modern military engineering, berm has come to mean the earthen or sod wall or parapet itself. The term especially refers to a low earthern wall adjacent to a ditch

BIAP: Baghdad International Airport

Bird: slang for helicopter

Black Hawk: helicopter

Body Counts: number of deaths

BOQ: Bachelor Officers' Quarters; building where they live

Bucca, Camp: a prison camp maintained by the United States military in the vicinity of Umm Qasr, Iraq

Bunker: dug out hole, reinforced with sandbags

Camaraderie: good spirits among comrades

CAT scan: this machine forms a full three-dimensional computer model of a patient's insides. Doctors can even examine the body one narrow slice at a time to pinpoint specific areas.

CBT: Cognitive-Behavioral Therapy; one type of PTSD treatment

CCATT: Critical Care Air Transport Team

CDR: Commander; navy rank equivalent to an Army lieutenant colonel

CDP: Center for Deployment Psychology

Chief Nurse: director of a nursing department in a hospital or medical center

Chinook: helicopter

Chopper: helicopter

CHS: Combat Support Hospital

CHU: Containerized Housing Unit (pronounced "choo"); a CONEX container

Citizen soldier-reservist: Common description for someone who serves in the reserves

Class A Uniform: Army green uniform like a civilian business suit (jacket with rank, insignia, and medals; shirt with a tie and skirt/pants)

CMS: Central Material Service which sterilizes instruments in a hospital

CMV: Center for Minority Veterans in the national offices of the VA

CONEX: a shipping container with a door; may also have a window, top vent, power, cabling, and air conditioner; version with a bathroom between two rooms is called a "wet chu" and a base with a large number is called "CHUville"

CRNA: Certified Registered Nurse Anesthetist

CSTS: Center for the Study of Traumatic Stress

CWCP: Civilian War Casualty Program

Daisy chain: sequential, multiple explosive devices

DCoE: Defense Centers of Excellence for Psychological Health and Traumatic Brain Injury with five component centers DVBIC, CDP, DHCC, CSTS and NICoE.

DEROS: Date expected to return from overseas duty

Desert Shield/Storm: "Operation Desert Shield" began on August 7, 1990, when U.S. troops were sent to Saudi Arabia due to the request of its monarch, King Fahd, after Iraq invaded Kuwait. On January 17, 1991, when it became clear that Saddam would not withdraw, Desert Shield became Desert Storm.

Deuce and a half: a truck in the 2 1/2 ton weight class, it was one of many vehicles in U.S. military service to have been referred to as the *"deuce and a half"*

DFAC: (pronounced dee-Fak) a dining facility where soldiers eat; older soldiers call it a Mess hall or chow hall

DHCC: Deployment Health Clinical Center

DVBIC: Defense and Veterans Brain Injury Center

EMT: emergency medical technician or emergency medical trauma room

ER: Emergency Room also known as the emergency medical unit

EVAC: evacuation hospital, or the patient/process of being transferred from one hospital to another treatment facility

Expectant: patients critically injured without hope of recovery

Fallujah: a city in the Iraqi province of Al Anbar

Field: area of combat

Firefights: gun battle

Flak Jacket: bulletproof vest

FOB: Forward Operating Base

Fobbit: service member who never leaves the base (goes outside of the wire)

Friendlies: member of the U.S. Army or Allied Forces

FST: Forward Surgical Team

Good copy: clearly received radio message

Green Zone: the common name for the International Zone of Iraq— a 10-square-kilometer (3.8-square-mile) area in central Baghdad, Iraq, that was the center of the Coalition Provisional Authority and remains the center of the international presence

GS: a civilian who works for the government

GWOT: Global War on Terrorism

Head Nurse: the senior nurse in charge of staff and patient care on a ward or in a clinic

Helicopter drop: helicopter never touches the ground/delivers troops

Hootch: tent or hut used for living quarters

Ibn Sina: American Military Hospital in Iraq

ICU: Intensive Care Unit otherwise known as a Critical Care Unit (CCU)

IED: Improvised explosive device

IG: Inspector General; their mission is to inspect, investigate, or inquire into any and all matters of importance to a command

Incoming: Arriving mortars

Installation: An Army Post or a Navy or Air Force Base

IV: Intravenous; method to inject fluids/medications

KAF: Kandahar Air Field, the main base of operation for the southern part of Afghanistan; a major transportation hub for airplanes, helicopters, and convoys

KBR: Kellogg, Brown & Root, the largest contractor serving Coalition Forces

Kevlar: A well-known component of personal armor such as combat helmets, Ballistic face masks, and Ballistic vests. The PASGT helmet and vest used by United States military forces since the early 1980s both have Kevlar as a key component, as do their replacements

KIA: Killed in action

KY Jelly: A water-based, water-soluble personal lubricant produced by Johnson & Johnson

LZ: Landing zone

M60: 60 caliber machine gun

M240: Machine gun

MACV: The United States' unified command structure for all of its military forces in South Vietnam during the Vietnam War.

MASCAL: An acronym used by the United States military for situations involving simultaneous, multiple hospital admissions that tax the hospital's capabilities

MBI: Maslach Burnout Inventory; recognized as a leading measure of burnout

MED EVAC: Medical evacuation of casualties

MEDCAP: Medical Civil Action Program

MOAA: Military Officers Association of America

Mosul: North of Iraq; second largest city in the country

MST: Military Sexual Trauma; veterans sexually assaulted by veterans

MVPC: Minority Veterans Program Coordinator at VA hospitals

NCO: Noncommissioned Officer (see Appendix E for the ranks)

NCOIC: Noncommissioned Officer-In-Charge

NICoE: National Intrepid Center of Excellence being constructed on the campus of the National Naval Medical Center Bethesda, Maryland, campus

Noncombatants: One that does not engage in combat: as a member (as a chaplain) of the armed forces whose duties do not include fighting. A civilian

Operation: a mission or job assignment

OEF: Operation Enduring Freedom (100701); OEF-A (Africa); OEF-P (Panama); OEF-HOA (Horn of Africa); OEF-TS (Trans Sahara)

OIC: Officer-in-Charge

OIF: Operation Iraqi Freedom is an ongoing military campaign that began on March 20, 2003, with the invasion of Iraq by a multinational force led by troops from the United States and the United Kingdom. OIF1 ends/OIF 2 began February 2004

OR: Operating room

OSCT: Operational Stress Control Training

PCS: Permanent Change of Station; reassignment of a soldier to another location

PH: Psychological Health

Plain of reeds: An area of land not significantly higher than adjacent areas with minor differences in elevation, commonly less than 500 feet within the area (Random House).

Pod: Individual living area (on p. 96)

PROFIS: Proficiency training

PRT: Provincial Reconstruction Teams; military, government departments, and civilian aid organizations who come to town to help to rebuild the country (construction projects and humanitarian)

PTSD: Post-traumatic Stress Disorder

PX: Post Exchange, like a department store

Quonset Hut: Living quarters for some Vietnam Army nurses; a lightweight prefabricated structure of corrugated galvanised steel having a semicircular cross section

R & R: Rest and recuperation time away from the combat area, like a vacation

Rear: Area behind the front lines for support operations

Red Zone: A term designating unsafe areas in Iraq after the 2003 invasion by the United States, Britain, and other allies

REMF: "Rear eschelon motherf**r"; a Vietnam-era phrase revived in Iraq as the "fobbit"

Rhino: Armored bus

ROA: Reserve Officers Association

ROTC: A college-based, officer commissioning program, predominantly in the United States. It is designed as a college elective that focuses on leadership development, problem solving, strategic planning, and professional ethics.

RRT: Rapid Resolution Therapy™; developed by Dr. Jon Connelly to treat past traumas

RSI: Rapid Saline Infusion

Saddam Hussein: His home was in Tikrit

Sandbox: Iraq

Sandpit: Iraq

SCI: Spinal Cord Injury

SF: Special Forces

Sick Call: Time and place designated for medical evaluations/care

SIT: Stress Inoculation Therapy; online course at www.essentiallearning.net

Strafed: Being fired upon with weapons

Stryker: Ambulance that holds 6 patient litters

Sweep: To look for explosives/mines

Tallil Airbase: 310 kilometers southeast of Baghdad

Tarmac: Airport landing area

TBI: Traumatic Brain Injury

Temper tents: Temperature controlled modular tents

TET Offensive: A major attack by the Viet Cong in 1968

Theater: Geographical area of operations

Tikrit: 140 kilometers northwest of Baghdad on the Tigris River; home of Saddam Hussein

TLF: Tricare for Life

TMC: Troop Medical Clinic

TOPS: The Officer Placement Service provided by members of MOAA

TRADOC: U.S. Army Training and Development Command

Triage: In a mass casualty situation with one health provider and two or more critically injured patients simultaneously, adhering to the maxim of accomplishing the greatest good, for the greatest number. Sorting categories:

- *Immediate:* demands prompt resuscitative care of short duration with minimal medical resources
- *Delayed:* requires moderate emergency procedures with little possibility of death from a treatment delay
- *Minimal:* requires minor treatment and could return to duty
- *Expectant:* massive injuries and questionable survivable requiring extensive medical resources and operating room time

Triage: Without regard to available resources, the most critical go first. Patient sorting by:

- *Priority 1:* requiring medical care within 6 hours or less
- *Priority 2:* requiring care within 12 hours
- *Priority 3:* care can be delayed over 12 hours

VA: Department of Veterans Affairs

VC: Viet Cong

WAQ: Warrior Adventure Quest; program designed to break down communication barriers among fellow platoon members

WIMSA: Women in Military Service

WRAMC: Walter Reed Army Medical Center located in Washington, D.C.

Zappers: Viet Cong guerrilla soldiers known for penetrating perimeters

10K generator: 10,000 kilowatt generator

11B: Army designation for an infantry soldier

APPENDIX E:
U.S. ARMY RANKS

RANK	INSIGNIA	DESIGNATION
Company Grade Officers:		
2LT: Second Lieutenant	Gold Bar	0-1
1LT: First Lieutenant	Silver	0-2
CPT: Captain	Silver Double Bar *(like railroad tracks)*	0-3
Field Grade Officers:		
MAJ: Major	Gold Oak Leaf Cluster	0-4
LTC: Lieutenant Colonel	Silver Oak Leaf Cluster	0-5
COL: Colonel	Silver Eagle *(sometimes referred to as a bird colonel)*	0-6
General Officers:		
BG: Brigadier General	One Silver Star	0-7
MG: Major General	Two Silver Stars	0-8
LTG: Lieutenant General	Three Silver Stars	0-9
GEN: General	Four Silver Stars	0-10
GOA: General of the Army	Five Silver Stars	0-11

ENLISTED RANKS

DESIGNATION	RANK
E1	PV1: Private
E2	PV2: Private
E3	PFC: Private First Class
E4	SP/CPL: Specialist/Corporal
E5	SGT: Sergeant
E6	SSG: Staff Sergeant
E7	SFC: Sergeant First Class
E8	MSG: Master Sergeant
	1SG: First Sergeant
E9	SGM: Sergeant Major
	CSM: Command Sergeant Major
	SMA: Sergeant Major of the Army

APPENDIX F:
MOAA SELECTED LEGISLATIVE GAINS
2000—2008

Active/Reserve Force Issues

- 46 percent cumulative pay raise (vs. 33 percent private sector) since 2000
- Raised ground forces manpower levels for the Army and USMC
- Raised maximum daily temporary lodging expense allowance to $290 *(previously $180)*
- Allowed two family separation allowances if both member spouses with dependents deployed
- Barred bonus recoupment/pay full bonus if member dies/separated/retired for combat injuries
- Extended full commissary privileges to Selected Reserve and 'gray area' retirees
- Allowed tax credit for small businesses paying salary differential for activated reservists
- Won new protections and benefits for wounded warriors and their families

Health Care Issues

- Authorized TRICARE for Life (TFL) for Medicare-eligible uniformed services beneficiaries
- Authorized TRICARE pharmacy coverage for Medicare-eligibles
- Defeated multiple proposals to impose large TRICARE fee hikes on retirees under 65
- Established a Military Medicare-eligible Retiree Health Care Trust Fund, making TFL an entitlement
- Authorized premium-based TRICARE for the Selected Reserve (TRICARE Reserve Select)
- Substantially reduced TRS premiums to actual 28 percent cost-of-care under program
- Won increases to Medicare reimbursements to physicians, overcoming scheduled rate cuts

- Raised TRICARE payment cap for active duty children with special needs to $36K per year
- Raised bonuses/special pays to attract/retain more health care professionals
- Authorized DoD to waive reserve dental copays if needed to ensure readiness
- Defeated proposals to charge VA enrollment fee/increase Rx copay for certain veterans

Retirement/Survivor Issues

- Eliminated Age-62 benefit reduction for Survivor Benefit Plan (SBP) annuitants
- Won 10-Year phase-out of retired pay offset by VA compensation for 50 percent > disabled retirees
- Ended retired pay offset associated with any combat/ops-related disability
- Raised death gratuity to $100K; SGLI coverage to $400K; won coverage for AD children
- Restored VA survivor annuity (DIC) for survivors who remarried after age 57
- Authorized new special survivor indemnity allowance for SBP/DIC widows
- Extended SBP coverage to survivors of all members who die on active duty
- Ended SBP premium payments for retirees who are at least 70 and paid into SBP for 30 years
- Allowed survivors to deposit military death gratuity in tax-favored accounts

Military Family/Veteran Issues

- Won Post-9/11 GI Bill: pays full state-college tuition, plus housing/book stipends
- Authorized transfer of GI Bill to spouses/child(ren) for additional service after 6 yrs.
- Established traumatic injury insurance rider (TSGLI) for certain severe disabilities
- Authorized 500 lbs PCS weight allowance for military spouses' professional items
- Expanded child care and career-assistance programs for spouses (licensing, credentialing, education)
- Authorized 10 days of paternity leave for new military fathers, in addition to normal leave
- Established funeral honors as a statutory entitlement

APPENDIX G:
MOAA PUBLICATIONS

MILITARY OFFICERS ASSOCIATION OF AMERICA

MOAA's Publications: Free for Members (nominal fee for the public)

Order at the Web site www.moaa.org or mail your request to:
201 N. Washington St.
Alexandria, VA 22314
1.800.234.6622

_____ Aging Into Medicare (1-907) Booklet

_____ Aging into Medicare & Tricare for Life (1-609) Pamphlet

_____ Auxiliary Checklist (1-610) Pamphlet

_____ Estate Planning (1-909) Booklet

_____ Financial Planning Guide: Investing in Your Future; Planning; Allowances;
Savings & Investing; Retirement Plans; Benefits (1-905) Booklet

_____ Focus on You: A Career Handbook for Military Spouses: Incorporating
Volunteer Experience; Dress for Success; Interview Questions; Networking;
Mentoring; Looking for a Federal Job (1-908) Booklet

_____ Guard/Reserve Retirement Checklist (2-221) Pamphlet

_____ Help Your Survivors Now: A Guide to Planning Ahead: Financial Benefits;
Continuing Entitlements; Personal Affairs; Worksheets; Forms (1-601)
Booklet

_____ Marketing Yourself for a Second Career: A Guide for a Successful
Transition (1-700) Booklet

_____ Military Entitlements: Benefits for Guard & Reserve: Your Reserve
Retired Pay; Taking Care of Your Survivors; Your Medical Care Benefits;
Your Non-Medical Benefits (1-603) Booklet

_____ Personal Affairs Workbook: Personal Information; Military Records; Financial Records; Survivor Assistance (9-981) Booklet

_____ Security on Call: Survivor Benefits for Guard & Reserve (9-970) Booklet

_____ SRB Made Easy: Active Duty Guide to the Survivor Benefit Plan (1-606) Booklet

_____ Survivor Benefit Plan: Security for Your Survivors: Important Changes to SBP; Factors to Consider; Myths & Realities about SBP; Enrolling in SBP; Benefits of SBP (1-602) Booklet

_____ Survivor's Checklist: First Steps for Moving On (2-220) Pamphlet

_____ TAPS: Your Guide to Military Burials (1-604) Booklet

_____ Turning the Corner: Surviving the Loss of a Loved One: What is Grief? Types of Loss; The Stages of Grieving; A Helping Hand; Signs You are getting Better; Survivor's Checklist (9-972) Booklet

APPENDIX H:
BIOGRAPHIES OF FORT HOOD, TEXAS, ARMY NURSE CORPS CASUALTIES

LTC JUANITA WARMAN, age fifty-five, had twenty-five years of active duty and reserve service as an Army Nurse Corps officer. This would have been her fourth deployment as part of the Missouri based 1908th Medical Detachment and she was headed to Iraq. The 1908th detachment is one of about eight U.S. Army Reserve combat-stress units around the United States. LTC Warman had a master of science in nursing degree from the University of Pittsburgh and was a certified psychiatric nurse practitioner specializing in post-traumatic stress disorder and traumatic brain injury.

When not deployed, LTC Warman worked at the Perry Point Veterans Administration Medical Center and actively participated in outreach events for veterans returning from deployments. She also assisted the National Guard with implementation of their Beyond the Yellow Ribbon Reintegration Program. LTC Warman is survived by her husband Phillip Warman, Esq., her daughters, stepsons, and six grandchildren. She was buried at Arlington National Cemetery in Virginia on November 23, 2009.

CPT RUSSELL SEAGER, age fifty-one, was commissioned as an Army Nurse Corps officer in the reserves four years ago and assigned to the 467th Medical Detachment (Combat Stress Control) in Madison, Wisconsin. He was headed to Afghanistan on his first deployment and planned to return to teaching after his active duty tour. CPT Seager's civilian job was as a Nurse Practitioner in the Primary Care Mental Health Integration Program at the Zablocki Veterans Administration Medical Center in Milwaukee, Wisconsin.

This talented nurse was also on the faculty of Bryant & Stratton College contributing to the medical assistant program and the nursing programs. CPT Seagar had earned a master's degree from Marquette University in Milwaukee, Wisconsin, and was working on a doctoral program to earn an Ed.D. This patriotic man once said, "I've always had a great deal of respect for the military and for service, and I just felt it was time that I stepped up and did it." He is survived by his wife Cynthia and his twenty-year-old son. He was buried in Wonewoc, Wisconsin, on November 16, 2009.

A psychiatric nurse, CPT JOHN GAFFANEY worked as a devoted Supervisor of San Diego, California's County Protective Services Department for over twenty years. After five years honorable service with the Navy (1973-78) and then fifteen years with the California National Guard, Major Gaffney retired. Military service called to his heart again after the tragedy of 9/11/2001, but he was prohibited from rejoining the military because of a hearing deficiency.

CPT Gaffaney's repeated requests for a waiver were finally answered affirmatively and he was allowed to join the 1908th Medical Detachment (Combat Stress Control) as a captain. This devoted nurse went to the home of his California patients for a more personal evaluation and he was headed to Iraq to serve our soldiers in the place where they were to be engaged in combat. He is survived by his wife Christine and his son Matthew. CPT Gaffney was buried on November 14, 2009, at the Fort Rosecrans National Ceremony in San Diego, California.

ACKNOWLEDGMENTS

This book came to fruition from seeds planted by my publisher Ross Hawkins several years ago. I thank you Ross for your unrelenting persistence, ultimate faith in me, and absolute belief in the integrity of the Army Nurse's voice. Given that I prayed for and claimed divine intervention for each step of this writing process, I give God all of the praise and glory for this bountiful harvest. Each morning I ask to be blessed, to be a blessing, and to have my work be a vehicle for God's love, joy, peace, grace, wisdom, comfort, and healing. Each evening, I thank God for the bountiful gifts given to me that day in the people that I met, lives that I touched, and work that I accomplished.

As I look back on what brought me to this point, I must first look to my family of origin. Thanks first to my loving parents, now together on the otherside, Bill and Helen Richie, who laid the foundation for the pursuit of excellence in each of their seven children: "Yes you can! You are a Richie, you have each other, and you are number one!" Special thanks go to my personal family writing team: my sister The Reverend Marsha L. Williams, my comprehension and interpretation specialist; sister Beverly A. Rohan, my grammar expert and ultimate spell-checker; sister Patricia L. Warren, my relentless, steadfast cheerleader, and to Cousin Denise Smith, my ultimate transcriptionist and research confidant for over twenty-five years. Thanks also to my brothers who always have my back and who provide the glue which binds us together: Bill Richie Jr., my "Rich," our rock; J. Curtis Richie, our moral compass, and Gregory K. Richie, our loving elder care specialist. Their spouses Cheryl Richie, Stanley Williams, Al Williams, Angela Richie, Edward Warren, and Deborah Richie are my sisters and brothers of the heart, always lifting and supporting me through life's joys and challenges. Thanks to their children, my nieces and nephews who are beacons of light in my world: Jason, Daina, Marisa, Clifton, Aaron, Brian, Marcus, Tiffany, Michelle, Nicholas, Gregory Jr., and Antonio.

Thank you also to Cousin Lionel Richie who saluted me as a captain in Europe, called my general's mom during the California earthquake and dubbed me "Three Times a Lady" when I was promoted to colonel at the U.S. Army War College. To my Aunt Evelyn and Aunt Shirley who always held down the fort and kept the home fires burning and the family close in Philadelphia. To my dear Aunt Mable Oglesby who is a blessing to me everyday. She has provided fifty + years of nursing service to her community and church and serves as my role model for expert, compassionate, holistic nursing care. She is indeed one of God's chosen few angels sent here to bless each of us.

I am also molded by my sister/friends from the nation's first all girls school in the nation. Now called the Philadelphia High School for Girls, it is known for its excellence in preparation for higher education and civic life. Yes, we are unique, powerful women raised and guided by the best in our pink marble hallways. Yes we wore white gloves, but underneath we were strong, righteous, and full of steel. I owe a special debt of gratitude to my classmates Imani Constance Johnson-Burnett, BeBe Moore Campbell (We miss you!), Peggy Beecham, Roz Watson, Jonelle Procope, and Oren Whyche-Shaw (WHF '83-84).

Wagner College gave me my first roommate and forever supporter, Navy nurse corps officer Mary Ann Pekaar-Murphy; my first adult employer (to baby-sit and do football play-by-plays for the radio station and newspaper) Brian Morris, and my first political action group with a strong conscience and dedication to our future African-American students, Black Concern. Perhaps most important in my life journey Wagner College gave me my freshman advisor, later promoted to lifetime Mum, Dr. Janet Rodgers. She took me to task when necessary, lifted me up on each step of my professional career and personal pathway, and gave me my Poppa Terry C., our Teddy Bear. My mum is still here for me and I am forever grateful.

I am blessed by my family of origin and also by my acquired family of godparents. My childhood was blessed by being an "only child" every weekend with my first godparents Aunt Mae and Uncle Ernie (I miss you both, still). When my mom died too soon for me, I didn't think I could go until the then Chief of the Army Nurse Corps Brigadier General Hazel Johnson told me about the godmother connection. She shared that when her mother passed on, she decided that she was entitled to have as many godmothers as she wanted and that I could too. She went on to explain that once someone accepted the position as godmother, they had the privilege of loving you totally and spoiling you in any way they saw fit. I took her advice and gathered a few godmothers for myself over the years like my "Mother Mary" Messerschmidt, Mom Rose Henry, Aunt Judy Melvan, and of course my dearest, around the corner, Mom who feeds my tummy and fills my heart with love, Barbara Melvan.

I am nourished today by the children of my heart; my global godchildren who fill my world with love and pride for their precious gifts to this world. Each was given to me by a mother who left this earth too soon or they are on loan to me to bless my life. Thank you to my first and forever godsons Jason and Aaron Williams of Houston, Texas; my miracle man Rahsaan Saladin Corbin who rose like a phoenix from the ashes and his children, my "grands" Prince Duce and Princess Sanai of Philadelphia, Pennsylvania; the gifted Dr. Sharon Maxwell, a The ROCKS, INC scholarship recipient; my sweetest star Melinda Baldridge Chasteen of Hawaii; the brilliant beauties Niveen and Nurmeen of Syria; the genius Jahaad of Abu Dhabi, United Arab Emirates; my whimsical hippie "Flippy" angel and pediatric nurse Tania Kilian of the United Kingdom; model beauty and teenage musician Melissa Gird of New Zealand; business leader extraordinaire with a loving spirit Cynthia Latimer of Atlanta, GA; chef Frani B. of Inverness, Florida; junior tennis star Malik Tahiri and his sister, the photogenic star Mirabelle Tahiri of Morocco/U.S.; my gifted, talented, gentle giant and high school basketball star, Paul Gombwer of Nigeria; and last but not least one of the Army's best and brightest shining stars, Cadet Shanley Lawler of the U.S. Military Academy at West Point.

Thank you from the bottom of my heart to all of my "forever friends," my family of military sisters and brothers around the world, and those here in Citrus County, Florida. There are far too many to call by name except for two ANC legends and my Angel Walk generals. First is trailblazer Margaret Bailey, the first African-American ANC officer to be promoted to colonel. The second is Dr. Joyce Johnson-Bowles who never showed me the Vietnam photos in her footlocker, but did write the critical question for my questionnaire, "Have you ever been to the wall?" From my first question about how to proceed with this book until the final manuscript review, I have been privileged to be guided by my very own ANC angels, General Clara and General Dot. Thank you both for your personal and professional support and for generously sharing your time and expertise. You are my role models and forever Global Chief Nurse leaders!

I deeply appreciate the hospitality of my military family members who gave me shelter, scrumptious food, transportation, and broad shoulders to lean on when I traveled to do the "Lean on Me" interviews. These trips are made possible because they are family funded and friend supported by folks like retired Brigadier General Vernon Spaulding and his wife, chef extraordinaire Paula; as well as Lieutenant General Robert Gray and the incomparable Mrs. Annie Gray. My dear friend Joyce A. Blowe-Jones graciously nursed me to health in the United Arab Emirates and hosted me in Augusta, Georgia. My lifetime prayer partner, spiritual advisor, life coach, military study partner and brother, the Reverend Milton A. Clarke, his wife Sheila and their daughters became my second family during my military career and are still there for me today.

Help in transitioning from my active duty Army life to civilian life and then through some of life's toughest challenges have been lovingly provided by my White House Fellow (WHF) sisters Ellen Colemire and Pricilla Douglas class of '81–82; as well as Paula Cholmondeley and Cathy Anderson class of '82-83. The WHF's program gave me another lifetime family and numerous role models who inspire me each day. There is no greater group of Americans who selflessly give of their time, efforts, and money to help our country rise to greatness. I am grateful to each one.

As I come full circle in acknowledging those who brought me to this point with *Angel Walk: Nurses at War in Iraq and Afghanistan*, I arrive at the three most important families in my life today: the Arnica Creative team, the Unity Church of Citrus County, and Mr. Michael Donald Melvan. First is my coauthor, '82-83 WHF classmate and professor at the University of Portland, Dr. Diane Vines. As psychiatric nurses, we have always shared a gentle knowing about our world and mutual respect that made for a very positive and rewarding working partnership for our writing collaborations. We complemented and challenged each other to ensure the best for *Angel Walk* and we are both proud of and grateful for the result. We both were blessed to have diligent, caring, and dedicated editors Gloria Martinez and Kathy Howard, who pushed and prodded us to ensure that we formulated a coherent, moving, and comprehensive manuscript that would be helpful to military nurses, wounded warriors, their family members, colleagues, and friends. My gratitude to the Arnica Creative team also extends to each person across the United States and around the globe who has volunteered to be a book ambassador for *Angel Walk: Nurses at War in Iraq and Afghanistan*.

My church family members at Unity of Citrus walked with me every step of the way in producing this book. From my first drafts and tearful transcriptions; to soul searching questions of whether this was really mine to do; my minister, fellow prayer chaplains, enlightened church leaders, and Silent Unity responders helped me to answer the questions, stay on task, and pray for the strength to go on. I am forever grateful and thank each of you.

Finally, I turn to the rock centered love of my life, Michael Donald Melvan. He is the ultimate Tao Te Cheng practitioner living a life of joy, integrity, peace, and balance while freely being of service to his family and community. I am blessed and honored by his absolute love, total support, and the little piece of heaven that he shares with me each day.

—Sharon Richie-Melvan

Both Dr. Sharon and I owe a great deal to Ross Hawkins for his perseverance with the book. He forced us to keep going when we were both too busy to spend enough time on the book. He believed in the book and in Dr. Sharon's ability to bring the people she interviewed to life—to make them real and engaging—so their stories would bring new knowledge and empathy to the readers. I owe a debt of gratitude to Dr. Sharon for taking me along on this journey to tell this important story. We owe thanks to our two editors, Gloria Martinez and Kathy Howard, and to the great creative design work of Aimee Genter. I also owe a debt of gratitude to my colleagues at the University of Portland School of Nursing for continually urging me to find the time to keep researching and writing. This has been a labor of love for many people who have donated their time and energy to helping us complete the book. I, like Dr. Sharon, pray often for our soldiers and their caregivers—for their safety and mental health in these difficult times.

—Diane Vines

REFERENCES

Abramson, Mark. "Marine Suicides Up Sharply." *Stars and Stripes,* October 9, 2009.

Alvarez, Lizette. "Wartime Soldier, Conflicted Mom." *New York Times*, September 27, 2009.

AMSUS. "Obama, Shinseki Cite Post-traumatic Stress As Priority." *AMSUS Newsletter,* August 5, 2009.

Army Behavioral Health. "Military Enlisted Now Online." U.S. Army Medical Department. http://www.behavioralhealth.army.mil/news/20081020medenlisted.html (accessed November 30, 2008).

Associated Press. "GI Suicides in 2008 Highest On Record." *Associated Press*, January 29, 2009. http://www.military.com/news/article/gi-suicides-in-2008-highest-on-record.html (accessed on March 22, 2009).

Associated Press. "Suicide Spotlights Troops' Mental Care." *Associated Press*, January 15, 2009.

Association of the United States Army. "Army Adopts New Strategy to Address Sexual Harassment, Assault." *AUSA News,* January 2009: 3.

Association of the United States Army. "Army Teams With NIMH to Research Suicide Risk Factors." *AUSA News,* December 2008.

Association of the United States Army. "Army Takes Closer Look at Rising Suicide Rates." *AUSA News,* February 2009: 12.

Bender, Bryan. "More Female Veterans Are Winding Up Homeless." *The Boston Globe*, July 6, 2009.

Bilmes, Linda J., and Joseph Stiglitz. "The U.S. in Iraq: An Economics Lesson." *Los Angeles Times,* July 2, 2009.

Boivin, Janet. "New Generation of Army Nurses Won't Suffer PTSD Under General's Watch." *NurseWeek*, March 14, 2005. http://www.nurseweek.com/news/features/05-03/chiefarmyrn_print.html (accessed February 16, 2009).

Caldwell, LTG William B. Letter to The ROCKS, Inc. on October 26, 2009.

Campos, Rene A. "Statement of the Military Officers Association of America Roundtable Discussion on Growing Needs of Women Veterans: Is the V.A. Ready?" 111th Cong., 1st sess. before the House Committee on Veterans' Affairs, May 20, 2009.

Cantrell, Bridget, and Chuck Dean. *Down Range: To Iraq and Back.* Seattle: Wordsmith Publishing, 2005.

Captain Barb. "Military Women Veterans: Yesterday, Today, Tomorrow." http:// userpages.aug.com/captbarb/ (accessed November 30, 2008).

Cardillo, Donna. "Show Support for Military Nurses." *Nursing Spectrum.* http:// www.dcardillo.com/articles/militarynurses.html (accessed February 16, 2009).

Carey, Benedict. "Military Stress Training Is Planned for U.S. Soldiers." *New York Times,* August 28, 2009. http://www.nytimes.com/2009/08/18/ health/18psych.html?_r=1&pagewanted=print (accessed on September 13, 2009).

Carpel-Miller, Vicki, and Ellie Izzo. "What Is Vicarious Trauma?" http://www. vicarioustrauma.com/whatis.html (accessed September 2, 2009).

Carroll, Edward M., and David Foy. "Assessment and Treatment of Combat-Related Post-Traumatic Stress Disorder in a Medical Center Setting." In *Treating PTSD: Cognitive-Behavioral Strategies,* edited by David W. Foy: 39-68. New York: Guilford Press, 1992.

Chiarelli, General Peter. "Rising Tide: 2008 OEF/OIF Army, Marine Suicides 28% of Overall KIA Casualties; Jan '09 Suicides May Surpass Month's KIA Count." *PBS NewsHour* interview with General Peter Chiarelli. January 29, 2009. http://ptsdcombat.blogspot.com/2009/01/riding-tide-2008-oefoif-veteran.html.

Collins, J., Richie, Sharon I., and Vines, Diane W. "Nurses and Policymaking: Washington Fellowships." *Nursing Economics,* July-Aug.1983.

Compassion Fatigue Awareness Project. "Compassion Fatigue Self-Test." http:// compassionfatigue.org/pages/selftest.html (accessed January 30, 2010).

Connelly, Jon. Revolutionary Trauma Treatment. http://www. rapidresolutiontherapy.com (accessed February 16, 2010).

Dao, James. "Vets' Mental Health Diagnosis Rising." *New York Times,* July 17, 2009.

Defense Centers of Excellence (DCoE). "Defense Centers of Excellence for Psychological Health and Traumatic Brain Injury." http://www.dcoe.health. mil/default.aspx (accessed September 2, 2009).

DeLuca, L. C. "Gender and Other Factors Known to Affect Post-Traumatic Stress." *Suite101.com,* July 28, 2009. http://post-traumatic-stress-disorder. suite101.com/article.cfm/ptsd_statistics_and_research (accessed on September 5, 2009).

Department of Veterans Affairs Undersecretary for Health Workgroup. Provision of Primary Care to Women Veterans. November 2008.

Duckworth, Tammy. "Coping with Unseen Injuries: From Battlefield to Homefront." Defense Forum sponsored by the U.S. Naval Institute and Military Officers' Association of America, September 16, 2009.

Duckworth, Tammy. "What Our Veterans Need." *Parade.* November 9, 2008.

Duin, Steve. "The Stress of Surviving, and Carrying On." *The Oregonian,* April 12, 2009.

Duncan, Alaine D. "Restore and Renew Wellness Clinic." Crossing Healingworks. June 9, 2008, Memo to Nurses Week Coordinators.

Foy, David W., ed. *Treating PTSD: Cognitive-Behavioral Strategies.* New York: Guilford Press, 1992.

Frankl, Viktor. *Man's Search for Meaning.* 1946. Reprint, New York: Pocket Books, 1997.

Freston, Kathy. *Quantum Wellness: A Practical and Spiritual Guide to Health and Happiness.* New York: Weinstein Books, 2008.

Friedman, Matthew J. "Posttraumatic Stress Disorder Among Military Returnees from Afghanistan and Iraq." *American Journal of Psychiatry* 163, no. 4 (2006): 586–593.

Harben, Jerry. "Warrior Transition Unit Resident Cadre Training." The U.S. Army, Nov. 12, 2008. http://www.army.mil/-news/2008/11/12/14088-warrior-transition-unit-resident-cadre-training.

Hart, Ashley B. *An Operators Manual for Combat PTSD: Essays for Coping.* New York: Writer's Showcase Press, 2000.

Hunt, Dave. "Communications from Speaker Dave Hunt." Oregon Legislative Assembly, House Joint Memorial 2 and 4, February 13, 2009.

Jackson, Kathi. *They Called Them Angels: American Military Nurses of World War II.* 2000. Reprint, Lincoln, Nebraska: University of Nebraska Press, 2006.

King, Lynda A. & Daniel W. King. "Traumatic Stress in Female Veterans." The National Center for PTSD. http:www.ptsd.va.gov/public/pages/traumatic-stress-female-vets.asp (accessed September 9, 2009).

Leipold, J.D. "Army, NIMH Begin Suicide Study." The U.S. Army, October 29, 2008. http:www.army.mil/-news/2008/10/29/13732-army-nimh-begin-suicide-study/ (accessed November 30, 2008)

Leveque, Phil. "Military Nurses: VA's Shabby Treatment of Forgotten Angels."
    Salem-news.com, May 28, 2008. http://www.salem-news.com/ articles/
    may282008/leveque_mj_5-27-08.php (accessed February 16, 2009)

Library of Congress, The. "Experiencing War: Stories from the Veterans History
    Project." Veterans History Project. http://loc.gov/vets/stories/med-nurses.
    html (accessed February 18, 2009).

Lintecum, Sarge & Leslie. "The Humane Guide to VA Benefits for Veterans with
    PTSD." Mr. and Mrs. Sarge Enterprises, 1998. http://ptsdhelp2000.com/
    ptsd1.html (accessed February 16, 2009).

Marcus, Mary B. "Veterans With Post-traumatic Stress Are at High Risk of
    Dementia." USA Today, July 13, 2009.

Maslach, Christina. & Jackson, Susan E. Maslach Burnout Inventory (MBI).
    Consulting Psychologists Press, 2009.

Matsakis, Aphrodite. I Can't Get Over It: A Handbook for Trauma Survivors. Oakland:
    New Harbinger Publications, 1996.

Maugh II, T. H. "Deployed Women Report Abuse VA study: 1 in 7 Seeking
    Postwar Health Care Allege Sex Harassment." Stars and Stripes, October 30,
    2008, 1-4.

McMichael, Willliam H. "Mullen Issues Call For More Community Support."
    Military Times, July 8, 2009.

McVicker, S.J. "The Invisible Veteran: The Women Who Served in Vietnam."
    Journal of Psychosocial Nursing 23, no. 10 (1985): 12-19.

Meagher, Ilona. Moving a Nation to Care: Post-traumatic Stress Disorder and America's
    Returning Troops. New York: Ig Publishing, 2007.

Meagher, Ilona. "The War List: OEF/OIF Statistics." PTSD Combat, April 6,
    2008. http://ptsdcombat.blogspot.com/2007/03/war-list-oefoif-statistics.
    html (accessed on September 9, 2009).

MinorityNurse.com. "Caring for Minority Veterans." Alloy Education. http://
    www.minoritynurse.com/print/49 (accessed February 18, 2009).

National Association of Social Workers. "Military Service-Related PTSD."
    National Association of Social Workers. http://www.naswdc.org/research/
    naswResearch/0907military/ (accessed February 16, 2009).

Nursing 211: Research Final Versions, Fall 2007. "Disadvantages of Nurses
    Strategies That Would Assist the Military with Post-traumatic Stress
    Disorder (PTSD) in Veterans of Foreign Wars." December 13, 2007. http://
    nurs211f07researchfinal.blogspot.com/2007/12/disadvantages-of-nurses-
    strategies-that.html (accessed February 16, 2009).

Operation Homefront. "Supporting Our Troops by Helping the Families."
Operation Homefront. http://operationhomefront.net/aboutus.asp (accessed
March 15, 2009).

Pfifferling, John H., and Kay Gilley. "Overcoming Compassion Fatigue." *Family
Practice Management* 7, no. 4 (2000): 39–45.

Point Man International Ministries. "PTSD." Point Man International Ministries,
2008. http://pmim.org/ptsd.html (accessed March 15, 2009).

PSPInformation.com. (2009). Overcoming Compassion Fatigue. PSP Information,
April 22, 2009. http://www.pspinformation.com/caregiving/thecaregiver/
compassion.shtml (accessed February 16, 2009).

PTSDsupport.net. (2009). Compassion Fatigue. http://ptsdsupport.net/
compassion_fatigue.html (accessed February 16, 2009).

Dr. Quintal and Associates. "Rapid Resolution Therapy™." http://www.
drquintal.com/RapidResolution.html (accessed November 4, 2009).

Raj, Shabu. "PTSD Among Military Personnel: A Review." *Ezine Articles*, October
12, 2006. http://ezinearticles.com/?PTSD-Among-Military-Personnel:-A-
Review&id=325701 (accessed February 16, 2009).

RAND Center for Military Health Policy Research. "Post-Deployment Stress:
What Families Should Know, What Families Can Do." Santa Monica: RAND
Corporation.

Richie, Sharon I. "Echoes from the Past – Lessons for the Future: A Vietnam Oral
History." Study project for the U.S., Army War College, March 30, 1988.

The Robert Wood Johnson Foundation. "Hospitals Implement Programs
to Help Nurses Overcome 'Compassion Fatigue.'" The Robert Wood
Johnson Foundation. http://www.rwjf.org/humancapital/digest.
jsp?id=8665&c=EMC-ND137 (accessed February 16, 2009).

Modern Medicine. "Modern Medicine." Advanstar Communications, Inc. http://
www.modernmedicine.com/modernmedicine/ (accessed March 15, 2009).

Rosenbloom, Dena, and Mary Beth Williams. *Life after Trauma: A Workbook for
Healing.* New York: The Guilford Press, 1999.

Rucker, Philip. "The Voice of a New Generation of Veterans." *Washington Post,*
September 3, 2009.

Ruff, Cheryl L. *Ruff's War: A Navy Nurse on the Frontline in Iraq.* Washington,
D.C.: U.S. Naval Institute Press, 2005.

Scannell-Desch, Elizabeth A. "Lessons Learned and Advice from Vietnam War
Nurses: A Qualitative Study." *Journal of Advanced Nursing* 49, no. 6 (2005):
600–607.

Schiraldi, Glenn. *The Post-traumatic Stress Disorder Sourcebook*. 2000. Reprint, Los Angeles: Lowell House, 2009.

Schoomaker, Eric B. "AMEDD: Keeping the Army Fit to Fight." *Army*, July 2009: 23-30.

Seal, Karen H., Daniel Bertenthal, Christian R. Miner, Saunak Sen, and Charles Marmar. "Bringing the War Back Home: Mental Health Disorders Among 103,788 US Veterans Returning from Iraq and Afghanistan Seen at the Department of Veterans Affairs Facilities." *Archives of Internal Medicine* 167, no. 5 (2007): 476-482.

Seal, Karen H., Thomas J. Metzler, Kristian S. Gima, Daniel Bertenthal, Shira Maguen and Charles R. Marmar. "Trends and Risk Factors for Mental Health Diagnoses Among Iraq and Afghanistan Veterans Using Department of Veterans Affairs Health Care, 2002-2008." *American Journal of Public Health* 99, no. 9 (2009): 1-9.

Shachtman, Noah. "Army's New PTSD Treatments: Yoga, Reiki, 'Bioenergy.'" *Wired*, March 25, 2008. http://www.wired.com/dangerroom/2008/03/army-bioenergy/ (accessed on February 16, 2009).

Shay, Jonathan. *Odysseus in America: Combat Trauma and the Trials of Homecoming*. New York: Scribner, 2003.

Shinseki, Eric K. "Remarks by Secretary Eric K. Shinseki." Keynote address, Military Officers' Association of America Luncheon, April 23, 2009.

Sipprelle, Carl R. "A Vet Center Experience: Multievent Trauma, Delayed Treatment Type." In *Treating PTSD: Cognitive-Behavioral Strategies*, edited by David W. Foy, 13-38. New York: Guilford Press, 1992.

Stouffer, Samuel A., Edward A. Suchman, Leland C. DeVinney, Shirley A. Star and Robin M. Williams. *The American Soldier: Combat and its Aftermath*. Princeton: Princeton University Press, 1949.

Steen, Joanne and M. Regina Asaro. *Military Widow: A Survival Guide*. Annapolis: U.S. Naval Institute Press, 2006.

Stetz, M., C. Long, B. Wiederhold and D. Turner. "Combat Scenarios and Relaxation Training to Harden Medics Against Stress." *Journal of Cybertherapy and Rehabilitation* 1, no. 3 (2008): 239-246.

Stirling, H. "Counseling for Nurse Veterans: ANA Professional Counseling & Placement Service, Inc., Enters Into Agreement with Veterans Administration." *The American Journal of Nursing* 45, no. 10 (1945): 824-827.

Stretch, Robert H., et al. "Posttraumatic Stress Disorder Among Army Nurse Corps Vietnam Veterans." *Journal of Consulting and Clinical Psychology* 53, no. 5 (1985): 704-708.

Sullivan, Julie. "The End of a Long, Valiant Fight." *The Oregonian*, July 19, 2009.

Sullivan, Julie. "Mental Illness in Vets Soars." *The Oregonian*, July 17, 2009.

Tanielian, T., Jaycox, L.H., Schell, T.L., Marshall, G.N., Burnam, M.A., Eibner, C., Karney, B.R., et al. *The Invisible Wounds of War.* RAND Corporation. http://www.rand.org/pubs/monographs/MG720.1/ (accessed September 2, 2009).

Thissen, Paul. "Returning Veterans Now Battling at Home." *Contra Costa Times,* July 15, 2009.

Tick, Edward. *War and the Soul: Healing Our Nation's Veterans from Post-Traumatic Stress Disorder.* Wheaton, Illinois: Quest Books, 2005.

U.S. Army. A Guide to Coping with Deployment and Combat Stress. https://www.militaryonesource.com/ (accessed February 16, 2010).

Veterans Administration. "Health Outcomes of Vietnam Era Women." *VA Research Currents*, Sept. 2009. http://www.research.va.gov/currents/default.cfm.

Veterans for America. About the Wounded Warrior Outreach Program. http://www.veteransforamerica.org/woundedwarrior/about/ (accessed March 15, 2009).

Veterans for America. Resources for Military Women. http://www.veteransforamerica.org/woundedwarrior/military-women/ (accessed March 15, 2009).

Walsh, Bari. "When Mommy Comes Marching Home." *Bostonia,* Fall 2008: 26-49.

Weisskopf, Michael. *Blood Brothers: Among the Soldiers of Ward 57.* New York: Henry Holt and Co., 2006.

Williams, Mary B., & Poijula, Soili. *The PTSD Workbook: Simple Effective Techniques for Overcoming Traumatic Stress Symptoms.* Oakland: New Harbinger Publications, 2002.

Worley, Cynthia A. "The Art of Caring: Compassion Fatigue." *Dermatology Nursing*, December 1, 2005.

Yeoman, Barry. "When Wounded Vets Come Home." *AARP Magazine*, July-August 2008.

Zoroya, Gregg. "Return of U.S. War Dead Kept Solemn, Secret." *USA Today,* December 31, 2003. http://www.usatoday.com/news/nation/2003-12-31-casket-usat_x.htm (accessed on September 17, 2008).

Zoroya, Gregg. "Troubled Soldiers' Treatment Criticized." *USA Today,* July 13, 2009.

Zucchino, David, and Rick Loomis. "The Fallen Get a Quiet Salute at Runways in Afghanistan, Iraq." *The Seattle Times,* June 26, 2008. http://seattletimes.nwsource.com/cgi-bin/PrintStory.pl?document_id=2008018050+zsection (accessed on September 17, 2008).

RESOURCES: WHERE TO FIND HELP

Alliance for National Defense. PO Box 22241, Alexandria, VA 22304, http://www.4militarywomen.org. Publishes reports, fact sheets, book reviews, and annotated bibliographies concerning the role of women in the military.

American Legion, The. http://www.legion.org. Offers veterans help transitioning into civilian life, family support, aid with VA claims, and a chance to connect with other veterans.

American Muslim Armed Forces and Veterans Affairs Council (AMAF and VAC). www.amafandvac.org. Serves warriors and veterans of the Muslim faith.

American Red Cross. www.redcross.org. Provides disaster assistance worldwide.

America's Heroes at Work. (866) 487-2365, http://www.americasheroesatwork.gov. Sponsored by the U.S. Department of Labor, offers help to veterans with PTSD and TBI and their employers.

AMSUS Association of Military Surgeons of the United States. Professional journal is *Military Medicine International Journal of AMSUS*.

Anxiety Disorders Association of America. 8730 Georgia Ave., Suite 600, Silver Spring, MD 20910, (240) 485-1001, http://www.adaa.org. Nonprofit organization that works to inform the public and health care providers about anxiety disorders. Provides information about anxiety disorders and treatments and therapies available.

Army Nurse Corps Association, The. http://www.e-anca.org. Provides network of support for Army Corps nurses.

Army OneSource. http://www.myarmyonesource.com/default.aspx. Provides information on health care, support for families, education benefits, and housing for Army members.

Association of the United States Army. Publishes the magazine of the United States Army, *ARMY,* and a newsletter, *AUSA News.*

Care for the Caregivers. 1035 Greenwood Blvd, Suite 205, Lake Mary, FL 32746, (407) 805-8566, http://c4conline.com. Helps caregivers find resources to relieve their unwanted pain, lower chance for injury, and increase levels of energy. Includes lists of related resources.

Centers for Disease Control and Prevention. 1600 Clifton Rd., Atlanta, GA 30333, (800) 232-4636 or (888) 232-6348, http://www.cdc.gov. Provides free information and referrals regarding health concerns and physical illnesses.

Coalition to Salute America's Heroes. 2 Church St., Suite 101, Ossining, NY 10562, (914) 432-5400, http://www. saluteheroes.org. Organization for communities to help veterans returning to America, provides emergency aid to veterans.

"Coming Home—A Guide for Service Members Returning from Mobilization/ Deployment." http://www.nmfa.org/ site/DocServer?docID=160. Brochure with information about adjusting to civilian and family life for veterans returning home.

Coming Home Project, The. 1801 Bush St., #213, San Francisco, CA 94109, (415) 353-5363, http://www. cominghomeproject.net. Offers group support for returning veterans and families from Afghanistan and Iraq, builds community within military and greater community.

Culture Project. (212) 925-1806, http://cultureproject.org/. A New York City theater company best known for producing work that sheds light on pressing human rights and social justice issues presented a performance of Temple University's acclaimed production *In Conflict*, a series of candid interviews with seventeen returning Iraq and Afghanistan veterans whose lives have been forever changed by their unpredictable experiences in war. Culture Project views *In Conflict* as an extraordinary opportunity for dialogue about the experiences of veterans and the issues they face upon returning home.

Defense Centers of Excellence for Psychological Health and Traumatic Brain Injury (DCoE). 866-966-1020, http://www.dcoe.health.mil/. Assesses, validates, oversees, and facilitates prevention, resilience, identification, treatment, outreach, rehabilitation, and reintegration programs for psychological health and traumatic brain injury to ensure the Department of Defense meets the needs of the nation's military communities, warriors, and families.

Deployment Health Clinical Center. Walter Reed Army Medical Center, Bldg. 2, 3rd Floor, Room 3E01, 6900 Georgia Avenue NW, Washington, DC 20307-5001, (202) 782-6563, http:// www.pdhealth.mil. Resource for caregivers and veterans, information provided about health and mental well-being of veterans.

Disabled American Veterans. PO Box 14301, Cincinnati, OH 45250-0301, (877) 426-2838 or (859) 441-7300, http://www.dav.org. A grassroots advocacy organization that offers representation for disabled veterans with claims before the VA and U.S. Department of Defense, support for disabled veterans of all wars.

Employer Support of the Guard and Reserve (ESGR). 1555 Wilson Blvd,

Suite 200, Arlington VA 22209-2405, (800) 336-4590, http://esgr.org/about.asp. U.S. Department of Defense organization to build employer support for Guard and reserve members of the armed forces and ease return of service members into the workforce.

Equine Assisted Growth and Learning Association (EAGALA). PO Box 993, Santaquin, UT 84655, (877) 858-4600 or (801) 754-0400, http://www.eagala.org. Nonprofit organization committed to providing assisted therapies using horses. Recruits volunteers to work with returning veterans and their families to improve their quality of life and mental health.

Gift from Within. 16 Cobb Hill Rd., Camden, ME 04843, (207) 236-8858, http://www.giftfromwithin.org. Source for those who suffer from, treat, or are close to those suffering from PTSD. Provides educational information and other support resources.

Give an Hour. PO Box 5918, Bethesda, MD 20824-5918, http://www.giveanhour.org. Connects mental health counselors, returning veterans, and volunteers from community organizations to provide free mental health treatment for veterans.

Hearts Toward Home International. 1050 Larrabee Ave., Suite 104, PMB 714, Bellingham, WA 98225-7367, (360) 714-1525, http://www.heartstowardhome.com/index.htm. Helps veterans and their families maintain healthy relationships as veterans come home.
HireVetsFirst. http://hirevetsfirst.dol.gov/. Offers variety of resources to help injured veterans find jobs, return to their previous jobs, work for the government, receive assistance for their families, and access benefits and support services.

Hooah 4 Health. http://www.hooah4health.com. Specifically targets Reservists. Promotes physical, mental, spiritual, and environmental health and provides information for families of service members.

Illyria. http://www.illyria.com. Collection of information about women who served in Vietnam. Suggested reading list of books relating to the Vietnam War.

International Conference of War Veteran Ministers (ICWVM). http://www.vietnamveteranministers.org. Members are war veterans as well as ministers.

International Society for Traumatic Stress Studies, The (ISTSS). 111 Deer Lake Rd., Suite 100, Deerfield, IL 60015, (847) 480-9028, http://www.istss.org. Organization of health professionals that share information about trauma and stress-induced disorders so as to better treat patients.

Iraq and Afghanistan Veterans of America (IAWA). 770 Broadway, 2nd Floor, New York, NY 10003, (212) 982-9699, http://iava.org. Forms local groups of service members and families, provides educational materials for families about deployment, promotes awareness of veterans' needs.

Marine Parents. PO Box 1115, Columbia, MO 65205, (573) 303-5500, http://www.marineparents.com. Helps Marine families connect with each other, support the Marine Corps, and stay connected with their loved ones throughout their deployment.

Mental Health America. http://www. mentalhealthamerica.net. Formerly known as National Mental Health Association. Advocates for the mentally ill, provide resources and referrals, lobbies for better treatment.

Mental Health Self-Assessment Program. https://www.militarymentalhealth. org/welcome.asp. Screening program which allows for personal understanding of one's mental health, tells whether a person ought to seek treatment.

Military Families Speak Out (MFSO). PO Box 300549, Jamaica Plain, MA 02130, (617) 983-0710, http://www. mfso.org. Organization opposed to the war in Iraq working to pressure a withdrawal of troops to prevent more injuries and deaths.

Military Family Resource Centre (MFRC). http://mfrc-ncr.org/english/. Local chapters work with military families to provide resources and support.

Military Health System. http://www. health.mil. Sponsored by the U.S. Department of Defense. Informs veterans of their health care benefits, connects them to health care providers worldwide, and participates in medical research.

Military Homefront. http://www. militaryhomefront.dod.mil. Official U.S. Department of Defense Web site for service members and families. Features online government resources and links.

Military Officers Association of America. 201 N. Washington St., Alexandria, VA 22314, (800) 234-6622 or (703) 549-2311, http://www.moaa.org. Largest organization of military officers from all branches of military in America. Advises and lobbies Congress on behalf of officers and military community, provides advice and assistance for all retired and active duty officers and their families.

Military OneSource. (800) 342-9647, http://www.militaryonesource.com/ skins/ MOS/home.aspx. Collection of online resources for military families.

Minerva Center, The. http://www. minervacenter.com. Studies women in the military, currently publishes the *Minerva Journal of Women and War*. Not an advocacy organization.

Minority Veterans Programs Coordinators (MVPC), http://www1. va.gov/centerforminorityveterans/ page.cfm?pg=13. VA program to help minority veterans by promoting VA benefits and services and advocating on behalf of minority veterans within their communities. There is a coordinator located in every state who can be reached through Regional Offices.

The Mission Continues. www. missioncontinues.org. Nonprofit organization aimed at uniting veterans and their fellow citizens in shared service to our nation. Awards fellowships to wounded and disabled veterans from Iraq and Afghanistan for volunteer service in their communities with the goal of providing service opportunities to wounded veterans who still have the desire to serve their country, but whose disabilities prevent them from continuing to serve in the military. Through the Veterans Tributes program, volunteers come together in service to memorialize members of our military who lost their lives in defense of our country. The Warrior in Service initiative offers group volunteer opportunities to "wounded warriors" who are still in the midst of their recoveries. These opportunities can be one-time engagements or recurring commitments, and they may serve as precursors to full-time Mission Continues Fellowships.

My HealtheVet (MHV). http://www.myhealth.va.gov. Service provided by the VA for veterans, provides access to Personal Health Journal, online VA prescription refills, links to benefits and VA resources, and other health information.

National Alliance on Mental Illness (NAMI). 2107 Wilson Blvd., Suite 300, Arlington, VA 22201-3042, (703) 524-7600 or (800) 950-6264, http://www.nami.org. Grassroots advocacy organization for those who are mentally ill and their families.

National Association of County Veteran Service Officers (NACVSO). http://nacvso.org. Established to help claimants approach the Department of Veterans Affairs. Services available for veterans, widows, widowers, and children.

National Center for Posttraumatic Stress Disorder. (802) 296-6300, http://www.ptsd.va.gov/. Working to advance the quality of clinical care and welfare of veterans suffering from PTSD, world's leading research center on PTSD. Offers links to other Internet resources about PTSD.

National Institute of Mental Health (NIMH). http://www.nimh.nih.gov/health/topics/post-traumatic-stress-disorder-ptsd/index.shtml. Provides detailed information about PTSD and finding treatment.

National Military Family Association (NMFA). http://www.militaryfamily.org. Online resources for military families. Runs Operation Purple Camps for children of service members. National Organization of Veterans Advocates, Inc (NOVA). 1425 K St., Suite 350, Washington, D.C. 20005, (877) 483-8238, http://www.vetadvocates.com. Professional advocates for veterans dealing with the government and VA.

National Suicide Prevention Lifeline. (800) 273-8255, 24-hour toll-free suicide prevention service. http://www.suicidepreventionlifeline.org. Connects people to local crisis centers and provides suicide prevention counseling on the phone.

National Veterans Foundation. (888) 777-4443, http://www.nvf.org. Veteran-run aid organization helps returning veterans receive education benefits, home loans, life insurance, and compensation.

Navy One Source. (800) 540-4123, http://www.militaryonesource.com/

MOS/Navy.aspx?MRole=Member &Branch=Navy&Component=Active. Information and referrals for Navy members and families.

Ombudsman Program in Support of Warriors in Transition. http:// medcomombudsman.amedd.army. mil. Provides volunteers that work as mediators for returning veterans and their families. Program established through the U.S. Army Medical Department.

ONE Freedom, Inc. PO Box 7418, Boulder, CO 80306, (303) 444-1221, http://www.onefreedom.org. Supports veterans, families, and care providers as they deal with stress. Offers program to aid in dealing with stress naturally.

Operation Comfort. 4900 Broadway, Suite 400, San Antonio, TX 78209, (210) 826-0500, http://www. operationcomfort.org. Provides living areas and family waiting rooms that are comfortable and assist in rehabilitation for injured veterans.

Operation First Response. 20037 Dove Hill Rd., Culpeper, VA 22701, (888) 289-0280, http://www. operationfirstresponse.org. Provides financial safety net for returning veterans and their families.

Operation Homefront. 8930 Fourwinds Drive, Suite 340, San Antonio, TX 78239, (210) 659-7756 or (800) 722-6098, http://www.operationhomefront. net. Provides emergency relief to veterans and their families in various forms, including food assistance, scholarship programs, housing assistance, vehicle, computer, and furniture donations, and financial assistance.
The Post-traumatic Gazette. Patience Press, http://www.patiencepress.com/ samples/1stIssue.html. Newsletter for trauma survivors, informs survivors about PTSD symptoms and recovery.

Proponency Office for Rehabilitation and Reintegration (PR&R). http:// www.Armymedicine.Army.mil/prr/ index.html. Office within the U.S. Army Medical Department, Office of the Surgeon General. Provides information about stress-related disorders in attempt to improve care and treatment of returning veterans.

National Conference of Vietnam Veteran Ministers, The (NCVNVM). (617) 278-4576, www.vietnamveteranministers.org. Conducts spiritual retreats for veterans and their spouses. Provides support of chaplaincy programs in veterans organizations.

Nurses Organization of Veterans Affairs (NOVA). 1726 M St., NW, Suite 1101, Washington, D.C. 20036, (202) 296-0888, http://www.vanurse.org. Focuses on improving the quality of VA medical care, specialist nurses.

Point Man International Ministries. PO Box 267, Spring Brook, NY 14140, (716) 675-5552 or (800) 877-8387, http://www.pmim.org. Constructs small groups of returning veterans to provide support systems for veterans returning, particularly those suffering from PTSD. Run by and for vets.

PTSD Help 2000. http://ptsdhelp2000. com. Offers veterans with PTSD help for dealing with the VA to receive benefits.

PTSD Help Network, The. http://www. ptsdhelp.net/index.html. Offers help understanding and diagnosing PTSD, receiving compensation from the VA, and finding treatment. Links to other resources.

Rand Corporation. www.rand.org. Provides pamphlets for warriors and families to assist in post-deployment stress, substance abuse, and mental illness.

Rapid Trauma Resolution at http:// www.cleartrauma.com.

Real Warriors Campaign, The. www. realwarriors.net. An initiative launched by the Defense Centers of Excellence for Psychological Health and Traumatic Brain Injury (DCoE) to promote the processes of building resilience, facilitating recovery, and supporting reintegration of returning service members, veterans, and their families.

Reserve Officers Association. www. roa.org. Represents all members of all service branches especially through policy development and advocacy.

Returning Veterans Project. 907 NE Thompson, Portland, OR 97212, (503) 933-4996, http://returningveterans.org. Offers support for returning veterans and their families, collection of health care providers that aid veterans in the Northwest.

Sidran Institute. 200 East Joppa Road, Suite 207, Baltimore, MD 21286-3107, (410) 825-8888, http://www.sidran.org. Offers educational resources and access to treatment for people suffering from PTSD and stress disorders.

Soldier's Heart. 500 Federal St., Suite 303, Troy, NY 12180, (518) 274-0501, http://www.soldiersheart.net. Provides variety of programs for returning veterans to aid in transition to civilian life, including healing retreats, clinical consultations for vets and their families, community-based support groups, veteran mentors, professional training, lectures, awareness, and faith services.

Soldiers Project, The. (818) 761-7438 or (877) 576-5343, http://www. thesoldiersproject.org. Provides free counseling for service members serving in Iraq and Afghanistan and their families. Includes links to other sites for psychological assistance for families and service members.

Still Serving Veterans. Werner Baker, 2939 Johnson Rd. SW, Huntsville, AL, 35805, (256) 883-7054, http:// stillservingveterans.org/Home.asp. Helps wounded veterans and their families reintegrate into the workforce and community via counseling, coaching, guiding, job transition, and assistance in obtaining all Veterans Administration (VA) benefits to which they are entitled.

Strategic Outreach to Families of all Reservists (SOFAR). PO Box 380766, Cambridge, MA 02236, (888) 278- 0041 or (617) 266-2611, http:// www.sofarusa.org. Free mental health counseling for all families of reservists and Guard members.

Treatment Trends. 18-22 South 6th St., PO Box 685, Allentown, PA 18105, (610) 439-8479, http:// www.treatmenttrends.org. Provides information for those suffering from addictions. Helps addicts receive treatment and helps families support those addicted in attempt to reduce addiction-caused violence.

Tricare Management Activity. Suite 810, 5111 Leesburg Pike, Falls Church, VA 22041-3206, http://www.tricare. mil. Provides information about Tricare benefits and policies.

U.S. Armed Forces Legal Assistance Locator. http://legalassistance.law.af.mil/ content/locator.php. Provided by the U.S Armed Forces Legal Assistance, provides general legal information to military community.

U.S. Army Center of Military History. http://www.history.army.mil. Records Army history and advises current Army staff on historical events.

U.S. Department of Veterans Affairs. (800) 827-1000, http://www.va.gov. Provides various benefits and services to veterans and their families.

U.S. Substance Abuse and Mental Health Services Administration (SAMHSA). http://www.samhsa.gov. Provides funding for programs and research for substance abusers and those with mental illness.

United States Navy Operational Stress Control Training (OSCT). http:// www.navy.mil/search/display.asp?story_ id=40964. Provides background information about stress control training for sailors.

USO Services. (888) 484-3876, http:// www.uso.org/whatwedo/usoservices. Offers programs and services to boost

morale among service members and build community on the home front.

VA Facilities and Locator Directory. http://www2.va.gov/directory/guide/ home.asp?isFlash=1. Locates VA facilities across the U.S.

VA Travel Nurse Corps (TNC). 650 E Indian School Rd., Phoenix, AZ 85012, (602) 200-2398 or (866) 664-1030, http://www.travelnurse. va.gov/. Provides information for nurses interested in temporary assignments working at VA centers across the country.

VA Watchdog. http://www.vawatchdog. org. Provides current information about the VA and Congressional action, advises the VA of veteran concerns and needs.

Valley Forge Return to Honor Workshops. 1601 Valley Forge Rd., Valley Forge, PA 19482, http://www. returntohonorworkshop.com. Offers transitional support to returning veterans by offering leadership and educational seminars. This organization does not provide mental health programs for returning veterans but instead provides a support group for veterans.

Vet Center. (800) 905-4675 or (866) 496-8838, http://www.vetcenter. va.gov/index.asp. Provides readjustment counseling and outreach services to veterans and families through 232 community-based centers across the U.S.

Veteran Improvement Program (VIP). 1240 E. 79th St., Chicago, IL 60619, (773) 374-9800, http://vetwins.com/ servicesforveterans.html. Aids veterans in finding VA benefits, housing, case management, job placement, job retention, legal assistance, and referral services.

Veteran Love. 930 Washington Ave., Suite 206, Miami Beach, FL 33139, (305) 673-2856, http://www.veteranlove.com. Provides financial and psychological help for wounded and disabled veterans returning from Operation Iraqi Freedom and Operation Enduring Freedom.

Veterans for America. 1025 Vermont Ave., NW, 3rd Floor, Washington, D.C. 20025, (202) 483-9222, http://www. veteransforamerica.org/home/vfa. Advocacy program working to ensure the government meets the needs of service members. Work includes advocating through more specific groups: National Guard Program, Purple Dog Tag Program, Wounded Warriors Outreach Program, Resources for Military Women.

Veterans for Peace. 216 South Meramec Ave., St. Louis, MO 63105, (314) 725-6005, http://www.veteransforpeace.org. NGO represented at the UN. Working to end the current wars, save VA health care, and defend veterans' rights.

Veterans History Project. http://www. loc.gov/vets. Collects firsthand stories from returning veterans to be shared with others through the Library of Congress.

Veterans Law Clinic. Widener University School of Law, PO Box 7474, Wilmington, DE 19803-0474, (302) 477-2070, http://law.widener.edu/ vetclinic/index.shtml. Offers free legal representation to disabled veterans and dependents appealing the VA, specializes

in appeals from the VA Regional Offices in Delaware, New Jersey, and Pennsylvania to the Board of Appeals. Veterans of the Vietnam War. 805 So. Township Blvd., Pittston, PA 18640-3327, (570) 603-9740, http://www. theveteranscoalition.org/home.htm. Originally established to provide services to Vietnam veterans. Offers wide range of programs including building community support, resources for veterans, and running the Beacon House for Homeless Veterans.

Veterans Outreach Center. 459 South Ave., Rochester, NY 14620, (585) 546-1081, http://www. veteransoutreachcenter.org. Aids veterans in restoring their well-being and reentering civilian life.

Vets 4 Vets. (520) 319-5500, http:// www.vets4vets.us. Organization of veterans to help those returning from Iraq deal with their experiences positively. Free services and support groups for returning veterans.

Vietnam Veterans of America. 8605 Cameron St., Silver Spring, MD 20910, http://www.vva.org. Advocate for Vietnam veterans and rights to health care, identify full range of disabilities, hold government-sponsored agencies accountable, improve the public perception of veterans, try to account for all POW/MIAs.

Vietnam Veterans of America's Guide on PTSD. http://www.vva.org/benefits/ptsd. htm. Assists in filing claims with the VA for PTSD, describes current compensation programs, provides suggestions for receiving the appropriate care.

Vietnam Women's Memorial. http://www.vietnamwomensmemorial.org. Provides educational information, films and articles about the Vietnam Women's Memorial and Foundation with stories, a "sister search," events, a library of articles, books, and films about women who served in Vietnam.

War-Related Illness and Injury Study Centers (WRIISC). VA Medical Center, c/o WRIISC-DC, Room 3B 203, 50 Irving St., NW, Washington, DC 20422, (800) 722-8340 or (202) 745-8249, http://www.warrelatedillness.va.gov/. Study and treat war-related illnesses and injuries among combat veterans. Offer services to combat veterans, families, and doctors.

Web MD. http://www.webmd.com. Provides free information about health problems, including PTSD and mental health issues, from recognized field experts. Offers information about treatment and referrals for finding help.

Women in Aviation Resource Center. http://www.women-in-aviation.com. Compilation of resources for women in or interested in aviation-centered careers. Resources include lists of museums, books, employment, and recent headlines.

Women in Military Service for America Memorial Foundation. (703) 533-1155 or (800) 222-2294, http://www.womensmemorial.org. Recognizes all women who have served America and documents their service.

Women in Vietnam. http://www.illyria.com/vnwomen.html. Chronicles the service of women in the Vietnam War.

Women Marines Association. PO Box 8405, Falls Church, VA 22041-8405, (888) 525-1943, http://www.womenmarines.org. Program offers support for women Marines and their families, organizes volunteers to service hospitalized veterans in VA hospitals.

Women Organizing Women (WOW) Veteran Advocacy. http://www.vetwow.com. Advocacy organization for women service members, educates government officials about MST in attempt to change policies, procedures, and laws surrounding military sexual trauma.

Women's Research and Education Institute, The. 1828 L St. NW, Suite 801, Washington, D.C. 20036, (202) 280-2720, http://www.wrei.org/default.htm. Studies women and equality within society, specifically issues important to military women, so as to report to Congress, the military, and the media.

Women's Trauma Recovery Program (WTRP). 795 Willow Rd., Menlo Park, CA 94025, (650) 493-5000, http://www.womenvetsptsd.va.gov/. Residency and out-patient programs for returning women from all eras. Aid for PTSD and MST available. Located with the Women's Mental Health Center.

Wounded Warrior Project. 7020 A.C. Skinner Pkwy, Suite 100, Jacksonville, FL 32256, (877) 832-6997, http://www.woundedwarriorproject.org. Raises awareness in the community regarding issues that veterans face when returning home, builds network for returning veterans.

LaVergne, TN USA
06 April 2010
178332LV00002BA/4/P